House Calls by Dogsled

To Darrel
Happy Birthday "80"
[signature]

HOUSE CALLS *by* DOGSLED

SIX YEARS IN AN ARCTIC
MEDICAL OUTPOST

Keith Billington

LOST
MOOSE
THE YUKON PUBLISHERS

Lost Moose is an imprint of Harbour Publishing Co. Ltd
Harbour Publishing Co. Ltd
P.O. Box 219, Madeira Park, BC, V0N 2H0
www.harbourpublishing.com

To protect the privacy of individuals, the names of some patients, staff and residents have
been changed.
Photographs from the collection of Keith Billington.
Edited by Betty Keller
Cover and text design by Anna Comfort
Map design by Roger Handling, Terra Firma Digital Arts
Printed in Canada

Harbour Publishing acknowledges financial support from the Government of Canada
through the Book Publishing Industry Development Program and the Canada Council
for the Arts, and from the Province of British Columbia through the BC Arts Council
and the Book Publishing Tax credit.

THE CANADA COUNCIL | LE CONSEIL DES ARTS
FOR THE ARTS | DU CANADA
SINCE 1957 | DEPUIS 1957

BRITISH
COLUMBIA
ARTS COUNCIL
Supported by the Province of British Columbia

Library and Archives Canada Cataloguing in Publication

Billington, Keith, 1940–
        House calls by dogsled : six years in an Arctic medical outpost / Keith
Billington.

ISBN 978-1-55017-423-6

        1. Billington, Keith, 1940– 2. Billington, Muriel. 3. Nurses—Northwest
Territories—Fort McPherson Region—Biography. 4. Midwives—Northwest
Territories—Fort McPherson Region—Biography. 5. Gwich'in Indians—Social life
and customs. 6. Gwich'in Indians—Medical care—Northwest Territories—Fort
McPherson Region. 7. Fort McPherson Region (N.W.T.)—Biography. I. Title.
RT37.B54A3 2008   610.73092   C2007-907570-3

DEDICATION

I would like to dedicate this book to the Gwich'in of Fort McPherson and all those who made my wife and me feel a part of the community. Of special note were the late William and Mary Firth who became our children's "Jijii" (grandfather) and "Jijuu" (grandmother), and to Rachel Stewart and Mary Teya who kept the nursing station functioning after hectic activities. The late William Vittrekwa took great pains to show me how to drive a dog team and camp out at minus 50, where to hunt and where to fish. But above all, I would like to thank my wife, Muriel, who shared all of these adventures with me and who has always been a source of encouragement and inspiration.

—*Keith Billington*

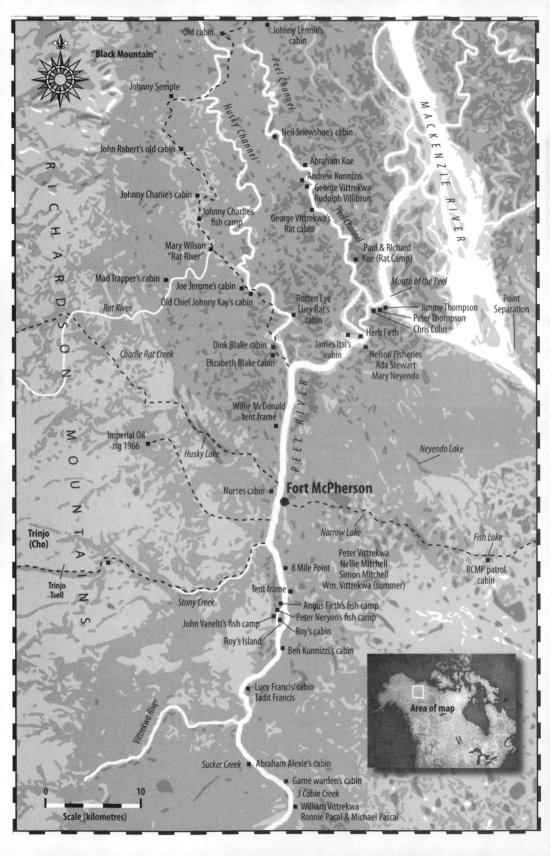

1

IT WAS OCTOBER 22, 1963, and snow had fallen during the afternoon. The usual sounds of Fort McPherson were now muffled, and my wife, Muriel, and I sat reading and listening to some soft orchestral background music. A few dogs barked in the distance, and as the evening wore on, we relaxed deeper into the cushions with our books.

Suddenly the garden gate banged against the fence, and we heard someone run along the wooden sidewalk that led to the back door. We glanced at each other as we waited expectantly for the knock on the kitchen door that was bound to come at any second. Instead, the door was flung open, hitting the wall with a crash. A slightly built young native man staggered into the kitchen with his bare hand clutched to his face, his parka shedding icy particles over the floor as he faced us.

"My eye, my eye, I've lost my eye!" he cried. Blood trickled from underneath his hand and ran down his face, where it dripped from his chin onto the wolverine fur of his parka hood.

I was on my feet even as the injured man opened the door, and I could feel my hands and feet go cold with the anticipation of what I was going to see. "It's okay now, you'll be all right. Just come with me," I managed to say calmly as I led him slowly down the corridor to the treatment room. I sat him down, feeling far from the calm that I was trying to portray to my hysterical patient.

Muriel was right behind me and told me later that she had felt

Looking north in winter to the nursing station on the east bank of the Peel River.

a bit nauseated at the prospect of looking at an eye-less socket. She had always detested eye injuries, and it had been the worst moment in her nursing training when she had to be the scrub nurse in the operating room for an enucleation—the removal of an eye. But now, swallowing hard, she put her hand comfortingly on the injured man's shoulder as I gently removed his hand from his face.

A stick had penetrated his eye through the upper lid, and the pencil-sized object was firmly embedded in the socket with about four inches protruding. I could not see the eyeball to assess the damage because the stick held down the rapidly swelling lid. I tried to visualize the damage and thought about how far the stick might have penetrated his skull.

While the patient moaned and writhed with the agony of the injury, Muriel started to prepare a hypodermic syringe with pain-killer. My toes literally curled up in my moccasins as I saw his suffering and, looking around the clinic, I almost despaired at our meagre supplies. What this young man needed was a properly equipped operating room, a neurosurgeon and an ophthalmologist.

Before Muriel could give him an injection, we had to find out his name and make sure that what he was going to be given was not going to put him into shock. Was he allergic to anything? How old was he? Who did he belong to? When he told me who his mother was and that his name was Frank, Muriel had his medical file out in seconds, read it and then finished preparing the injection.

I asked him how the accident had happened. He waved his head around slowly as he told me that he had been driving his dog team toward the village in the dark, and he couldn't see the willow branches that hung over the trail. As he got closer to the village, the bright lights had diminished his night vision some more, and then suddenly he felt a searing pain when the stick punctured his eye. He fell off his toboggan and lay there for a short time before he staggered up the trail to the nursing station. He did not know where his dogs were but still had the presence of mind to say that they would probably go home.

Since our patient was only seventeen, we had to get a message to his mother. However, we couldn't wait until she gave permission for his treatment so he was given the injection and we made him as comfortable as possible on one of the beds.

Our local communication system was primitive but effective. A battery-powered buzzer could be activated in the home of the nursing station's janitor and handyman, William Firth, two houses north of the station, by simply pressing a button on our clinic wall. One ring meant "come when convenient," two rings "come as soon as possible" and three rings "emergency."

Muriel pressed the button three times.

I went to get my parka and was pulling my mukluks on when William, looking alarmed, came into the station. Quickly I told him what had happened—that there had been a serious eye injury and that a dog team was wandering about without a driver—and sent him to get our patient's mother. I did not give him the details of the injury so that neither he nor the parent would be able to let their imaginations go wild. William showed his concern on his face, but after years of caring for the nursing station, he was used to shocking events and took the news of death and disability without a murmur. He went quietly out into the night.

Leaving Muriel with the patient, I ran the half-mile (.8 km) to Fort McPherson's RCMP office and hammered on the officers' door. The ready smile on Corporal Jim Simpson's face vanished when he heard about the accident, and he immediately called the Inuvik detachment on his single sideband radio, asking the officer at the other end to call a doctor at the hospital and to be prepared to relay a message to him. While we waited, Jim's wife, Phyllis, brought us some coffee, and we sipped the scalding liquid as we talked about this and other accidents. After about 15 minutes and just as Jim was trying to explain to me how a single sideband radio worked, the radio crackled and the Inuvik RCMP officer—in a high voice that sounded as though the owner had been breathing helium—came on the air with the Fort McPherson detachment's call sign. He told us that a doctor was standing by to receive a message.

Conscious that most of the RCMP units in "G" Division would be listening in, I told the doctor what had happened and what we had done. I took a deep breath and waited for a reply. Nothing happened. The radio seemed dead.

"Take your finger off the transmit button!" Jim said in a stage whisper. I looked down and saw that I was grasping the microphone tightly with the transmit button held down.

"Oops! Over," I said, feeling the sweat run down my neck. This was an emergency and I was suffering from stage fright!

The doctor asked a few questions and then relayed instructions for medication and continued care. He promised that he would radio again at first light and send a plane to evacuate the patient to the hospital in Inuvik nearly 120 km away.

Daylight north of sixty diminishes rapidly in the early winter, so that dawn would not come until 9:30. To complicate things further, the regularly scheduled Pacific Western Airlines planes were not flying; they were in Edmonton where they were undergoing their annual mechanical overhaul and being equipped with skis, and they would not return until the ice was strong enough to hold them, probably in early November. Until then we relied on a true northerner, Freddy Carmichael, the owner and pilot of Reindeer Air Services, to risk his neck for us.

By 9:15 the next morning I was sitting in the RCMP detachment office sipping another cup of hot coffee. During the night Muriel and I had taken shifts in sitting with young Frank, and even in his drugged state he had moved and groaned with the pain and we had to prevent him from trying to put his hand up to the dressing that covered his eye and the stick.

"No change in condition," I reported as soon as the doctor called from Inuvik.

"Okay, we are going to fly in with Reindeer Air Services, and Freddy thinks that he can land on the sandbar out in front of the village. We'll be there in about two hours. Over and out."

Jim Simpson, having one of the few four-wheel drive trucks in the village, said that he would organize the transportation for us. He promised to pick us all up at the nursing station as soon as he heard the plane overhead. We prepared Frank for the medivac, strapping him to a stretcher and covering him with warm blankets, while his worried mother spoke to him soothingly in Gwich'in. Muriel had another hypodermic ready for him but delayed giving it until we heard the plane so that the effects would last for the one-hour flight to Inuvik.

Forty-five minutes after the radio conversation with the doctor, Jim arrived at the clinic door. "Let's go," he said, placing himself at one end of the stretcher. "The plane is just over the point now." He indicated with a nod of his head to the north. He was referring to a point of land about 12 miles downriver where the Peel swings to the east and disappears from view.

"Wait!" Muriel called out and quickly pulled aside a corner of the blanket, cleaned a piece of Frank's exposed skin and injected the painkiller.

Jim had been busy. He had collected a few volunteers (who, he told me later, just happened to be standing outside the store), driven them down to the sandbar, detailed them to cut small spruce trees on the riverbank, then mark out a winter landing strip. The sandbar that Freddy had used previously had been covered with debris when the ice had briefly backed up, and now the men had to walk a considerable distance along the strip to clear any driftwood or other obstacles from it.

A small blue Cessna 185 swooped low over the snow-covered sandbar. "Don't worry," someone called out. "Freddy can land on a dime!" The ski-equipped plane banked sharply, throttled back, flaps down, and then within seconds it was down on the strip in a flurry of snow. As soon as the engine died, the door of the small plane opened and out jumped Freddy Carmichael, smiling shyly around him as he was greeted like a long-lost friend. He ran his fingers through his long curly black hair and then reached into the plane.

"I brought some of the First Class mail, but I didn't have time to get the other stuff."

Cries of delight came from all around at this unexpected pleasure in the middle of freeze-up, and willing people soon formed into a chain gang to move the heavy blue mail bags from the plane to the side of Jim's truck. Then when all the bags were out, a large figure in a snowmobile suit emerged, and Freddy said, "This is the doctor from Inuvik." Everyone made way for him, and he came over to where Muriel and I were standing by the truck. After quick introductions, he held what we considered a case conference, finding out Frank's latest status, and then doing a perfunctory examination so that he both introduced himself to our patient, established his authority, and learned in general what he had to deal with should an emergency occur on the way to Inuvik.

He gave one final nod to us and said, "Good. Now we had better get him to the hospital fast." I don't think Frank was really too aware of what was happening, and he lay quite still while the stretcher was angled this way and that in an effort to get it securely into the small plane. When it was strapped down, Frank's mother came over and put a brown paper bag of his personal belongings by his side. She did not touch him or say anything; just stood still and looked at his sleeping face for a few seconds before stepping back to let the doctor climb in beside the stretcher. Freddy buckled up his seat belt, reached over to close the door, and everyone moved back.

The Cessna's engine was still warm, and after two revolutions of the propeller, there was a puff of blue smoke as the engine fired and then a loud roar as Freddy revved it up prior to take-off. Almost as one person we turned our backs as the snow was whipped up around us, and we missed seeing the plane leave the ground. When we turned around, it was climbing steadily, heading northeast towards Inuvik and the hospital.

Feeling light-headed from lack of sleep and the excitement of the last 12 hours, Muriel and I declined an offer of a ride from Jim, and after seeing him off up the trail with a load of mail bags, we walked slowly back towards the nursing station. Muriel admitted that what she remembered most was Frank rushing into the kitchen yelling that he had lost his eye, and she had pictured an eyeball all on its own, lying in the middle of the trail, looking up at the stars! We talked about the possible outcomes of his injuries, and then our talk wandered into philosophizing about our work and responsibilities. Were we up to what was expected of us in this remote northern village? And just what *was* expected of us? And then we talked about all the "what ifs" in our new life. We realized that there would be other cases like Frank's and maybe the outcomes would be worse, but we both knew that we were glad that we had come to Fort McPherson, and that we were going to stay. What we did not fully realize was that we were starting out on a long-standing relationship with a people and a place.

We heard later that, when they arrived at Inuvik, Frank and the doctor were met by an ambulance and rushed to hospital. X-rays gave the doctor all the information he needed, and within quite a short time Frank was having the stick removed from his skull under a general anaesthetic. The doctor called us from the operating room telephone to ask us to pass on the information to Frank's mother that, miraculously, the young man was not going to lose his sight and apart from severe bruising the eye was not damaged! We could hardly believe it. The doctor went on to tell us that the stick had perforated the upper lid and then, possibly because of the entry angle, had severely compressed the eye, then gone through the flimsy bony structure that held the eye, narrowly missing the nerve and blood supply. It had stopped short of doing further damage within the skull. He added that he was keeping the stick in a jar of saline on his desk just to show what could penetrate someone's head without killing them! He was very impressed with the way Frank had behaved and his tolerance of what must have been incredible pain. Six weeks later, when scheduled aircraft were operating again, Frank climbed out of the plane into the gloom of a Fort McPherson winter day. He had no more to show for his ordeal than a pair of dark sunglasses covering his eyes and a painful memory.

MEDICAL EMERGENCIES continued to give us an adrenaline rush every time they happened, and in the years that we spent in the Northwest Territories they came day and night, summer and winter. The exciting life in an isolated northern community more than fulfilled our expectations as Fort McPherson became our home and the Gwich'in people became our family.

2

BACK IN THE SIXTIES, northern Canada was opening up to mineral exploration, and oil companies from the south pushed seismic roads into areas that may have previously seen only a few trappers and hunters but certainly not the big drilling rigs that sprouted up suddenly and then just as quickly disappeared again. The roads abandoned by the exploration companies left only long, straight cuts through the tundra that turned in on themselves as the unprotected permafrost melted. As these incursions were made into this once isolated country, people in the south began to focus on the plight of the bands of Indians in the western Arctic and the Eskimo in the east. Tuberculosis and other diseases had ravaged these native residents, and the government wanted to improve health services.

Far away in England, Muriel and I were nearing the completion of our nurses' training, Muriel as a nurse-midwife, and me—one of the few males in the profession—in general nursing with an emphasis on surgery and the operating room. As the final exams came closer and we thought about our future together, we would put down our textbooks and turn to the professional journals to look at job postings in exotic parts of the world. A plan to go to Iran fell apart because of the political unrest there, and then the same thing happened when we thought of going to the Congo. The far north of North America had appealed to me since, as a young boy growing up in the Welsh mountains, my friends and I had built shelters and teepees. I had devoured adventure books from the mobile library at the school and over the years read everything I could about the early explorers of North America. I read and re-read books such as *The Young Fur Traders* and *Cache Lake Country* and pictured Canada as a land of rivers, lakes, trees, Indians, log cabins and backwoods trails from one ocean to the other. Thus, it seemed like a natural progression for me first and then Muriel to get excited when we read of nurses being urgently required in outposts to care for the Indians and Eskimo of Canada's north.

Before our exam results were in, we applied to the Canadian government for positions in Canada's north; we were interviewed and accepted, pending our successful completion of training, our marriage, and emigration to Canada. We both passed our exams, got married in May 1962 and set sail for Canada in September.

Five days on an ocean liner from Liverpool to Montreal, followed by three days on a train to Alberta, and a year of work in Edmonton gave us time to adjust to the country, obtain Canadian nursing registration, and travel the western provinces to acclimatize ourselves in general to our new home. After a year of working at the Charles Camsell Indian and Eskimo Hospital in Edmonton, Muriel and I felt that it was time to move on and explore the homeland of some of our patients, people who had picturesque names: "Mary Strikes-With-A-Gun" was from a reserve in Alberta, "Johnny W3594" was an Eskimo from the Barren Lands who only had a disc number for a surname. They and other patients described their land with a far-off look in their eyes as they told of travelling over the tundra, seeing large herds of caribou, or of living in canvas tents that could house whole families, or of journeying for days by dog team or riverboat. By comparison Edmonton seemed crowded and impersonal and we ached, like our patients, to see the north country.

We were interviewed in Edmonton for outpost nursing positions that might become available with the Northern Health Services of National Health and Welfare, and after some delay and a number of impatient inquiries, we were called to the Northern Health Services centre. Winifred Roscoe, the regional nursing supervisor, smiled at us and said that there were two openings available that would be suitable for a couple, and the choice was ours. "We don't want tourists," she said bluntly. "We want people who are dedicated." Muriel and I looked at each other and felt slightly guilty. After all, we were tourists of a kind but we were also prepared to dedicate ourselves to working in the north, and though it was not appropriate to admit at our job interview, we also intended to enjoy whatever experiences came our way.

One of the positions offered was located on the Alaska highway in the town of Watson Lake in the Yukon Territory; the other was in the Northwest Territories in a remote village on the Mackenzie Delta where about a thousand Loucheux Indians resided and lived off the land. Mrs. Roscoe explained to us that the Indian band there were Takudh-Kutchin or "People of the Slanting Eyes" which translates into "Loucheux" in French, the name by which they were known in the sixties and seventies. (In the 1980s, these people changed their name to "Gwich'in" rather than Kutchin in order to be phonetically correct.) My heart leapt as she described Fort McPherson and the people, and when I glanced over at a smiling Muriel, I knew what our choice would be.

"Look at this map," Mrs. Roscoe said, pointing to a large map of Canada on the wall of her office. "You see where the Yukon Territory takes a jog in the northeast? Well, Fort McPherson is about 50 miles (80 km) north of there on this long river, the Peel River, which goes into the Mackenzie River and then the Beaufort Sea."

We gazed at the map. "Where is Edmonton?" I asked. Mrs. Roscoe's finger traced downwards and then finally stopped. "Right here. They say it is about 1,700 miles (4,500 km) south, but don't worry—there is a hospital at Inuvik, just here." She paused and located a spot about 75 miles (120 km) north of Fort McPherson. "And someone from this office will try to be up to see you quite regularly." We sat down again, hardly able to contain ourselves.

"There are also a few Indians in the village who are not registered, that we call 'non-status.' They are usually the native children of a white man and an Indian woman because, if a registered Indian woman marries a non-Indian, she loses her status. It's not fair but that's how it is, and we look after their health anyway. There are also some non-Indian government workers, but most of the people are hunters and trappers, and the place is quite isolated. You will live at the nursing station there and you will also look after the people who live in another village about 40 miles (64 km) away. You will have to make local arrangements for travelling there and, you know, it could be quite exciting."

She looked at our excited faces knowingly and added, "And I think that you will both like it!"

"Are the living quarters furnished? Do we have to take our own household things? Is there a store?"

"Whoa! We will go over the things that are there, but maybe you should take your own linens and other household goods with you because I'm not exactly sure what there is for personal use."

We were excited as only naïve young people can be. We didn't even think of the great responsibility that we were undertaking and the people's lives that would be in our hands. Both of us were in our early twenties, but we were ready to take on the world!

We began our preparations to go north by shopping for long underwear during the blistering hot days of August. Shop clerks looked at us pityingly as we wiped our sweaty brows and assured them that, yes, we really did want winter weight "longies." Some Edmonton stores were quite used to shipping supplies north and did not bat an eyelid when we asked to have our purchases "crated up and shipped to Waterways for furtherance to Fort McPherson by Northern Transportation Co. Ltd. (NTCL) barge." We found out there was a local Canadian Broadcasting Company (CBC) radio station but it played mostly country music, so for days I recorded classical music on reel-to-reel tapes, thinking that tapes would travel better than the long play records that we were used to.

Meanwhile, we continued working at the Charles Camsell

Hospital, but now we were given opportunities to visit different departments and learn techniques and procedures that had not been included in our training in England. There was an afternoon with a dentist to learn how to give dental anaesthesia and how to best extract teeth; a talk with the hospital orthopaedic surgeon and an afternoon in the plaster cast room; a day with the X-ray technician who showed us the art of X-ray photography and developing films. The days passed quickly as we tried to absorb all of the medical information that was thrust at us, which seemed to be intended to make us instant experts! Then on top of everything else, we were given immunization boosters to help protect us from communicable diseases, and these gave us both high fevers. As we were recovering from our shots, we were called to the office to be measured for our uniforms. When we saw them, the greyish-blue colour reminded us of airline stewardesses or Esso gas station attendants. Oh well!

By mid-September we were as ready as we could be, and friends drove us to the Edmonton Industrial Airport, where they admitted to being more apprehensive about our future than either of us were. Our first plane ride ever was on a Pacific Western Airlines DC6B, a large propeller-driven plane, which took us from Edmonton Industrial Airport via Fort Smith, Yellowknife and Norman Wells to, finally, the gravel airstrip of Inuvik. It had taken nine hours to transport us from a busy metropolis in the south to an arctic town of 5,000 people, but here we were in Inuvik, which seemed as hot as Edmonton had been—until the sun went down. A very friendly nurse from the Inuvik Health Centre met us at the airport and drove us in an old Willys jeep the few miles along the dusty road into town where we were immediately struck by the cheerfulness of the multi-coloured houses. In response to our questions, Joy told us that she thought that all the pastel shades were designed to give some visual relief when everywhere else seemed black and white in the winter time. Another very obvious part of the landscape was the box-like structure that snaked along by the side of the road, sometimes branching off and going under the road, but because of the

The utilador system in Inuvik NWT. Because of the permafrost, all water and sewer services were carried in above-ground insulated tunnels.

permafrost the road had to go up over the structure, making a series of huge "speed bumps."

"*That* is the infamous utilador system," Joy said, pointing. "It's the umbilical cord of the community. Well, for most of the community. It carries water and heat to the government houses and the navy base, but it doesn't go to the native village at the far end of town. The water circulates continually to stop it freezing, and it carries power to the houses and then takes the sewage out. It's heated all of the time because of the permafrost." She pulled up in front of a large building and turned off the motor. "And this is where you will be staying tonight. I'll come and get you and take you to your plane tomorrow." We unloaded our travel bags, and after Joy had introduced us to our hosts, she said goodbye and drove off in a cloud of dust. A few mosquitoes flew around us, but they were nothing compared to what we would learn to live with during subsequent summers.

As there was no room in the nurses' residence or the hotel (the latter referred to locally as "the Zoo"), we had been invited to spend the night in the Anglican hostel, which was supervised by Mr. and Mrs. Holman. He was a large man with a very large moustache, but both he and his wife made us feel very welcome. We found that being dwarfed by him was not the only time that we were made to feel small in this Land of the Midnight Sun.

The next morning Joy picked us up at the hostel and gave us a whirlwind tour of the hospital and a quick introduction to some of the staff. We were asked if we would mind taking two babies with us to Fort McPherson because they were ready for discharge from the hospital and could only be sent on the plane with an adult. We bundled up the babies and then Joy rushed us down to the east branch of the Mackenzie River where a blue and white float plane was being loaded at the dock.

"That's Pacific Western Airlines, and that is how you will be going to Fort McPherson," Joy told us, helping us down to the dock with our bags and the two babies. Before we knew it, we were fastening our seat belts as more freight was pushed in between the two rows of seats.

We didn't see very much as we flew along in the noisy single-engined Otter as the babies needed feeding and fussing over. And then there we were! We caught a tantalizing glimpse of Fort McPherson as we flew overhead, but two large pieces of plywood—part of the freight for the village—and the two babies prevented us from totally viewing our new home from the tiny window. The pilot, Wray Douglas, landed the float-equipped plane very smoothly on the Peel River and soon it was tied up at a floating dock.

As soon as it was convenient, we passed the two babies out to Alex Forman, the local Scots entrepreneur who was the airline agent and owner of a small trading post. He passed the babies to one of the waiting white women on the dock who, in turn, passed each baby to one of the native women standing on the riverbank. When we emerged from the plane, we struggled up the bank towards the crowd of people who stood watching the unloading of the plane. We

Fort McPherson lies along the Peel River with the Richardson Mountains forming its western backdrop.

felt, rather than saw, that we were being critically eyed by the women, who wore multi-coloured scarves over their shining jet black hair. The men in their wool pants, checkered shirts and flat caps were also non-committal in their welcome, and we wondered what they were thinking as they saw this very young couple step off the plane—Muriel, at five feet three inches tall (160 cm) with her short auburn hair in a pixie cut, and me, five feet ten inches (177 cm) with short brown hair and a full beard. But whatever the people thought they kept to themselves.

However, when we were greeted by Lorraine Bode and Liz McCormick (the nurses we were replacing), they were more than enthusiastic. We were escorted up to the nursing station with lots of revelry and laughter, with one piece of conversation that kept on being repeated—they were just delighted that we had arrived before freeze-up because they would now get "outside." We soon learned that "going outside" or "coming in" had nothing to do with indoors or outdoors but referred to going or coming from that great civilization down south. We had just "come in" and Lorraine and Liz were primed to "go out." The two nurses were eager to show us the village and introduce us to some of the more influential people—the chief, the old people, other government people, the storekeepers and others, and we found it difficult to absorb all the names that they told us.

Then Liz asked, "By the way, how was your flight in with Pacific Western?"

Lorraine laughed before we could think of an answer. "D'you know what everyone calls good old PWA?—'Pray While Aloft' or 'Please Wait Awhile.' But they haven't let us down yet!" And then after a short pause she repeated, "Yet… and we don't want them to start now, do we, Liz?"

As we followed the two excited nurses along the river trail towards the village, we noticed that they both wore colourful beaded moccasins that came up over their ankles. The dark beaver trim accentuated the colour of the beads. We had seen native women with this same style of moccasin and soon found out that they were called Crowboots, perhaps because they originated in Old Crow in the Yukon. Most of the men wore their moccasins low cut, just like the natives down south, though a few of the older men wore a low style with a wrap-around moosehide upper, but while the ground was wet, everyone wore rubber overshoes commonly called "moccasin rubbers."

We passed some houses made of plywood, very simply built and designed with very little imagination. Next to these were several log houses that, to my way of thinking, had a lot more character because they fitted in with what I thought a northern house should look like. The smell of woodsmoke hung in the air and we could see it drifting up from a few metal chimneys.

My thoughts were interrupted by Liz. "I said, what do you think of your village?"

"Eh? Well, to be honest, we haven't seen very much of it yet. When we were coming in on the plane there was so much stuff on board neither of us could see through the windows!" Muriel explained about our trip in and added, "When we got up the first morning in Inuvik and looked out of the window, we wondered what sort of country we had come to because right outside the window there was this *huge* St. Bernard dog gnawing on a *huge* bone—from a moose, I think—and all around were those *huge* black ravens all making really strange sounds, sort of like an echo down a long pipe!"

Liz and Lorraine laughed and one of them said, "Hey, wait until you experience our mosquitoes. *Then* you'll know what big is!"

We were led through a gate in a low chain-link fence and down a wooden sidewalk to a beige-painted, shingled building roofed with the standard red shingles that all government buildings seemed to be blessed with. "Ta-daah!" Lorraine held her arm out toward it. "Welcome to the Fort McPherson nursing station!" There was evidence of grass in the yard, and a small area on the south side had been fenced with white pickets for a garden. At the far end of the property was an old building that Liz explained had housed a generator before the community had a power source, and there was also a large well-built shed where ice blocks were stored for the winter water supply. Two more buildings were located in the yard, one a storehouse for the year's supply of drugs and groceries and the other a Nissan hut—referred to as "the igloo"—where tools, old furniture, and miscellaneous junk were stored.

But Muriel and I focused our attention on the building that was to be our home for how long exactly we did not know, but we had committed ourselves for at least two years. As it turned out, it was to be ours for the next six years.

The staff door was the back door and it opened into the furnace room, so the first thing we saw in our new home was a huge blue furnace. Obviously the building was designed to be practical, not beautiful. The furnace room also housed the ice-melting tank, a heating oil storage tank, the staff bathroom, the X-ray darkroom and the clothes washer and dryer. There were also some big storage cupboards along one wall.

We toured the adjoining spacious kitchen, small dining room, living room and bedroom. All the staff rooms were furnished with an orange shade of Vilas maple furniture, staple furnishings that we found in every government house in the north. The walls were painted institutional green. Lorraine then took us down to the "business end" of the building that included the office, two small wards, each with two beds and infant cribs, a cubbyhole-sized examining room and even smaller waiting room. Then she said in an apologetic voice, "What you see is what you get!" It was true that the station was not much to look at by city standards, but we thought that it was quite adequate.

FORT McPHERSON WAS just how we had mentally pictured a northern community. When we arrived there on September 17, 1963, the trees, grasses and fireweed were still various shades of yellow, red and green. The evening sky above was deep blue, which lightened into an orange hue as it got closer to the western horizon, and our sitting room window, which faced the Richardson Mountains, was to show us many beautiful sunsets. As the nursing station was situated on a high riverbank to the north of the main community and close to the Hudson's Bay store, it had a wonderful view to the west where the distant mountains—with snow gleaming on their numerous peaks so that they looked like a row of shark's teeth—were a backdrop for a range of hills that appeared to cascade down to the Peel River, where the mood of the sky was reflected in the murky waters. It was not a picture book pretty place, but it had a hardiness that intrigued and enthralled us. So often we had read about beautiful places in books only to be disappointed when we saw them for ourselves later; this village offered isolation from the noise and pollution of the world outside and we were soon to find that our work was professionally challenging while life itself was physically challenging.

Finally it began to dawn on us that we two were, though barely into our twenties, the new recruits for the Fort McPherson nursing station, the only medical facility in a geographic area of thousands of square miles, and we were to be the only professional medical staff. The responsibility that we had assumed awed and excited us, but we had the confidence of the young. This was our new home!

When the rest of our boxes and bags finally arrived on the last float plane from Inuvik before freeze-up, the level of the river had dropped so much that there was not enough water by the dock for the plane to reach it, so Alex organized a local flat-bottomed boat called a scow to go out into the main channel of the Peel River to meet the plane. They had to unload the freight swiftly as both the pilot and the boatmen had to keep a wary eye on the plane's propeller, which had to be kept turning so the plane would not be swept by the current onto the sandbar or into the far bank of the river.

When Alex brought our baggage to the nursing station, he explained in his soft Scots brogue that "there was a black duffle bag that fell into the water. Have a look at it and see if you want to make a claim." Apparently the big canvas kit bag that contained my music tapes had been pitched out of the plane by a too-enthusiastic helper, been missed by the boatman, and landed in the river, where it was quickly retrieved, though not before it had a good soaking. Alex apologized for what had happened.

"Don't worry about it," I said as Muriel began to open the bag. "And by the way, thank you for bringing our stuff up to the house."

"All part of the service," he said with a grin, then turning to Liz he asked, "When are you girls leaving?"

"When's the last plane before freeze-up?" Liz asked.

"Saturday, the 28th, is what they are saying in Inuvik, but it depends on the weather." He looked up at the sky. "I don't think that you'll have any trouble. It's still warm."

"We want you to guarantee it," Liz joked.

"Okay, anything to get rid of you!" he laughed. "Well, I've got to go. Someone around here has got to work."

"Wait, Alex," Muriel called. "I've looked in the bag and its okay... Oh, and how appropriate!" she added as she lifted out the first and rather wet box. It was labelled *Handel's Water Music*. Some of the tapes were wet, but after we had carefully dried and played them, we found that the music was unspoiled and we were able to enjoy many hours of relaxing music in the coming months.

3

BEFORE LIZ AND LORRAINE "went out," they took us to see the chief of the Indian band, John Tetlichi. He was a big man and his tanned, lined face spoke of the many hours he spent braving the elements at his distant trapline at Road River. His handshake was firm and friendly, and he said he would invite us to his next council meeting to introduce us to the band councillors and we could tell them about ourselves. He took us into his log house where we met his wife, who seemed to be quite shy; she did not say very much but shook our hands in the way that most of the people did, with one shake.

We visited the two RCMP officers and had coffee with them at Corporal Jim Simpson's house, where we met Phyllis, his wife. Then on we went through the main part of the village, waving to some people and shaking hands with others, and we noticed that now people smiled and called greetings to us, quite a different attitude from when we first arrived on the plane. We paid a quick visit to the Peter Warren Dease school, where we met Otto Tucker, the principal, and his wife, Ruby, then over the road to the school hostel. By the time we had been introduced to Al Jackson, the hostel supervisor, our heads were spinning, and I thought that for a small community there were an incredible number of people whose names we would have to remember!

Then in spite of our protestations, Liz dragged us over to one of the government offices at the far end of the village. "You must meet this man because you will need him in many aspects of the work, and he has a lot of financial influence with the band." Ray Hunter was the Indian agent who gave out welfare to those who needed it and planned the housing and infrastructure for the Indians. He was broad-shouldered and had a barrel chest, but for all his size he had a pleasant smile. He was one of the few people who liked to visit the camps on the Peel by riverboat, a duty which the people appreciated. He pumped our hands enthusiastically and his firm grip confirmed his renowned strength.

We had not been back home for more than 15 minutes when William Firth, the nursing station janitor and handyman, came in. We had met him briefly the day we arrived, but now over coffee we were able to sit and talk to him, and it wasn't long before this coffee-time break became almost a ritual. William would come into the kitchen and pour himself some coffee, then taking off his base-ball cap and putting it with his gloves on the floor under his chair, he would run his fingers through his neat salt-and-pepper-coloured hair before lowering his slender frame to the chair with an audible sigh. He sometimes smiled behind his hand as people do who should wear false teeth but don't. (Later on, when he was comfortable with us, when he laughed at something, he would throw his head back and slap his knee, and then his head would come down so that his hand could go over his mouth again.) Because he was slightly deaf, we all spoke loudly, first to William, and then found that we spoke to each other the same way! He was already 65 years old when we met him but able to carry out all of his work without help and would have been quite insulted if I were to ask him if he could manage.

When we arrived in the village, he fussed around us, making sure that we were comfortable, and could not wait to tell us about everything and everyone in the village. He was not malicious. He just wanted us to know what everyone was like, especially any shady characters, so that we would be forewarned in some way. (He prob-ably translated back to the people just what *we* were like too, but we never got to hear that side of the story.) It would have been much harder to adapt to life in Fort McPherson had it not been for William taking upon himself our northern education.

WILLIAM FIRTH was an old "Bay man"—a Hudson's Bay Company employee who had come up through the ranks from store clerk at Lapierre House and Rampart House to post manager at the main Fort McPherson store after his father, Chief Factor John Firth, died. William had also worked at several other winter outpost stores along the coast and had travelled hundreds of miles by riverboat and dog team and on foot. As the history of the village intrigued both Muriel and me, whenever he came into the nursing station for coffee, I plied him with questions. One day when he came in, he handed me a large envelope containing pages of handwritten notes along with some

Our daughter, Helen, with her mother and William Firth, the nursing station's caretaker and Helen's "Jijii" (grandfather).

old photographs and some printed works by Richard Slobodin, an anthropologist. After reading all of this collection and discussing some of Dr. Slobodin's papers with other people, it became obvious that he had been revered by the old people because he had been interested in them and had visited them in their camps and lived amongst them for quite awhile.

The information was fascinating and helped us understand the great changes that the Gwich'in had already seen in their country, and how the coming of white men had been both a blessing and a curse. We learned that prior to the establishment of a fort and trading post there, the Gwich'in Indians had lived in the southern parts of the Richardson Mountains and wandered over a large area from the headwaters of the Peel and Blackwater rivers as far as the eastern part of Alaska. They went where the caribou went and migrated as the caribou migrated—north in springtime and south in the fall. They lived in skin tents, which were partially underground, and ate the fish and game that usually abounded in their territory.

Then in September 1826 Captain John Franklin's expedition discovered a tributary of the Mackenzie River, which he named the Peel River, in honour of Sir Robert Peel, secretary of state for Britain's Home Department. The Hudson's Bay Company moved quickly to exploit this new territory, and within a year the Council of the Northern Department of Rupert's Land had directed Peter Warren Dease, chief factor at Fort Good Hope, to look at the possibilities of establishing a post on this newly discovered river. Reports of hostile Indians in the area prevented further action until 1840, when John Bell, having found a large camp of Indians further up the Peel a year earlier, established a Hudson's Bay Company post on the Peel River. The Indians moved to the post to help with the construction, but as the location was later found to be on a flood plain, the fort had to be moved four miles downriver to its present site. "The Company," as the Hudson's Bay Company was usually called, had wanted to build on the higher ground on the west bank of the river, but the Indians said that they would be unable to see any approaching Eskimo war parties from there and convinced the Company to build on the east side. The new post was first called Peel's River House, a name still used in the Tetlit Gwich'in language, but it was later changed to its English form to honour Chief Factor Murdoch McPherson.

John Firth came to take charge of Fort McPherson in 1893 and stayed until his retirement in 1920, and there is no doubt that he was a figure of authority. Very early in his tenure at Fort McPherson, the Company became concerned with the advent of whaling ships on the coast because the captains and crews of the ships, while wintering in the ice, had begun to deal for furs with the natives in the area, thus threatening the Company's income. However, since all of the mail in the north was handled by the Company, Firth used this as a basis for negotiations with the whalers. "We will deliver your mail if you leave the furs to us," he told them. Mail was of sufficient importance that the whalers agreed. A report sent by Firth in May 1897 showed that, within a very short time after his negotiations, fur trading by the whalers was virtually non-existent:

On the 30th October 1896, I left this place [Fort McPherson] on a visit to the whalers at Herschel Island. It took us eight days to reach the coast at Shingle Point. At this place there was a little trading post that had been put up the year before by Captain James McKenna for the purpose of trading meat and fish for his two ships wintering at the island… There were thirteen ships wintering at the island, seven of which belonged to the Pacific Steam Whaling Company, two to Captain James McKenna and four were employed by Roth, Blum and Company of San Francisco.

There was also an old ship stranded on the beach that had been abandoned as unseaworthy. The P.S.W. Company have had a station on the island for the past five years. There were about 500 men at the island besides quite a number of natives who hang about the ships all winter. Within the last five years a number of Eskimo from the west have come to the island and are employed as deer hunters for the ships... 17 Lapierre House Indians arrived at the island while I was there. Each man had about 100 to 150 pounds of fresh meat for trade, besides some moccasins and mittens for which they were well paid by the quantity of stuff that I saw them carry off. So far as I could see, none of the captains gave any encouragement to the Indians to bring furs (except Nyuth). Of the thirteen ships at the island none had got more than two whales all summer, but two ships belonging to the P.S.W. Company that were wintering up east of Cape Bathurst got ten whales each, and as these ships had found good wintering there, it is thought that most of the larger ships will winter there in the future, but they will still have to come to the island for their supplies as usual. After staying at the ships for five days, I left on my way back, and in reaching Shingle Point, I found that all of the natives that I had seen there had left, and as I left the coast at this place, I saw no more of the whalers.

Born in Stromness in the Orkney Islands in 1853, John Firth had developed physical strength and a natural independence as he grew up. In 1871, when he was just eighteen years old, he set off for the new world. It took him a year to travel, first by ship, then by horse, ox-cart, dog team and finally on foot to reach his destination on the Peel River, where he was to learn his trade from the ground up. His first salary amounted to 22 pounds a year, but he worked hard and won the respect and confidence of his superiors. When he was 33, he married the half-Gwich'in daughter of his countryman, Alexander Stewart, and was sent to temporarily replace the manager at LaPierre's House; his salary was now raised to 32 pounds per year.

During a period as post manager at Rampart House, another incident occurred that displayed the character of this innovative and stalwart man. One day a powerful but disreputable Gwich'in chief by the name of Senatee came from Fort Rupert to Rampart House because there was a beautiful young girl there whom he thought to marry. Although he had been a strong chief and a renowned hunter, he was said to have more than 18 wives already and he had also been suspected of both murder and rape in the past.

The marriage custom of the time was simply for the marriage relationship to commence, so Senatee made his way to the girl's lodge. Now, even though he was getting on in years, he was not one to be easily crossed, but the girl's parents were not about to give up their daughter so easily, and to avoid the inevitable they simply refused to go to bed and stayed up all night. The next day they asked John Firth for help. A feast was organized for Chief Senatee and, being the honoured guest, he had to attend. While he was at the feast, the girl was hidden away. Later that night he returned to the lodge to take up from the previous night, only to find the girl missing. In a rage, he made preparations to follow her and bring her back, but John Firth intervened and pointed out that it was not appropriate for so great a chief to leave in such undignified haste and that a fitting farewell was to be organized. Senatee was impressed and agreed to wait, and John Firth made the preparations with as much delay as possible. After much food and many speeches, Senatee finally left the post to drum beats, a fusillade of shots and the yells of the population. As soon as he was safely out of sight, the girl was brought home again. Some time after this Senatee renounced his old lifestyle, much to the relief of the missionaries and very much to the relief of John Firth.

In 1893 John Firth was sent to Fort McPherson as chief factor, responsible to the Company for a huge territory that was noted for its highly valued furs. Although this post was not on the coast, the Eskimos could reach it via the Mackenzie and Peel rivers to trade, and at one time there were between 300 and 400 Eskimos camped on a sandbar below the post, and their large skin boats—called umiaks—and their kayaks filled the waters around it. The Eskimos were reported to be bigger than their eastern brothers, standing well over six feet tall and weighing over 200 pounds. They apparently looked quite formidable, and yet the Gwich'in disdained them, referring to them as "Huskies." In football games, using a bladder stuffed with moosehair and refereed by one of the Scots clerks from the

Company, the Gwich'in could run rings around the Eskimo. "Too fat," they said sarcastically.

The ongoing animosity caused John Firth a lot of worry. However, dealing with the unexpected was part of his life, and he learned to react quickly when circumstances warranted it. Once when he was trading with an Eskimo chief who was a well-known bully, the man became so domineering that Firth ordered him out of the house. Half an hour later, in response to a knock on his door, he unlatched it carefully, and the Eskimo chief attacked him with a long snow-knife. Firth slammed the door as the blow fell and the knife became buried four inches into the wood, then he quickly whisked the door open again, bringing the Eskimo headlong into the house to land on his face. Grabbing hold of the man, Firth ran him to the edge of the bluff overlooking the river and kicked him over it.

Expecting a reprisal, John Firth collected his men together and waited. Soon the whole Eskimo band, led by the chief, was seen climbing the bluff, but to everyone's surprise the chief laid down his weapons in front of Firth as a sign of peace, and Firth went out alone to meet him. The chief proceeded to tell Firth that he was now the strongest man in the land and that he loved him like a brother and had given the band instructions to go up to the post to trade. The whole affair blew over in gales of laughter and handshakes all round.

In 1920, fifty years after signing on as a servant of the Company in far-off Stromness, John Firth retired from the position as chief factor, having added trust and prestige to the Company to which he had dedicated his life. He is buried in the church cemetery in Fort McPherson, but his name lives on in his many descendants, and his strong characteristics have been passed on, too. William Firth carried on in the Company's service in the footsteps of his father; John's grandson, Walter Firth, was a Member of Parliament, representing the Northwest Territories for many years. More recently, the world class cross-country ski champions, Shirley and Sharon Firth, have shown that John Firth left a real legacy in the north.

THE FOLLOWING POEM, contained in a letter to John Firth, was written by Joe Hodgson, "The Mackenzie River Bard":

> These weaklings now who ape our places
> Hard would be to save their faces;
> Not one of them could eat dog traces,
> Or fill his guts on snowshoe laces.
> It stirs one's spleen to hear them talk
> And strut around: I can't say walk
> In well brushed suit and standing collar
> Though in their pockets not a dollar.
> When travelling round no snowshoe blisters
> The toes of these perfumed misters
> But each warmed clothed, well fed, doth loll
> Most dignified in carriole;
> A man ahead before his dogs
> And then, to carry all his togs,
> And grub and razors, portmanteau,
> And extra bedding not a few,
> A second sled brings up the rear,
> That he from want may well be clear.
> To tell of all the various foods
> I will not try: t'would do no good.
> A few I'll mention: fruit and jams,
> Much potted meats and potted hams,
> Currant cakes, and even custard,
> And sandwiches, done up with mustard.
> In your day, John, a slab of meat
> Was about all one got to eat,
> And sometimes when the food ran short,
> And men with packet left the Fort,
> To make grub run, they got a gun!
> But to such men t'was only fun.

These pygmies now would wear no smiles,
If marching thus three hundred miles.
(Joe Hodgson, circa 1890)

Our nursing station's handyman, William Firth, John's oldest son, had signed on as a "Company man" at an early age, but one year when the muskrat trapping had been so good that trappers had to bury some of the pelts in the permafrost until they could get around to stretching them, he took a year's furlough from the store and went trapping himself. Money was plentiful in Fort McPherson at that time and people gambled their houses, their schooners, their guns and—some even said—their wives at the throw of a dice. (Whenever William told us about the wives, he would throw back his head, slap his thigh and, covering his mouth with his hand, laugh as though this was the biggest joke.) William recounted how Tsell (Small) Remi of Arctic Red River had lost a brand new schooner on the throw of a dice even before the boat had been unloaded off the Hudson's Bay supply vessel *Distributor*. Then before the day was over he went on to lose his house and everything in it, but he just shrugged and said in his distinctive way, "Never mind, here, soon get 'nother one, here, that one house he was getting too old, see, here!" When we met Tsell in the mid-1960s, he was no richer and no poorer than any of his neighbors, and he still spoke in this unique style.

After William's furlough as a trapper, he realized that some of the Company's dealings he had seen and heard of were very one-sided and always to the Company's benefit. When an Indian who was not used to bartering and haggling over fur prices came to the store and asked how much a new rifle was worth, the manager would indicate that when he had piled mink furs one on top of the other until they reached the height of the gun the gun could be his. According to William, many guns were sold this way, and with mink pelts selling for such a high price, each of those guns was sold for what today would be a small fortune. He also told us that when chewing tobacco was first introduced into the country, the Gwich'in were not familiar with it, so the store manager instructed his assistants to give out a plug of it with every order of winter rations. The Indians were instructed in its use and came to like the taste of it. Very soon most of the Indians couldn't do without it, but the next fall when the hunters and trappers came to collect their winter grubstake, there were no plugs of tobacco included. When they inquired where it was, they were told that this year the tobacco was going to be added to their credit and they could pay for it with furs, just as they did for their other necessities.

However, the Company also had its good points, and William told us that he was frequently called upon at all hours to provide the services of banker, lawyer, doctor or undertaker, and that this was expected of him by both employer and customer. And he was

Tsell (Small) Remi of Arctic Red River.

quick to point out that the Company had always tried to care for the health of the people. This was long before the days of refined medicines and antibiotics, but they kept a record of all the sick people seen, their symptoms and diagnoses, the treatment given and the outcome of the case, if known. On one of our visits to the house of the Bay manager, George Seaton, we were given the opportunity to look at one of the old records, which showed the severe limitations of the managers in both diagnosis and treatment of disease. A six-month-old infant was brought to the manager's house with all of the symptoms of what we would now know to be meningitis. The manager decided that, because the baby was arching its back and appeared to be straining, it must be severely constipated. When the child died after all attempts to relieve it had failed, constipation was given as the cause of death. (We were soon to be reminded of this incident, which made us wonder how much progress had really been made in our modern world.)

After his brief period of freedom from the Bay, William decided not to go back and instead did any work that came his way in order to earn enough money to live on between trapping seasons. When the federal government decided to put a nursing station in the village, he helped to assemble the prefabricated building and afterwards got the job of full-time janitor and handyman. The nursing station became his personal responsibility, his baby, and he did everything that had to be done weekdays, weekends, and holidays—it was all the same to him. Stocking supplies, maintaining the buildings, painting, gardening—he did all these, sometimes with my help, but more often than not on his own. And after freeze-up when the ice was thick enough, he looked after cutting ice blocks down on the river then hauled them up from the river by dog team and stacked them in the icehouse or in the yard adjacent to a large water tank that was located under the utility room. Every day he would throw about two dozen of these 30-pound (13.6 kg) blocks of ice into the tank where they were melted down by two big electric immersion heaters. This provided us with our water supply.

WE WERE JUST STARTING our journey towards understanding
the Gwich'in people when an incident occurred that showed us how
difficulties could arise because of the differences in communication
between two cultures. Then we had to rely on our own resources and
training.

Old Fred Brown and his wife had moved to their winter trapping cabin just before the ice started running on the river. With them
went their son and his wife and child. They had loaded their riverboat with a quantity of food, dogs and toboggans, clothes, fishing
gear, gas, a new wood stove, and what seemed like an endless supply
of other necessities for life out in the bush. Then they pushed the
boat out into the Peel River, and with only a few inches of freeboard
it moved slowly downriver with the current. A small 3.5 horsepower
outboard motor—referred to as a "kicker"—kept the boat headed
in the right direction and helped the crew manoeuvre around the
sandbars that lurk just below the surface of the river, ready to mire
any boat with an unwary skipper.

On journeys like this there never seemed to be any hurry, and
if the people did not arrive at camp that night, they would simply
make camp at some convenient spot, and then carry on the next
day or the next or whenever they felt like it. If they were fortunate
enough to shoot a moose on the way, they might stay camped by
the river for a week. This freedom made us quite envious when we

compared it to our lifestyle, where we consulted a watch to see if we were hungry or to see if it was time to go to bed. But if we had had any doubts about the physical strength and resourcefulness of the Gwich'in people at the beginning, it was soon to be dispelled, and time after time we were reminded of the difficult living conditions under which they lived without complaint.

The Browns' trip took them about eight miles (12.8 km) down the Peel River, then west on the Husky River. The cabin to which they were heading was not too far down the Husky, but by the time they arrived, their boat was pushing through the thin ice that was forming on the sluggishly moving water. So it was with some relief that Fred Brown unloaded the boat that evening, and with everyone helping, they soon had everything put away in the rapidly warming cabin.

One evening five days after the Browns left Fort McPherson, our clinic being finished, we had eaten supper, washed the dishes and put them away, and Muriel and I were relaxing in the comfortable chairs in the nursing station, reading as usual, when the inevitable ring of the doorbell roused us. Reluctantly putting my book down, I walked to the clinic entrance and opened the door. To my surprise, Fred stood outside indicating that he wanted to come in, which in itself was unusual because he rarely came to the station even during regular clinic hours.

"That baby is sick. You should send a plane," he said bluntly.

"Why? We can't just send a plane at freeze-up without knowing what is wrong with the baby." I felt a little irritated by his attitude. "What's wrong with him?"

"It's like he can't go out." Gwich'in people had a very polite way of describing the body's elimination functions. When they described a bowel movement, they said that they "went out with food" and described urination as "going out with water."

"Why can't he go out?" I did not feel as though I was asking the right questions, and I did not know where Fred was trying to lead me.

"He can't go out with food."

"Oh, I see, he's constipated!"

"Yes."

I asked the usual questions about regularity and diet, but Fred was very vague, probably because he was the grandfather and would not normally be associated with child-rearing activities. "It's like he can't go out but he's straining real hard," Fred persisted, and I could feel the communication block between us. I was not happy about my conclusion that the baby was severely constipated because the Brown family would have known if it was only constipation, and when I asked Fred how he had come into town, his answer only added to my doubts about the diagnosis.

"The Husky channel was frozen over," he said, "and I couldn't break through with the scow so I carried my canoe to the Peel and then paddled and jumped from ice to ice and landed way down the Peel because of the current, and then I just walked up through the bush." He made it sound as though it had been a stroll through the park, but it could have easily cost him his life if the canoe had been holed when a pan of ice had crashed into it. And since the Gwich'in people never wore life jackets, if he had fallen into the river, he would soon have died in the icy cold water. I was sure that he would not have made this journey for a slight problem like constipation, but although he was a bit agitated, he could not give me any more information.

Muriel and I sat down and listed all the facts. "I hate to call Wayne [Dr. Wayne Wright of the Inuvik General Hospital] with such a thing," I said, "but I think it will be the best, and we'll let him worry about it." Whether or not Wayne would worry, I knew that whatever happened we would still worry, but then at least it would be a worry shared. I told Fred to wait while I contacted the doctor in Inuvik.

I spoke to Wayne on the radio phone at the RCMP office and gave him the small amount of medical information I had, emphasizing the fact that this particular man would not have come to us unless it was really urgent. Wayne asked me if the symptoms could be meningitis, and I told him that we had wondered the same thing after hearing Fred describe the way the baby arched his back when "straining to go out." As it was already dark, Wayne said that there was nothing that any of us could do until daylight and this would give him time to think more on it. I relayed the gist of my conversation to Fred, whom I had left waiting patiently drinking coffee with William Firth, who had wandered in to see what was happening. Fred said that he would come back in the morning.

Shortly after daylight Wayne radioed to say that Freddy Carmichael of Reindeer Air Services knew the area where Fred's cabin was and would fly him to the spot later that morning. He said that they might be able to land on a frozen sandbar close by. Again Fred joined us and we all sat around drinking coffee and waiting. Almost two hours later, we heard Freddy's plane zoom over the village and we went to the window to see him land. The RCMP truck was down at the strip by the time he had set the plane down, and we knew that they would bring the doctor, the baby and whoever else straight to the clinic.

Doctor Wayne Wright entered the nursing station, brushed the snow off his mukluks and shook hands with us. But just as he started to talk, we heard the plane take off again and we looked inquiringly at him. "Freddy is going back to the Husky," he said. "The sandbar was too small for the plane to land with two of us on board, and he said that he didn't want to take a chance at landing and then have to leave me there. Besides," he added, turning to Fred, "there was a message written in the snow for us. I'm sorry to say that the baby is dead."

Fred did not say anything at first, then as we digested this unwelcome information, he picked up his hat and gloves and walked to the door. "I'll be down at the house. Maybe I'll come back when the plane gets back." William Firth also got up and went out, indicating quietly to us that he would accompany Fred, for which we were thankful, being at a loss what to say to this old man.

We fed Wayne a late breakfast, and as he ate and we drank yet more coffee, we discussed what might have happened to the baby. Wayne's conclusion was that the baby had meningitis or had succumbed to some other massive infection.

The plane returned to Fort McPherson before Wayne had finished eating, and once again we waited for the RCMP to bring the pilot and the small body up to the nursing station. This time it was Constable Frank Dunne who walked in carrying the small bundle wrapped in a blanket. Behind him came Freddy Carmichael. While Muriel gave Freddy a cup of coffee, Frank took the baby to the clinic for Wayne to make a cursory examination and prepare an official report for the police files. Frank, Wayne and I gathered around the pathetic bundle on the examining table. I removed the baby's clothing, and then Wayne made a physical examination. The baby looked quite normal. There were no marks on him and he was well-nourished. Our files indicated that he had just started his immunizations a few weeks earlier and that there had been no reaction to the vaccine.

Wayne stood back and looked at Frank. "I'll have to do an autopsy before I can give you any official report. I think I'll do it here though because with the river freezing up, if we take the infant to Inuvik, it might be some time before we can get him back here for burial." He turned to the sink and started scrubbing his hands while I wrapped the baby up again, and Frank made a few entries in his notebook. Each one of us had been affected by this small bundle that now lay lifeless in front of us, and it was easier for us to keep our words to a minimum, rather than let our emotions show.

As soon as we had everything together, Wayne carried out the autopsy and collected tissue samples to send to the pathology laboratory in Edmonton. We dressed the body in some new clothes that had been brought by unseen hands and left in the waiting room. William Firth already had some men working on a tiny coffin but it would not be ready until the following day.

Then Freddy came to tell Wayne that they would have to start back to Inuvik before it got much later, and within minutes they were putting on their parkas and waving goodbye to us. Frank took them down to the plane in his truck, and we stood on the riverbank and watched as the plane started up, went to the end of the runway, turned in a cloud of snow, and with a roar of the engine leapt forward, the skis skimming a few feet over the moving ice. Then the plane gained altitude and headed off into the late afternoon sky.

Muriel and I were left feeling tired and disturbed by the events of the day. Our books still lay upturned by the chairs that we had vacated when the doorbell rang the night before, and we did not feel like picking them up again just yet. We wondered about the parents, still down on the Husky River, and worried about how they were faring. William told us that the river would probably freeze over during the night and could be safely crossed shortly after that if the cold weather continued. True to his prediction, it was frozen over by the next morning, and by noon the following day we heard that someone had already crossed it. Arrangements were made to hold the funeral as soon as the parents reached town. Our last job was to place the baby in his coffin and send him with his grieving relatives to the little white church to await burial.

Weeks later we received notification from an Edmonton pathologist that, although the tests were inconclusive, they and the report from Wayne's examination indicated that the baby had died from meningitis. Although Fred Brown had been unable to communicate the problem to us, it was his bravery and commitment that had alerted us to the possible seriousness of the baby's illness. The parents told us that their child had died shortly after Fred had left the camp, and certainly before he had arrived at the nursing station. But this information was cold comfort to us and to the parents who had lost such a beautiful son.

5

PEOPLE GO NORTH FOR a variety of reasons; some stay for a lifetime while others can't wait to leave at the end of whatever term they have signed on for. The north tends to be either loved or hated with equal passion. In a study done for National Health and Welfare in the late 1950s, Dr. J.S. Willis was cited as saying that people go north "because they are young, enterprising and need the money." The description was certainly true for the hundred or so years that the "Honorable Company of Gentlemen Trading into Hudson's Bay" was recruiting young men from the north of Scotland. They lured them with the offer of adventure and what seemed like good money compared to the work and wages available in Scotland at the time. Most of them seemed happy with what their adopted country offered them and many stayed to raise families—some official and some less so.

Dr. Willis also wrote that some who go north are "people with a greater or lesser degree of missionary spirit" and that they are "people who are impressed by the need of the Northerners for religion, health, economic assistance, housing, education, etc. They like the challenge." There are "those who see in the north a place to escape... having failed to reach their objectives in the south." Then there are "visitors... who will tell you how much they would like to be able to spend more time in the north... whilst some of them will be thanking God in their hearts that they do not have to visit too often!"

Keith, all iced up after making home visits on a cold day.

For Muriel and me, going north gave us an opportunity to practice our skills in an isolated and adventurous location. We were young, idealistic and needed the money; we were impressed by the (apparent) need of northerners for health care, and we liked the challenge. Perhaps Dr. Willis had seen us on the horizon!

There were many things we had to adjust to, and most of these seemed to be at the social level. In the north the non-native people were hospitable and visited back and forth for a cup of tea or coffee at any time during the day or night, but as a recently married couple, we were still learning how to entertain. In addition, as recent European immigrants (and tea drinkers), we still had to learn how to make a good cup of coffee and cook a steak. We discovered that we still had a long way to go when after giving a visitor a cup of coffee, which he seemed to enjoy, he thanked us for the nice cup of tea!

Television was unknown in Fort McPherson and there was no phone service, but we could receive the radio station signals from

CHAK Inuvik. The government had supplied us with a "Hallicrafter World" radio but, apart from CHAK, reception was poor, even from Alaska. And whenever the Bay or the RCMP used their single side-band radios, a harsh, garbled noise that we were unable to decipher would break into our reception. We would sometimes listen carefully to see if we could make out anything but it was impossible, and one of the policemen told me that was why they used that system!

We had an eclectic supply of books on hand, and after we had read them all, they were circulated around to others, and every time we visited other people in the village, we invariably came back with a new supply of books or magazines. Periodically during the winter the school would have a movie sent in, and we would all gather there to watch whatever was showing, socializing when the large film reels had to be changed or, as frequently happened, the film had to be spliced after a sudden break. The classroom would become almost unbearably hot with the crowd of people, all dressed for the cold weather, pressed together. When it was over and we would stream outdoors, the cold seemed to bite right into us, though by the time we reached home we had adjusted again and were thankful for the warm winter clothes.

Outdoor activities were not hampered by the cold, and we tried cross-country skiing but, not having the right equipment, we soon gave that up and looked for more local and traditional sports. We had tobogganing parties on bright moonlight nights when a group of us "transients" would get together for coffee and snacks. One night someone suggested that we have a major sled run down the steep 50-foot (15.5 m) bank in front of the nursing station, so I got Williams' dogsled and we packed eight people on it like sardines and I stood on the back, holding onto the backrest. It took a lot of shouting, wiggling, and pushing but finally the sled took off over the bank. We were all blinded by the flying snow, and as the sled took a sudden turn, everyone was thrown out into the cold powder snow. Back in the nursing station we emptied snow out of pockets and shirts, and the noise was incredible as the sledders shrieked when the snow melted and ran down hot skin, and bystanders yelled as the snow from discarded clothes was flung over them. In spite of the mayhem the run was declared successful but by popular vote it was decided we would not have a repeat! This sort of winter recreation was not practised by the Gwich'in, who probably thought that white people were a little strange playing in the snow like children! But for us it provided some relief from our responsibilities, and it was good for our souls to let our hair down in this way.

It was several weeks after arriving in Fort McPherson that we started getting social visits from the native people. They would come, the men singly, the women usually in twos, and knock on the door and say quietly, "We've come to visit," then be quite happy to sit quietly and sip hot tea. Even if the temperature inside the house was 70 degrees F (20 C), they seldom removed their parkas. They would make a few observations but never seemed to feel the need to fill silences with a lot of pointless chatter as we did. We would ask about the beautiful Mother Hubbard parkas that the women wore or the wolverine trim on both men's and women's parkas. We would ask about the weather, dog team travel, anything, if it would fill the void of quietness. Our visitors would nod or say, "Aha, aha," and maybe giggle at each other as they sipped the hot tea, and then after about half an hour they would get up, thank us for the drink and visit and leave. We were left wondering if they had come for something specific, and it was only later that we came to realize that people would call in "to visit" and not necessarily to talk!

6

THE UNIFORMS THAT WE had been measured for during our orientation down south arrived in a huge parcel from Edmonton. We opened it with some trepidation and found that they would be of some use and we would just have to ignore the colour! Muriel modeled a skirt and blouse and a couple of pairs of slacks and she looked quite smart. The hat she was issued was similar to a Canadian forces wedge hat and not at all practical for the north. It could only have been worn in the warm south or on a very official occasion.

My share of the package included a couple of pairs of slacks, some white shirts and a pair of ski-pants, all of which I found practical, but my hat was exactly the same as Muriel's! "I don't really expect that they will want me to wear this!" I said, donning it and pirouetting around. "If you do, I'll pretend I don't know you!" Muriel said, laughing. "Now take it off before someone sees you!"

Parkas were necessary items of clothing, and we thought that it would be wise to have ours made in Fort McPherson in the fashion and style worn by other people in the village. William told us that his wife, Mary, could make them for us and, if we wanted, he would ask her to come to the nursing station later in the day. That afternoon as we were having a coffee break, there was a tap on the door and Mary Firth came into the kitchen. She seemed very shy and spoke in a soft voice. "William said that you wanted to see me." She didn't say that she had come about the parkas; maybe she

Muriel in her official uniform—minus the wedge hat—in the nursing station clinic.

thought that would be presumptuous. We invited her to come in and drink tea first. She answered our questions about the parkas, smiling quietly at our ignorance, and when she laughed, she covered her mouth just like her husband William did when he laughed! Like all of the women and girls in Fort McPherson, she wore a silk head scarf which kept slipping down her black hair and she would keep self-consciously hitching it back up again, but never took it off as I would have done.

Mary wore a "Mother Hubbard" style of parka that had a flowered print shell over Grenfell cloth. It was calf-length and had narrow strips of different coloured material sewn in a band all around the bottom. Around the hood there was a ruff of wolverine fur and attached behind this was a thin strip of wolf fur that stood up and framed her face like a halo when she pulled up the hood. She asked Muriel if she would like a "parkie" like hers or one like the one she was going to make me, a pullover three-quarter-length coat with wolverine trim on the hood and the bottom. Muriel really wanted a Mother Hubbard parka but decided that for her work it would be better to have one like mine. Mary made it sound as though making a couple of "parkies" was just a minor job and she said that she could have them ready for us in a couple of days if we would buy the material at the Bay right away.

After Mary had quietly whisked herself away and William came back in, we asked if he would select a wolverine skin for us from either Alex Forman's store or the Bay, and then we went up to the store and bought the measured amount of duffle and waterproof Grenfell cloth that Mary had recommended. That evening when she called around to see us, she laid the material out on the floor, then as we stood in front of her, she pulled out a big pair of scissors and with quick periodic glances up at us commenced to cut out the pattern of the parka. "You don't use any measurements?" Muriel asked, trying not to show any concern as Mary rapidly cut the material. "No, no need," she answered, putting one set of cut material aside and starting to cut out the next. "I've got enough bits at home for the Delta trim."

"What's Delta trim, Mary?" Muriel asked. As a seamstress herself, Muriel knew all the sewing and material terms, where they were a mystery to me. "That's this," she said, pointing to the multicoloured trim around the bottom of her parka. "Everyone in the Delta does this. We can usually tell who made it and where it comes from. People do it different." She folded the cut-out material, tucked it under her arm and headed for the door. "Thank you, I'll see you tomorrow." The native people who visited, who brought us things, or did something for us, were always so polite and thanked us, and Mary was typical of this attitude. It seemed backwards to us; we should be the ones to say "thank you" and I could not help thinking that the world would be a better place if people adopted this polite custom.

True to her word, Mary was back late the next day, carrying the two new parkas. The navy blue covers had a two-inch-wide Delta trim of red, blue and yellow and a hood trim of wolverine fur, which had been cut so that the light-coloured fur from the diamond pattern on the animals' back was centred in the middle of the hood and the legs and claws hung down on the chest. Mary had made them so that they were pulled over the head because they were warmer, and when we tried them on, they fitted us perfectly and we were delighted with them. The only problem that affected us both was the static electricity in the fur that made our hair stand up when we took the parkas off! A few months later we had zippers put in to make it easier for us to remove the parkas when we were called out to an emergency or when we went to visit someone and we didn't want to look as though we'd been caught in a wind storm.

We asked Mary how much she charged for making the parkas and, even though she probably knew exactly what her time and skills were worth, she told us to pay her what *we* thought they were worth. This was a new way of bargaining for us, but Muriel and I estimated the hours that she would have worked—and late into the night too—and settled on a price. When we told Mary what we thought her work was worth, she exclaimed that it was too much, but after

Muriel and Helen, wearing traditional Mother Hubbard parkas, enjoy a new litter of pups.

another cup of tea and a little pressure she accepted the cheque and seemed quite pleased. We could hardly wait for an excuse to go outside in our new northern parkas and headed down to the river at the first available moment, but by the time we had been outside for 20 minutes we were both perspiring and wishing for colder weather.

Not everyone in Fort McPherson wore the very fashionable Northern-style parkas. One lady wore a large man's wool jacket and tied a leather belt around the waist. Roy Wright always wore a tattered old parka with ripped pockets and oil stains on it, but it suited the type of work that he did. He had come north when the Hudson's Bay supply boat *Distributor* was in need of great quantities of cord wood for its hungry wood-burning steam engine. He had stayed on in Fort McPherson and now kept the village's motors and engines working and the roads open in wintertime. We could tell if he was walking down the road because he always seemed to have his overshoes on, the sort that came up past the ankles and fastened with metal clips—except that Roy never fastened the clips and as he walked they jangled just like John Wayne's spurs in western movies.

Like his parka, Roy's truck and Caterpillar tractors had seen better days—they had been hammered, welded, and bolted together numerous times—but they worked well and could be relied on. His Cat no longer had a canopy on it to protect him from the elements, and after a heavy snowfall when the temperature had plummeted, you could count on Roy—his hood pulled up over his peaked cap—to be out clearing the road. I don't think that he could see much further than the blade on his Cat, though glasses would not have helped him in the cold weather, so I often wondered how he managed to clear the roads so close to the wooden sidewalks without taking them and the power poles out with the blade.

Always busy, one of Roy's sidelines consisted of taking his Cat and a stoneboat—a heavy sled on skis—into the frozen bush to get dry firewood to sell to the villagers. On one of these forays he was crossing a frozen lake to a particularly good stand of dry spruce when about halfway across the Cat suddenly broke through the ice,

55

sinking to the bottom of the lake with Roy still sitting at the controls. After what seemed like an eternity to Roy but was probably only a few seconds, he looked up through the waters and saw the hole just a few feet above him. Freeing himself from the encumbrances of the Cat, he kicked upwards with all his might and clung to the edge of the ice. Then with a Herculean effort he crawled out of the water onto the firm ice, threw off his soaked parka and ran squelching back to a cabin that was about fifteen minutes' run away. By the time he reached the cabin, ice had stiffened his wool overpants and he was shivering uncontrollably. Fortunately, there was someone there when Roy burst in, and after the startled occupants had overcome their initial shock at the intrusion, they opened the stove vent, and as the stove began to roar, they helped Roy out of his saturated clothes. Hardly a word passed between them until Roy was sitting by the stove wrapped in a sleeping robe and grasping a hot mug of tea. He wasn't sure what had happened as the ice should have been strong enough, but it wasn't long before he was telling anyone who would listen about his adventure and eliciting their help to raise the Cat out of the lake.

We were never sure how true this story was and how much had been added before we heard it, but if it did happen, you can be sure that Roy raised his machine, stripped it down and—no doubt with grunts and curses—rebuilt it. I do know that the Cat he was driving when we knew him certainly looked as though it had been on the bottom of a lake!

7

THE BASIC SUPPLIES that Fort McPherson was going to need for a year were brought in by the Northern Transportation Company's barges during the short summer and then tractors, trucks, wheelbarrows and broad shoulders moved vast quantities of supplies to the various warehouses and storage rooms in the community. As we surveyed the boxes and cartons of food that were stacked in the nursing station warehouse, we saw that the food supplies ordered by Liz and Lorraine included items that they obviously enjoyed themselves, but the olives and pickles were something that we rarely if ever ate. I had never eaten canned lobster pieces either and, after mentioning this to one of the RCMP members, we unloaded about eight cases in his

A year's supply of goods arrives on the barge *Pelican Rapids*.

direction. Then one day I happened to open a can by mistake, tasted it, and found that lobster was sublime! Fortunately, we still had quite a few cases left, but Muriel never did get to like it.

Although we were a newly married couple who had lived most of the time in hospital residences where meals were provided, we were suddenly confronted with the next year's grocery shopping list that was to supply both us and an estimated one and a half in-patients per month with grocery, dry goods and pharmaceutical supplies for a whole year. When we sat down to make up the grocery list for the upcoming year, Muriel sensibly listed the nutritious items that we should be eating, while as I looked through the government catalogue, all I could see were the soft drinks, candy and desserts that were available. Then as we read and reread the instructions, we realized that we were not allowed unlimited amounts of food. We had to deduct the amounts that were already on hand in the warehouse and, as things were grouped together into classifications, we saw that in the vegetable class we might be stuck with only tinned green beans

George Seaton, the Hudson's Bay manager, and Les Wilderspin, Indian agent, oversee supplies being off-loaded from the barge *Pelican Rapids*.

The nursing station storeroom with an 18-month supply of foodstuffs on its shelves.

for half of the year. However, the hospital in Inuvik had fresh food flown in monthly from the south, and then if a chartered plane was going to one of the villages, they would send the nursing stations small amounts of fresh produce. It would last for a few weeks and we counted ourselves very fortunate to get it.

When we ordered drugs and medical supplies, we were inclined to order items that we were familiar with, but we also knew that a government pharmacist would review the order and, as he knew what sort of medications the doctors would be requesting, he would add or delete as he saw fit. Narcotics had to have a doctor's order, and when they arrived the RCMP were requested to visit us and we sat for hours counting and recording every vial and tablet in the narcotic register.

The nursing station warehouse was soon full of both food and enough medical supplies to last for over a year. Every week William

Firth went to the warehouse and turned the crates of eggs over. When we received them they were "fresh"—that is, only a few weeks old. We were still eating eggs from that supply several months later, and before using one we would always break it into a cup to see if it was green. If either the smell or the colour was not too strong, we would cook and eat it.

One old-timer decided he would have a go at raising his own chickens and have a reasonable supply of fresh eggs all year, so one summer he ordered some chicks from Edmonton, and they were flown in. He put his days-old chicks into a well-insulated shed and fed and watered them carefully. As the year progressed, he put a light bulb into the shed to provide light but later, after exchanging the light bulb for a heat lamp, it was decided that with the extreme cold temperatures expected in the months ahead, the chickens required a kerosene stove if they were to do anything productive. They grew well in this comfortable environment and eventually it came time for them to lay eggs. Everyone was as anxious and as excited as expectant fathers with this unique project and never failed to keep track of their progress.

Then one night when the mercury was hovering at 20 below F (-28 C) and not many people were venturing out, the raucous sound of the fire siren pierced the after-supper peace of the village. Fire in the north was a devastating experience, especially during the bitterly cold winters, and the usual procedure when the siren sounded was for everyone to grab a couple of fire extinguishers and run to the fire so that as much help as possible would be available. But the activity the siren aroused sometimes had a touch of the Keystone Cops in it because Fort McPherson did not have a fire truck, so the water delivery truck was used in the capacity of a pumper-truck. The problem was that even if it arrived at the scene of the fire, it was doubtful that the two-stroke pump could be started in the very cold weather.

When the siren sounded on this occasion, the volunteer firemen were ready for anything because they had made a few practice runs in the fall. They converged on the garage that housed the truck, climbed aboard and started the engine, then the driver confidently pulled out of the equipment yard and swung the heavy truck around the corner onto the main road. However, in his eagerness he stamped too hard on the gas and the truck spun around and then settled into the deep snow in the ditch. It took nearly two hours to pull the truck out of the ditch, and this was only accomplished after emptying all the water out of the truck!

We had run out of the house after pulling on our winter parkas and grabbing the essential fire extinguishers. No sign of a fire anywhere, but a lot of people were heading up the road so we followed them like sheep, running whenever we had enough breath and feeling the cold stab at our throats and lungs every time we exerted ourselves. A hundred yards down the road we met another group of people heading our way.

"Is the fire out?" we asked breathlessly.

"We don't know! It's down your end of the village!" We turned to look toward the north end of the village from where we had just come, but we could not see anything indicative of fire or smoke other than what was coming out of the house chimneys. But as the group we met seemed adamant that the fire must be at our end of the village, we turned, and with them, raced back up the road. By the time we reached our gate again, my lungs were misbehaving in an alarming manner, and I was gurgling and wheezing like an old steam train.

"Mind you don't freeze your lungs!" someone called out.

A bit late, I thought but I told Muriel I had had enough and she came back to the nursing station with me.

An hour or so later William Firth came by to make sure things were settled before he went to bed, and as I had recovered from my coughing fit by then, I was anxious to hear what the cause of the alarm had been.

"Oh, that!" William said. "That was way up at the other end of town. That chicken house burned down. The chickens are all roasted!"

Never before, and probably never since, had a small flock of chickens been the concern of so many people. Most of the villagers had been milling around, looking for a fire to extinguish and help whoever was in distress. The next morning when we came to the kitchen for a coffee break, there was a neat package on the table addressed to us. We opened it and found inside a plucked and cleaned chicken, very slightly singed, and ready to cook. It seemed a little incongruous to be living in a village where people survived on caribou meat that the first gift of fresh meat we received was chicken, and even more incongruous for us to then roast it after having tried to save it from just such a fate. The chicken episode amused everyone in the village, and even the owner saw the funny side when, instead of going outside in the cold to feed them, he sat in the warmth while they fed him!

A FEW MONTHS BEFORE our arrival in Fort McPherson, the Hudson's Bay Company had a new store built there because the old store had outgrown the burgeoning population. The manager had been getting the new store ready for a grand opening and the bright new shelves were almost filled with supplies. Then one night the wail of the village siren alerted everyone to a fire, and its location was spotted easily because the flames were already shooting high into the air. The old store was on fire and in a very few minutes the roof had caved in amidst a shower of sparks. The old dry logs burned fast and by morning only the tall chimney was left standing like a lonely sentinel in the smouldering embers.

For years, smoke rising from this chimney would have been the first sight of the village that weary travellers saw, whether coming from LaPierre House up in the mountains or from Aklavik or Tuktoyaktuk down on the coast. The welcoming sign would have beckoned men, women and excited children to come and explore the store's interior where they could trade for much-sought-after merchandise. Although we never got to see it, we were told that it was a typical HBC store and had character etched into it. For generations men had stood around the old pot-bellied stove to discuss the price of fur or the location of the caribou herds, or they had just listened and stared while they smoked their white clay pipes. Furs had hung in bundles at the back of the store; bolts of duffle and Grenfell cloth and brightly coloured material had sat side by side with rifles, traps and snowshoes; and every inch of the walls was covered with something that was for sale. Now it was gone.

The new store was large, with big windows and plenty of counter space, but there was no longer a wood stove to gather around and, according to the old men who used to gather at the store, it now seemed sterile and inhospitable. The staff remained the same, but, even though they enjoyed the new working space, they knew that a small piece of history had slipped from view and into memory.

IT IS SAID THAT FIRE is a good servant but a terrible master, and nowhere was this more true than in the north where fire was so necessary for survival. But in the bush it can literally mean life or death. If you are able to escape from a burning cabin with your life but all your clothes and food are destroyed, and if you are several days' journey from your nearest neighbour, the saved life could very easily turn into a very miserable death. But death by fire sometimes happened in the camps as well, especially when alcohol was involved. Thirty or so miles (48 kms) north, where the Peel River flows into the mighty Mackenzie, there was a camp where a small number of people stayed in the summer to fish and in the winter to trap. For a long time we had thought that people were going to visit "Martha Peel" when they moved downriver, and it was not until there was a fatal accident at this camp and the police came to tell us that two people had been killed in a house fire at the "Mouth of the Peel" that we realized that "Martha Peel" was a place and not a person! These two fatalities followed a homebrew party in a cabin, and the two occupants did not get out when the house burst into flames and was quickly demolished. We had to certify that the people were indeed dead, and to us there was no doubt about it when we saw the charred remains that were brought to us. When the RCMP investigated the cause of the fire, they found that open cans of gas had been stored under a bed quite close to the stove, which explained why the fire had been so devastating.

WHEN THE MEN OF Fort McPherson went out on hunting expeditions or when families went to meat camps, they would stop the dog teams every two hours or so for a rest, light a huge fire and make tea. These campfires were not the sort where every care is taken to preserve firewood, but where each person went and cut down a couple of small dry trees, each about 10 to 12 feet (3.6 m) high, and brought them to a place where they had scooped the deep snow away. The trees were then piled horizontally and set on fire. Open pans, used as tea pails, were balanced on a couple of the trees and tended with a long stick. It took a lot of snow to provide enough water for a few cups of tea, and after travelling with the Gwich'in, I learned to scoop the top layer of snow away until I came to the crystalline snow below. This had more water content, and the pail did not need filling up quite so often. I also learned to keep my eye on my pail to make sure that the drops of snow water did not evaporate; this lesson was learned the hard way one day when, after neglecting my duties, I found my pail reduced to a blob of aluminum at the bottom of the fire!

Many dozens of cords of firewood were used by the native people over a winter because most of them used it for both heating and cooking. Not very many collected a winter wood supply in advance because, they said, maybe it would get "borrowed" or—because the people considered staying in the village a very temporary thing (they often referred to it as "camping in town")—it was not thought to be a necessary thing. Why go to the trouble of gathering a lot of wood if you were not going to be around to use it?

William Firth wanted to make sure that Muriel and I would be able to light a fire if ever we were stranded on our own or if a plane crashed in the bush and we survived. (It was this last part about

A typical lunchtime fire to warm the travellers, cook their food, and—for the unwary—melt the teakettle!

surviving that troubled me more than lighting a fire!) Instead of just telling us how to light a fire and risk us feeling belittled over such a simple thing, he simply told us to go over the frozen river and try to light a fire in the snow. Being outdoor types, we thought that this would be a simple task, and that very afternoon we set out with an axe and a box of matches. He told us not to take paper because we might not have any with us in an emergency. This seemed fair enough, and I recalled an incident from my childhood in Wales when I had used a whole box of matches trying to set fire to a gorse bush. When I came to the last match and still had not managed to get the bush alight, I struck the match and flung it disdainfully into the bush. It started to burn and then set the next bush on fire, and the next, and the next, and so on until the whole mountain looked to be on fire. Then I knew I was in trouble! The secret had been in finding some dry part of the bush, so I knew that now, when we crossed the Peel, all we had to do was find some dry grass or something like it and we would soon have a fire going.

We followed a dog team trail across the Peel River, carrying a bag with a Thermos flask of hot tea, some sandwiches and, of course, a big box of matches. We then climbed up the slippery riverbank, but as I reached the top I slipped down again, dropping the bag with the tea and sandwiches. I gathered everything up and tried again and was finally able to join Muriel at the top of the bank where she was waiting patiently for me. We looked back at Fort McPherson. The houses could be seen clearly all along the riverbank; a frost haze, mingling with the smoke from the wood fires, hung over them. Well, William should be able to see the smoke from our fire once it was lit.

The snow was very dry and powdery, reminding us of loose sugar, but sticking up out of the snow was some dry grass. Just what was needed. After kicking aside the snow, we gathered up a few handfuls of grass and I placed it carefully in a small depression. We broke off some willow branches that grew all around us and arranged them like a little teepee over the grass. The first match I used would not set even a single piece of the grass on fire. My hands grew cold as I used match after match, and then while I put my fingers into my armpits to thaw them out, Muriel tried lighting the fire. After using a few matches unsuccessfully, she put three or four of them together and tried that. The matches were wooden so they burned well and some of the grass caught fire but it went out as soon as it got away from the source of the flame. Well, if this was an emergency situation, anything would go, so out came a few pieces of tissue paper, and I stuffed them under the grass and set them on fire. The grass burned quickly and went out.

We collected more grass but we discovered that, as we handled it, the heat from our hands was melting the frost in the grass, and it was getting wet. We broke off some bark from a dead tree that was lying on the ground and tried lighting it, but all to no avail. By now we were getting cold and annoyed, and after using the last few matches to set the match box on fire, we conceded defeat and decided to eat our sandwiches and warm up with the hot tea. Muriel opened the Thermos and started to pour then suddenly stopped and peered into the flask. "Guess what?" she said sadly. "When you fell down the bank, the Thermos broke. We can't drink the tea. It's got glass in it!" Feeling even more frustrated and very thirsty, we went home to thaw out our cold and stiff bodies.

William knew that we would now listen to his instructions on how to light a fire in the bush, without laughing at him. Of course, it sounded simple when he told us how to do it, and when he also told us what not to do, we recognized right away that we had been doing all the wrong things. He told us not to use any green trees for kindling—just because a tree doesn't have any leaves on it doesn't mean that it is dead—and in the extreme cold even green wood will snap off like dead wood. Find a standing dry tree, he said, cut it down, cut it up and make some kindling from it. Try to use some pieces from the centre of the tree for kindling and use one or two pieces to make feather sticks, that is, sticks from which shavings are partially cut and feathered out.

After the snow has been scraped down as close to the ground as possible, two feather sticks are placed together and some small dry kindling placed on them. One match is lit and touched to the feather stick, and as the flames grow, more kindling is added and bigger and bigger wood is put on the fire. If they are available, dry dead branches, which seem to accumulate on the lower parts of spruce trees, can be broken off, crunched together and used in place of the feather sticks. Even in rain or snowy weather, these small branches remain dry and catch fire easily. We have tried using the pine sap balls which solidify on evergreens but discovered that they get lost in the snow; however, they do burn well on a solid surface like a slab of wood or on bare ground in summer time. After William's lesson in fire-making, we tried it successfully close to home and learned another lesson about wood fires: the wood makes you warm at least three times—once when you cut it, once when you split it or stack it, and finally when you burn it!

8

ON ONE OF THOSE DAYS in early winter when the sun crept over the southern horizon with difficulty and stayed only long enough for us to admire the golden glow on the frost-shrouded trees, Muriel and I decided that we would take advantage of an abnormally quiet clinic and go for a walk along one of the many trails leading from the village and do a little exploring. We pulled on our new duffel socks, over which went our equally new mukluks made of moose-hide and stroud, and then tied the thongs around the ankles and the drawstrings around the calves to keep out the snow. We had heard that there were a lot of rabbits and ptarmigan around, so I took my .22 calibre rifle, hoping to get something fresh for supper.

We followed a trail going north and, judging by the amount of dog feces beside the trail, it was well used. The trees were heavily laden with snow and very picturesque, and all around us the willows formed a dark tangled web emphasized by the contrasting whiteness of the snow. The trail was firm to walk on, and we enjoyed the brisk air. There didn't seem to be a lot of rabbit signs, and though we would stop now and again to listen, all we heard was the sound of our hearts beating. All other sound had been muted by the snow, and we felt completely alone.

Suddenly a rabbit darted across the trail! I walked over to where I had seen it disappear into the brush and saw a well-used rabbit trail. "I'm going to see where this goes," I called to Muriel and stepped off the trail. To my surprise I found that I was nearly waist-deep in crystalline snow. "It's quite deep," I called out. It was obvious that it was deep, but somehow or other I wanted to reassure myself that all was well.

As I fell I had plunged my rifle into the snow, filling both the barrel and the bolt. I was still convinced that I would see a rabbit, although in reality every living thing except Muriel was now well hidden, scared by my thrashing around in the snow and willows. Still I struggled forward on the great rabbit hunt, but after taking ten paces and finding I had barely moved forward at all, I admitted to Muriel that walking through the bush in this part of the world was a physical impossibility. I had to stand on one leg and force the other one forward through the loose snow, lunge forward, then repeat the whole process. More often than not I slipped backwards. The exertion was making me uncomfortably hot and I began to feel as though I was in a sauna with a sweater on.

Back on the trail, we decided that we had better discuss this problem with William. Other people went hunting out in the bush, broke trail for the dogs, and generally got around. We wanted to know how to accomplish this. William, of course, was glad to help us. He did not laugh when we told him how hard we had found it walking off the trail though he sometimes smiled behind his hand.

"I'll bring some snowshoes for you to try," he said as he put on his cap and silently withdrew from the kitchen. Within fifteen minutes he was back again with two pairs of snowshoes.

"These are poor," he said, picking up the smaller pair. "They are what Mary uses when she is ratting, but you'll see if you can use them." They were about three feet long with the rounded front end slightly upturned. The rawhide, or babiche, lacing was very fine in the front and the back, but much coarser in the middle where the foot went. William bent down and fastened them onto Muriel's feet by adjusting a narrow piece of lampwick around her ankles.

"Is that really lampwick, William? The stuff that we put in lamps?"

"Yes, everyone uses it. It's cheap at the store and it stays on your foot better than that leather stuff you buy. Some people use a piece of inner tube, but it splits too easy in the cold. You will soon learn how to put your foot into the harness without even using your hands. You'll see. Keep the lampwick tied like this, and then you can just slide your foot in and out whenever you want," and he demonstrated the movement to us.

William had brought his son's snowshoes for me to try on. They were store bought, and the front was curved up and came to a point. The babiche was heavier and coarser than the locally made snowshoes. William told us that the finer babiche was good in the granular snow, and those bought in the store were good when the snow was wet, "but anyway, they will be good to try out."

After we had tried them out in the kitchen, we all sat around the kitchen table and William told us about snowshoes. "Alfred Charlie and Ronnie Pascal are the best snowshoe makers in Fort McPherson, but I don't think Alfred can see too well now. Ronnie, he makes his out of birch that he chooses and cuts himself. He soaks it well and then shapes it on a frame, just like the shape of Mary's." He pointed to the snowshoes on the floor. "Ronnie will sit there for hours and whittle away, and he can tell just by the feel if it is right. His wife, she makes the babiche from moose or caribou, whatever she's got. She scrapes off all the hair, then hangs it out in the frost for a few weeks. Then she brings it in and cuts it into thin pieces about that thick." He indicated a thickness of about three millimetres with his finger and thumb. "She measures it with her thumb nail as she cuts it, then when that's done, Ronnie laces up the snowshoe. He's very clever." When I looked at the intricate work, I agreed that it was a work of art and skill.

Saturday finally arrived, and we had a fast breakfast and dressed appropriately for the minus 20 F (-30 C) temperature. We decided to set off on the same trail and put on the snowshoes where no one could see us. We slipped our feet into the harness as William had taught us to do and took a few faltering steps off the trail. I found

Muriel on the snowshoe trail, Fort McPherson, NWT.

that I had to keep my legs a little apart and walk with a longer stride than usual. My confidence surged until I stood on the tip of one snowshoe with the other and crash-landed into the snow. It was a struggle to get up but once I was upright again it didn't take too long to get the hang of it, and within a few minutes we were walking through the bush slowly and carefully, thrilled that we could now walk practically anywhere. We walked to the river and slid down the bank, then found a dog trail leading back to the village.

We were so exhilarated that we tried running along the trail and had managed a short burst of a few yards when we both tripped and fell. My snowshoes dug into the snow and the ends flew up behind me, catching my back a painful blow. My pride was hurt now, so I got up quickly and tried again. Crack! down I went again. This time I had got the toe of one snowshoe caught in the mesh of the other.

Muriel caught up with me. "Better just to walk in them," she cautioned. "It's faster in the long run."

I was contemplating how it could be better to walk if it was a long run but gave up with a laugh and staggered to my feet, rubbing my hip, which had come into contact with a large piece of ice.

In spite of the falls, we enjoyed the novelty of walking in the snow and making giant footprints in the unbroken crust. We hadn't been out for too long but, when we turned around, the sun was already going down and we began to make our way home and, of course, give a report of our progress to William. He had just made coffee when we got back. "I guess you both fell a few times by the look of you." His wrinkled face broke into a grin. "You look like a couple of snowshoe rabbits!" and he laughed silently at his little joke.

"I guess we've got a lot to learn, William, but we sure enjoyed ourselves. Do you think you could get Ronnie to make us some snowshoes?"

9

THE WOMEN OF FORT MCPHERSON worked hard, and some of the frail bodies that we saw belied the strength and skill within them. Once when I made a routine public health visit to 95-year-old Annie Vaneltsi, who weighed maybe 88 lbs (40 kg) for her four-feet-five inches (134 cm), she was on her knees splitting wood outside her cabin. I greeted her and then, pointing to the wood, offered to split some for her. She smiled with little enthusiasm but I took the axe and let fly with all the male ego I could muster. Swinging the axe high over my head, I aimed for the log, missing several times and burying the blade into the earth, but I finally managed to get the axe to chew into the log. I stopped then and wiped the sweat off my brow, and old Annie immediately picked up the axe and swung at the log. "Pop!" the log split, and I just stared at it. I beat a shame-faced retreat, hoping that not too many people had seen my pride get axed!

We were told that before white men brought dogs into the Mackenzie and Peel river regions as they ventured toward the Yukon's gold that it was the Gwich'in women who used to haul the sleds, meat, children and camping supplies from place to place. The men would walk on ahead to the hunting grounds, cook and eat the products of the hunt first, and then the women and children would eat afterward. Early travellers and later a number of anthropologists reported that a woman's lot in life was so hard in those old days that female infanticide took place so that the girls would be spared the suffering in adult life. The Gwich'in also practiced polygamy, perhaps because the women died at such an early age from overwork, undernourishment and child bearing. It would also be nearly impossible for one wife to raise the children, make and break camp, get firewood, make clothes and footwear and do the hundred and one other chores that made up Gwich'in life.

When the native people adopted the use of dogs as freight animals, it must have come as a great relief to the women. When food was scarce, the dogs were left to fend for themselves; when it was plentiful, the dogs could gorge. They were supposed to be tied up, but they were strong and were continually lunging at their chains, and then the chain would break. One loose dog created more loose dogs as they all strained to get at the lucky one who invariably ran madly around barking and looking for food. Throughout the north there were stories of loose sled dogs who not only fought each other but would attack anyone who was close. It was devastating to have to try and sew up a person who had been savagely mauled by a pack of dogs, and adults as well as children sometimes died from these vicious attacks. Consequently, everyone was wary of loose dogs.

Once when I was away in Arctic Red River and Muriel was busy with some routine chore, RCMP officer Frank Dunne arrived at the door with a young native boy who had been attacked by several loose sled dogs. He had been severely mauled and was in a lot of pain, but like a lot of the young people he did not make much noise in spite of his wounds. He let Muriel know that he was hurt by looking at her with big eyes and letting little sobs escape periodically. Muriel treated him for shock and set about cleaning the multiple wounds. Some of the flesh had been torn by the savage dogs, and in other areas it was bitten almost through to the bone. He would need some time in hospital, and there was always the danger of rabies although neither Muriel nor the RCMP were aware of any recent sightings of rabid animals.

Frank had stayed to see if Muriel needed any help, and when

she said that the boy would have to be evacuated to hospital, Frank told her that the RCMP plane was in the village and that she could use it to save time. It was one of those rare instances when there was enough daylight, a plane ready to go, and someone willing to go along as an escort. The plane was already on its way to Inuvik before Muriel had time to phone the general hospital there to tell them that an emergency case was on its way.

Mel Peletier, one of the other constables, tried to capture the dogs with the intention of tying them up to see if they developed the outward signs of rabies, but the dogs were so vicious that neither he nor anyone else could get close to them. So Mel got out his rifle and, standing on the riverbank, aimed at the dogs, which were now cavorting on a frozen sandbar below the nursing station. Using his telescopic sight, he zeroed in on the closest dog, which looked to be a half-mile (0.8 km) away. Crack! the rifle spat and the dog dropped dead. He fired twice more and each time a dog dropped. Later he re-trieved the carcasses and had the grisly job of cutting off their heads and sending them, frozen, down south for examination of the brains for any evidence of rabies. It came as a relief for all when the news was received from Edmonton that the dogs did not have the disease, but in the meantime the boy had been given the first few shots of rabies vaccine.

On a later occasion I was given the task of accompanying a group of politicians who were making one of their lightning trips to the village along with an entourage of aides and reporters. As usual some of these visitors were friendly and likable, but some of the oth-ers were filled with their own importance and their arrogance was difficult for us to bear.

"Oh, look at that cute dog with its puppies!" A woman reporter pointed at one of the dogs tied up close by a house, and she started to walk over to it. A dozen voices immediately called out to her to be careful and stay away, but she just laughed and kept on walking toward the dog. It wagged its tail, expecting to be fed or released for a run with the toboggan, but its behaviour changed as it caught the scent of a stranger, and then as the woman came towards the puppies, the dog's tail went down and its hackles went up. Its ears flattened against its head and a rumbling sound came from its throat. Still the naive reporter kept getting closer as she was determined to pet the pups. The bitch, on the other hand, was out to protect its young and suddenly shot forward until the tethering chain snapped taut, but not before the dog's front legs had struck the woman, knocking her down.

"Stupid dog!" she shouted as she struggled to her feet and backed away from the growling dog. "They shouldn't be allowed to keep dogs like that!"

Now that she was safe, everyone was relieved, and someone at the back of the crowd shouted out, "No, they should keep poodles!" Everyone except the reporter laughed. I thought it was a pity that it took a near accident to teach people a lesson, and then I got to thinking how many near accidents I'd had before I learned—and was, in fact, still learning—about northern dogs.

THE SLED DOGS of Fort McPherson were not of any known breed. They were just "sled dogs" or sometimes they were called northern huskies. The RCMP used Siberian Huskies and had a dog breeding station in Arctic Red River that supplied dogs to all the western Arctic detachments. The Siberians had a good temperament and worked hard, and when I later acquired a team, I ran two Siberians along with four northern sled dogs. Most of them behaved themselves around people but, given the slightest provocation, would fight amongst themselves.

Some of the old-timers in Fort McPherson had their dog preferences, too. Andrew Kunnizzi had tried to breed some Collie into his team because he had heard that the breed was very obedient and trainable, but for some reason the mixture turned out very vicious dogs, and it was only Andrew who could handle them. Peter Thompson liked to run dogs that were about eight to ten years old because they were then usually well-trained and had slowed down

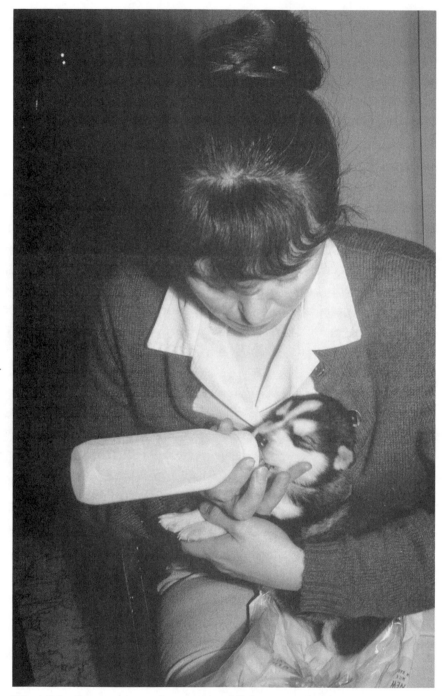

Muriel feeding an unusual patient—a Malamute puppy!

a bit. Peter was in his late sixties so he said that he neither needed nor wanted a fast team. "Lots of time!" he would say with a big smile creasing his round face. William Vittrekwa had great big hairy dogs that were also fairly slow but would pull him for days if need be. He was very fond of his dogs and took great care of them.

During our first winter in Fort McPherson, Muriel and I spent lots of time dashing to the nursing station window. "Listen, there's a dog-team coming!" one or the other of us would shout when we heard the jingling harness bells, and we would peer out at the team as it rushed by. We should have known, of course, who would be called upon when a favourite dog was hurt, and we were not long into winter when we answered the clinic doorbell and found Andrew Kunnizzi on the step holding one of his dogs wrapped in a blanket. What else could I say but "Come on in, Andrew. What can we do for you today?"—although I didn't really want to know the answer.

"My lead dog, he got a bad leg, got it all messed up in the harness. Now he can't stand on it." He added that he did not want to shoot it because it was a good dog, and it would be a waste if the leg was really all right.

We agreed that I would X-ray the dog's leg as long as Andrew would hold the dog, and that he would try and muzzle him because we knew that Andrew's dogs were vicious around strangers.

The X-ray turned out very well, but we found that a dog's anatomy is completely different from that of a human! I held up the X-ray plate for Andrew to see.

"Look at this, Andrew. There are no bones broken, but he's got joints all over the place, and I can't tell if anything is dislocated or if they are supposed to look like that."

"Andrew, you will just have to decide on your own," Muriel told him, keeping one eye on the quiet dog because she didn't trust even the quiet ones. "You are no better off really, except for knowing that there isn't a break."

"That's okay. Thank you very much Mr., Mrs. Billington." And he picked the dog up carefully and went out, calling back his thanks as he went down the steps.

Two or three weeks went by before we happened to meet Andrew walking through the village.

"How's the dog?" I asked.

"Oh, hello, Mr., Mrs. Billington. Oh, nothing wrong with that dog now. I just tie him up one week and then he get up like nothing was wrong. I take him to camp at Stoney Creek last week. I guess that X-ray fix him real good." He was quite serious but it was a popular misconception: many of our patients believed that they would not get better if we did not X-ray them.

Constable Mel Peletier and his wife, Lorraine, came to the clinic one Saturday morning with the news that his pet dog had been in a fight and was injured. Mel was used to handling the RCMP sled dogs but this one was the family's pet Keeshond. "Sorry to bother you this morning, but my pooch seems to have a hole in his chest, and we were wondering if you could sew it up?" The dog's normally perky tail hung down, making him look very dejected.

"Put him on the table and let's see what we can do." I could hear air bubbling through the wound, and it did not take long to find the chest wound. "I don't really know what to do, Mel. I haven't got any anaesthetic to put him under, and I really don't want to operate on your dog—even if I did have it." I did not tell him that I was scared stiff of doing anything. My dilemma was that if I refused to do anything, the dog would die and I could lose a friend, but if I did do something and the dog died, I would lose credibility. (I could just imagine people saying, "You know that man down at the nursing station, he couldn't even fix a *dog!*")

I had seen dozens of people operated on in hospital operating rooms—lungs biopsied, lungs removed, and all sorts of tubes, bone grafts and even wax put into chest cavities—but to start fixing up a dog with a punctured chest was a bit beyond my scope! "Mel," I said, "if you want me to just sew up the wound, I'll do it, but he's got a pneumothorax, and I just don't know what the outcome will be. He really needs a tube into the lung and a vet's care."

Mel looked at his wife and then turned to me. "That's fine, Keith. We know it's a lot to ask but if you can sew him up, we would be very thankful."

So I carefully cut the hair from around the wound and cleaned the area with some antiseptic. During the fight the other dog's teeth had penetrated the chest wall, leaving a jagged tear when he had been pulled away. I injected some local anaesthetic, keeping my eye on the dog's head in case he objected to the treatment, but maybe as an indication of the seriousness of his injury or due to Mel's soothing words, the Keeshond lay quite still while I worked. I then probed around the wound, identified the different tissues and slowly began sewing up the layers, finishing with some nylon sutures on the skin. I dabbed some collodion on as a dressing, knowing that a gauze dressing would soon be chewed off.

"Good luck then, Mel. I'll give him a shot of antibiotic, and then all you can do is watch him carefully." I turned the patient over to Mel, drew up a syringe of penicillin and, again with great care, I injected the dog. This time he struggled as the fluid forced its way into his muscle, but as soon as I had finished, he relaxed again.

Neither Muriel nor I gave much thought to Mel's dog for the rest of the day, but when we got up on Sunday morning, we found that an envelope had been pushed under the door. It contained a generous cheque from Mel and Loraine, with a note extending their gratitude for our services. We didn't want the cheque—it was not our own supplies that had been used, and the job had been done for friends—so we tore it up.

A few days later we met Mel in the store, and I could not help but ask how his dog was. "Oh, he died the next day," he said, then seeing my crestfallen face, he hastily added, "But we are very grateful. We know you did everything you could." It was only later that I realized that I had not mentioned his cheque. He would probably understand what happened when he got his bank statement later.

The fact that I had lost a patient shook me, and just because this patient happened to be a dog didn't make me feel much better. Muriel was more practical. "We would have felt much worse if we had kept that cheque," she said and I knew that was true. I did not feel guilty about that, but was my reputation as a "vet" now ruined? Had my career really gone to the dogs?

A FEW DAYS AFTER the ice stopped running on the river and the big ice pans stuck together, we would hear of people heading up or down the river to their trapping cabins. In every direction dog team trails led from the village, all of them beckoning us to follow to see where they went. This flurry of activity made us realize that to go anywhere in the wintertime we would have to travel by dog team, and after observing men, women and even children handling the teams without any apparent difficulty, we decided that it was time that we learned how to drive one.

We consulted William. He gave us a walk-through first, telling us that in spite of what books said, we did not start the dogs off by calling out, "Mush!" He said the only mush that dogs understood was when they ate it! Instead, the commands were All right! Whoa! Hee! and Cha! He then explained about the harnesses, which were made from leather with yoke collars similar to those worn by freight horses. The dogs were harnessed one behind the other in tandem hitch so that they could manoeuvre around the trees. William also explained that the dogs had differences in character, just as humans did, and we should try to recognize these differences because some dogs made good leaders and others were just followers. The wooden toboggan that the dogs pulled was about 18 feet (5 m) long and made of oak with a large curl at the front so that it would crest the deep snow, and it had a canvas wrapper or carriole that served to carry freight or belongings.

William's instructions took all evening because he kept us entertained with stories connected with every part of a dog and its harness. He told us of a dog that had an annoying habit of chewing its leather harness, a habit that could prove to be a life-or-death matter out in the bush. He said that the only way that he could cure this dog was to jump on it when it was actually chewing the harness, and then, using his axe file, he would file the dog's teeth enough to cause pain. He only had to do this twice before the dog learned his lesson.

This story then led William to tell us how he had used a file on his own teeth. He had been up on the coast trading furs when he developed a terrible toothache. When he was travelling, the Arctic wind would blow in his mouth, nearly driving him crazy. One day he could stand it no longer and, using a mirror, he found the offending tooth, a molar, and decided it would have to come out. He looked through his small tool supply and decided to use the sharp handle end of a file, jammed the point down into the gum and levered the tooth out with one quick motion. He told us that just as he passed out, he saw the tooth go flying!

William returned the next morning to make sure that we still wanted to try out a team, and after we had confirmed our wishes, he hitched up a team for us and brought the dogs round to the nursing station. Muriel sat in the toboggan on a sleeping bag, and I stood behind William as we drove down to the river, then William said we were on our own. Once on the river the dogs, not having worked all year, didn't seem too eager to go and when I looked at the heavy toboggan and thought of the combined weight of Muriel and myself, wrapped up as we were in heavy arctic clothing, I could understand their resistance to pull.

"All *right!*" William did not really shout but the words came out very forcibly. To my amazement, I was pulled off my feet and went down the snowy trail on my stomach, gripping the toboggan lazy-back as though my life depended upon it. The dogs did not look back and ran off happily, much to William's amusement! But this surge of power was short-lived. Coming to a place where several trails converged, and not being given any direction, the dogs stopped and investigated all of the different smells that passing teams had left. I picked myself up, scooped the snow from under my parka, and tucked in my shirt. Muriel stuck her leg over the side of the toboggan so that she could apply some braking power in case the dogs took it into their heads to start off on their own again, and we laughed over our initiation into dog-team travel!

As soon as we had gathered our composure, Muriel wrapped herself up in the sleeping bag and I stood on the back of the toboggan and gripped the handlebars firmly. I gave the command to go, and we zipped smoothly across the snow for a few hundred yards until the dogs slackened their pace again. Another hundred yards and the dogs were down to a walking pace, and they kept looking back at me. I felt guilty about riding on the back, so I jumped off and jogged behind the team. The dogs were now able to keep going slowly but steadily. We were going to visit the closest camp, which was only three miles (4.8 km) up the Peel River, and by the time we reached it, I was soaked with sweat and the poor dogs looked all in. How people moved with all of their camping supplies, family members and food out to traplines a hundred miles (160 km) away was beyond our comprehension.

We were welcomed at the camp with handshakes and laughter, and the kettle was immediately filled and put onto the wood stove for tea. We were asked to stay for some lunch, and we felt so pressed by the insistent invitation, that we agreed. As the meal was being prepared, we talked about dogs and travel and answered the inevitable questions about health. (We were to find that whatever conversation we had in the north, sooner or later it came round to the subject of health, and we had to be careful that we did not get into a full clinic every time we visited a house.) We were handed bowls of chicken noodle soup and some bannock. The chicken noodle soup had something in it that looked curdled and, seeing me look at it critically, the lady of the house said, "It's good, but in this weather you need something extra, so we put some caribou blood into it." I didn't want to look at Muriel at that instant because I knew that she would be having a hard time controlling her stomach but, putting mind over matter, I drank the soup and ate a lot of bannock so I didn't taste anything but chicken. I was surprised to see Muriel had finished hers, too, but we both refused second helpings.

We said our farewells, turned the dogs around, and set off in the direction of home. We had only gone a short distance when I found that the dogs could not pull me. As soon as I jumped on the back of the toboggan, they stopped in their tracks, but when I jumped off and shouted "All right," they would get up and start off at a walking pace again. I jogged for about two miles (3.2 km) behind them until, as we came around a corner in the river, we saw another dog team come out of the bush about 200 yards (182 m) in front of us and head off in the direction of the village. Our dogs also saw the team ahead of us and quickened their pace to a trot and I had to run to keep up. When they began to run faster, I jumped onto the toboggan. It had no effect upon them at all. In fact, they went faster, and as they gathered speed and caught up with the team ahead, I was apprehensive of the dogs fighting, so I yelled out "Whoa!" No effect.

"*Whoa!* You stupid dogs!" I yelled at them. Still they pulled hard. I gripped the handlebars tightly and straddled the toboggan, digging my feet into the deep snow in a vain attempt to slow them down. Those "poor, tired dogs" bent their backs and pulled harder than ever, ignoring me completely. In a desperate effort I swung the toboggan onto its side, and Muriel, who had been sitting quietly clutching the canvas sides of the carriole, flung out her hands to save herself as the toboggan tipped over. She let out a wail as she called my name, and then all was quiet as she was plunged into the deep, cold snow. Now, with her body half in the toboggan and half under the snow, she acted like a snowplow and eventually this made the dogs slow down. I slipped on some ice and was once again pulled along on my stomach, but at last the dogs stopped.

I was too breathless to tell them what I thought of them, and Muriel was busy extricating herself from the snow, emptying her parka and pockets of snow. Then I reached the lead dog and held

My faithful wheel dog "Adaijoh" (Whiskers).

him tight while Muriel straightened out the toboggan and emptied it of snow. She climbed back in, and I let go of the lead dog.

"All right!" I commanded and they set off, but with the other team now out of sight, our dogs slowed down and began to give me those imploring looks again, as though to say "Please get off. We can't possibly pull you."

This time I stayed on the toboggan, but I pulled off my belt and, gripping my pants with my knees, I hit the side of the toboggan with the belt. Muriel jumped but so did the dogs, and every time they slowed down, I hit the toboggan with my belt again. They continued to pull reasonably well and within a short time they had pulled us up the riverbank and straight into William's yard. While he unhitched the dogs, we recounted our experiences.

"Gotta show who's boss with dogs, otherwise they're no good," he said. "Use a whip if you have to. But never mind, it was a good lesson for you." I think that he was quite pleased that our first trip was not without incident so that we would not be overconfident on future trips.

Sled dogs tend to bring out the worst in the person driving them and the term "gone to the dogs" took on a whole new meaning for us. Later on, when I had my own dogs, I learned that each one had traits that endeared it to me one moment and infuriated me the next. In this sense they were like children who can be loving and happy as long as you treat them right, but they sometimes have minds of their own and will try and get out of their responsibilities if you ignore them for a moment!

10

WE WERE ALWAYS VERY busy in the nursing station, and being the sole providers of medical care gave Muriel and me some very pleasurable moments, but we knew that our patients were appreciative. Our work also took us into the village houses on a daily basis. Emergencies had to be responded to whenever they occurred, be it day or night, so whenever we visited someone socially for any length of time, we would take our emergency bag along, and more than once we have used a host's bedroom as a temporary clinic to examine or perhaps suture an accident victim.

We averaged two births a month at the station, and usually these were quite happy affairs. There was the time when the Anglican minister's wife gave birth to a long-awaited son (after three daughters), and we shared their joy. Peggy had insisted on staying in Fort McPherson for the birth so that Muriel could deliver her baby and would not listen to our pleas for her to go to Inuvik. The general policy was that all first and fourth babies should be delivered in a hospital because of the higher risk of complications, and we did not want to set a precedent or make the local mothers-to-be feel that we were favouring a white woman. But after Peggy's uncomplicated delivery the family made us feel that we had specifically designed it for them to have a boy. We told them that we were just like the post office and delivered whatever was sent!

One young lady came into the nursing station during the regular

An outstanding Gwich'in lady, Jane Charlie, with her warm, comfortable and satisfied new baby.

clinic hours and said she would like to be examined because she was pregnant. It was my duty roster to be doing the clinic, and as mid-wifery was not my specialty, I picked up the chart to work out her dates. We tried to encourage women to come to the clinic early in their pregnancy so that we could monitor both the mother and the baby's progress and give any supplements to the mother that were required. My patient that day did not look particularly pregnant, and with loose clothes and a Mother Hubbard parka on, I could not tell at a glance what stage of pregnancy she was in.

"When is the baby due?" I looked casually at her figure as she removed her parka.

"November."

"When in November?"

"The twenty-first."

I looked at the calendar. "That's this month!" I exclaimed, and then looking quickly at the calendar again, I said, "You were due last Monday!"

"Yes," she replied, a sudden look of concentration coming to her face. "I think I'm going to have it now!"

"*Muriel!*" I called. Fortunately my wife was working close by in the office. "This patient is for you!" And as I guided the patient into the labour room, I quickly explained the cause of my consternation.

When everything was ready, Muriel called me into the room. The woman lay on her back ready to give birth. She perspired a little when the contractions came and grasped the metal bar at the head of the hospital bed. The time for the birth came, she smiled, then grasp-ing the bar tightly, she gave a big push, waited, took a big breath and pushed again. Muriel held the baby and a loud cry pierced the quiet of the clinic. This large baby—10 pounds 9 ounces (5 kg)—had been born with less trouble than I could have imagined!

"Hey, Muriel, what's all this fuss that you make about labour and giving birth?" I teased. "It doesn't look that bad!" And the patient, who was now holding her crying baby, said as though to acknowl-edge my comment, "It wasn't so bad!"

Muriel just looked at me. "If only you could try it, my dear!" she said.

A YOUNG WOMAN WHOSE baby became ill during the small hours turned the tables on us one cold night when she felt it necessary to come down to the nursing station with her baby. Her faint tapping on the door barely disturbed our sleep, but its persistence finally registered in my tired brain and I lay there for a few seconds trying to analyze the sound. Then finally deciding to investigate, I jumped out of bed and felt around in the dark for my housecoat. It was then that I heard another light but definite knock on a door. Struggling to find the armhole in my housecoat so that I could pull it around my naked body, I walked quickly to the bedroom door, jerked it open and walked out, only to collide immediately with a young woman whose hand was poised ready to knock on the bedroom door again.

I was startled. The woman, just as startled, backed away, clutching her baby to her chest.

"What's wrong?" I asked, recovering my voice and still trying to cover myself with my housecoat. "Why didn't you ring the doorbell?" I persisted.

"I'm sorry. It's the baby," she said quietly.

"Well, why not ring the doorbell like anyone else?"

She looked at me sorrowfully. "I'm sorry," she said again. "I knew that you would be tired, and I didn't want to wake you!"

I couldn't think of an apt reply to this naive and completely innocent statement so rather resignedly I told her to come down the hall to the clinic with me. "And next time come to the clinic door and ring the bell. Then you won't be embarrassing either of us!"

I examined the baby and found she had a mild fever, the origin of which was not yet evident. So after prescribing and dispensing some infant fever medication, I told her to watch the baby carefully and bring her back during the day if there was no improvement in her condition or if something else developed.

I watched as she dressed and bundled her daughter up, then deftly swinging the baby onto her back, she wrapped a red tartan shawl around both the baby and her shoulders. She tied the shawl in front, picked up the medication, then after thanking me and muttering abject apologies for disturbing me, left by the clinic door.

I went back to bed and lay there thinking about the poor woman's predicament of wanting the baby examined but not wanting to disturb us. I smiled in the dark, turned over and went to sleep.

11

EVERY YEAR THERE WAS a certainty that there would be a white Christmas in Fort McPherson, but while the snow was "deep and crisp and even" by the festive season, rarely did we experience the heavy, wet snowstorms of Canada's more southern latitudes. In fact, when the annual precipitation is compared with some of the acknowledged world desert areas, the Mackenzie Delta could actually be called a desert, and though there is an impression of lots of falling snow, in reality it is the wind moving the fine crystals from "here to there." Every morning William Firth would come over to the nursing station to sweep any new snow from the sidewalk. If we heard him using a shovel, we guessed that the wind was either blowing hard or it had snowed heavily.

Periodically a chinook would occur and for a few brief hours the temperature would climb up to around zero (32 F) or even above zero, and the sky to the west would become an artist's palette of swirling colours as the high winds chased clouds from the Yukon out over the Delta. However, the snow would become very wet and slushy, making travelling almost impossible. At such times people out in the bush would stay in camp and do all the chores they had not had time to do previously, such as putting fresh spruce boughs down on the tent floor, and the newly warmed boughs would give off a pungent, aromatic odour, which I loved as much as I did the smell of freshly smoked moosehide. Snowshoe lacings were repaired or replaced, and mukluks mended with sinew. If the camp was a meat camp, the bones of the caribou were split and the marrow removed and rendered down to provide much-needed fat, which was used like butter. This was a time of waiting and watching. The natives knew that the warm weather would only last for a short time and that after about twenty-four hours the wind would shift to the north and the mercury would plummet. After a day or two of zero temperatures, the renewed cold of thirty or forty below was very noticeable.

But neither blizzards nor chinooks would keep people from travelling from their camps to Fort McPherson for Christmas; the weather might delay them but they would always get to the village in time to get into the festive spirit. Parents who had left their school children in Fort McPherson while they were out at camp would always try to get home in time for the school concert when, clad in their heavy parkas, they would sit in the hot and humid school gymnasium watching their offspring perform a variety of skits that were only limited by their teachers' imagination. As in other parts of North America, relatives watched the performances with pleasure and sometimes embarrassment, as some little tyke forgot his lines when he became entranced by all the people he could see through the glare of the lights or a child would stand picking his nose or playing with the zipper of his jeans. The evening's entertainment climaxed with Santa's arrival outside on a snowmobile. He would parade down the centre of the gymnasium with a sack of toys on his back, the little children gazing in awe at the sight and the older ones trying hard to guess who Santa was this year—peering closely at the perspiring face of the community volunteer and yelling out who they thought it was.

ONE SATURDAY MORNING just before our first Christmas in Fort McPherson, Alex Forman, the airline agent and trading post owner, unexpectedly called at the nursing station. We were busy arranging a turkey supper for the old age pensioners, an activity that had become a tradition in the village and something that, we were told, they all looked forward to.

"Hello there, Keith and Muriel," he said as soon as he came into the kitchen. "You both seem to be as busy as everyone else in this God-forsaken place." He wiped the frost from his greying beard and then took his glasses off and held them over the oil stove to thaw out. He looked at us vaguely with the sort of sightless eyes that short-sighted people have when they are not wearing their glasses. "The Community Club here puts on a Christmas party for all of the children," he continued, "and everyone gets a present, so they asked me to come down here and find out what the names of your children are." He looked around as he put his glasses on again. "By the way, where are they? You sure keep them quiet."

Muriel and I looked at each other, both wondering if this was some kind of Scots humour. "Oh yes," I said, "we keep them really quiet, especially considering we don't have any! What are you talking about, Alex? Have you started celebrating early or something?"

"No, really, where are they?" he persisted. "I haven't seen you with them since you arrived, and neither has anyone else."

Muriel was looking at him as though she expected him to suddenly break out into a laugh and tell us he was kidding. With a small, patient smile on her face she said, "Alex, we haven't got any children."

"C'mon, Muriel, you're pulling my leg! I saw them and everyone knows you've got two little kids tucked up in here someplace."

"No, Alex, really we don't," I said. "We've never had any, so I don't know what you saw. Maybe someone else's kids…"

"The day that you two arrived here, I was down on the dock and you passed the babies out to me first, and then you climbed out, right?"

The memory of that day came back to me, and as I looked at Muriel I saw the same inspiration flash across her face, too. We started to laugh. "Oh," I said. "Now I know what you are talking about!" It was Alex's turn to look puzzled. "You *did* see us pass two babies out of the plane sure enough, but they weren't *ours*. We were just escorting them back here from the hospital. We didn't even know who the parents were, but Lorraine made sure that they were delivered safe and sound."

Alex stared at us for a moment as the words sank in, then he gave a chuckle. "Well, well," he said, "just wait until they all hear this. Everyone was sure that you had children here, but no one ever saw them or heard them. Do you know," he added, "that people have been coming to the clinic and straining their ears listening for baby noises? We were wondering what the secret was to keeping your little ones quiet all day!"

"The secret is just don't have any children in the house, then it will remain nice and quiet! Now, would you like to join this childless couple for a cup of coffee?"

No one ever mentioned "our children" again, but had it not been for Christmas and the Community Club, our family would have been one hundred percent bigger and we would not have known a thing about it! We did wonder why he had not asked William or Maria, who was our nursing station housemaid, unless, of course, this really was Alex's sense of humour, but if it was, he wasn't telling!

MOST OF THAT HOLIDAY period was quiet for Muriel and me because people were having too good a time to remember their small aches and pains, but if a party got out of hand, we were called to do the suturing of cuts and bandaging of battered limbs. We were distressed to find some people spent the holiday in an alcoholic stupor, and their poor children had to find their own food and drink unless some kind neighbour or relative took them in for a while. Most of the children who could walk would go to find refuge in someone else's house, carrying the younger children with them, and never once did we hear of such children being turned away, so the bad elements were balanced by the good.

On the last day of the year, the chief or one of his councillors would call at every house in the village and ask for a donation of food for the New Year's Day Community Feast. We gave a sack of flour, a case of canned fruit, a sack of sugar, rice and anything else that we thought might be useful or which was surplus. This was all hauled up to the village and handed out to the various families who would be doing the cooking. In Fort McPherson, the women invariably did the cooking, as they did the child raising, although traditionally it had been the Gwich'in men who had been the cooks. After a successful hunting party the men would prepare the meat, cooking it and then eating their fill before the women and children ate.

At midnight New Year's Eve we heard a lot of rifle shots, and we would have thought that the village was under attack if William Firth had not had the foresight to call around earlier to explain to us that this was a custom from long ago when people would fire into the air and make a lot of noise to frighten away the evil spirits from the New Year. However, I have a notion that this tradition was started by the white men who came to teach Christianity to people whom they regarded as pagans. The shooting went on intermittently for about an hour, then tapered off completely. I estimated that several hundred dollars worth of shells had been fired during the shooting period, and yet I am sure that no one else gave it a thought, and when I tried analyzing this later, I was reminded of the many senseless ways that I had also wasted money in the name of "fun."

(In the coming years only once was I called out on an emergency sick call just before midnight on New Year's Eve, and as I walked along the riverbank and heard volley after volley of rifle shots, I wondered if I would make it to the patient's home and back without being shot. All I could do was hope that they were shooting straight up into the air and not out over the river, but I was also conscious that those people who were doing most of the shooting would not be too sure which way was up!)

Most of Fort McPherson's population must have been up all night, but at ten the next morning our clinic doorbell rang. When I opened the door, the chief stood there and behind him there was a long line of men.

"Happy New Year, Keith! Happy New Year, Nurse!" the Chief said with a big grin on his face as he shook my hand, then Muriel's.

"Happy New Year, John," I replied and then, as he moved on into the house, my hand was seized by the next man who gave it the customary single shake, and so on for all 140 men and youths who entered after him, walked through the clinic to the kitchen and let themselves out the back door.

It was a delightful experience, and we appreciated that we had been included in the ritual. The fact that it was cold and snowy outside and that everyone wore mukluks meant that we did not have to mop the floor after they had gone. Instead we quickly swept up any loose snow before it melted. No sooner had we sat down when the clinic door buzzer rang again. Curious, we both went to the door and there stood the chief's wife with a long line of women behind her, and we went through the hand-shaking routine once again. The women were quieter than the men had been and there were little nervous giggles as they shook our hands and went on through the house. Even when Mary Firth, William's wife, came through, there was no conversation, just a big grin, a quiet "Happy New Year" and she was gone. We felt that perhaps we should not try to make conversation, but after the 300th greeting I would have liked to have said something more than "Happy New Year" for a change. By the time the last young lady had passed through the house, we were quite cold and the snow on the floor didn't even begin to melt, so as the furnace tried to bring the temperature back up, we stood around the cook stove and drank hot coffee.

The rest of the day was spent visiting and being visited, as we all waited for the sound of rifle shots that would tell us to go to the community hall for the big New Year Feast. William had told us to each take cutlery and a bowl and that was all, so when we heard a rifle being fired—about an hour after we had been told to expect it—we were all ready. Everyone from the village was in the community hall and they sat around this large room on chairs, benches or the floor. The ladies served the food from huge cauldrons, carrying them around and ladling out as much as each bowl could hold. Caribou soup was served first, followed by caribou and moose meat,

Annie Bonnetplume Robert serves caribou stew at a Gwich'in feast in the community hall.

caribou stew and rice, bannock with butter and jam, dried fruits and rice and gallons of tea. I found that the food was quite bland, having been cooked without salt, and we had not brought any with us. And I had a hard time chewing some hunks of caribou meat because I could not stand eating gristle. Some stewed fruit was being ladled out and I received a good helping to mix with the rice, but unfortunately the fruit was cooked without sugar and it was very sour so I ate only small amounts that lasted me a long time.

As soon as the food was finished and cleared away, a dance was held, the music being provided by a fiddle player and guitarist. The two men played for hours without taking any breaks, and people never hesitated for a minute to get up and dance one of the many jigs where

At Gwich'in dances Charles Koe would play the fiddle for hours.

the men do a lot of fancy footwork and the women do a gentle shuffle on their tip-toes. It was fascinating to watch, but it would be several years before I was brave enough to try dancing myself.

As SOON AS CHRISTMAS and the New Year's holidays were over, people began to leave the village to travel back to the trapping camps, and every day we saw heavily laden toboggans pulled by straining dogs going by the nursing station, the dog-team driver jogging behind on the flat trail and jumping on as the toboggan started to ride easily down toward the frozen river. Though the fur was at its prime around the Christmas season and fetched good prices, the people were not eager to stay out in the bush and miss all the fun, so they just made do with a slightly lower price for their furs after Christmas and hoped that, when the spring muskrat trapping season started, they would be able to make up the loss.

After the parties and other social activities were over, and the majority of the people had left the village, it seemed very quiet as the rest of us settled into our routines. For us, this meant doing the never-ending government paper work and preparing inventories prior to ordering our medical and food supplies for the next barge season. In quiet moments Muriel and I continued to read as much as we could about the local history from books like *The Golden Grindstone*, and we took full advantage when old-timers came by to question them about early life in the north. They never tired of talking about the old days and we were always willing listeners. Over the years we were able to get a comprehensive picture of Delta history and the people who lived there.

BACK ON DECEMBER 6 the sun had set and we did not expect to see it again until mid-January, and during this period we experienced the coldest temperatures of the year in Fort McPherson. A cold haze hung over the village, and the houses all had their heaters turned up to the maximum, sending up columns of smoke and vapour from the chimneys. Whenever an outside door was opened, a fog would sweep across the floor as the frigid dry air melded with the moist indoor air. The dog teams used to get firewood from the bush would return to the village coated with frost, and their steaming breath hung over them in a cloud.

Our furnace could not keep up with our requirement for heat, and when I investigated, I found the fuel oil oozing like thick molasses through the pipe from the outside tank, its flash point almost non-existent. One day I checked the temperature outside and saw that it measured minus 75 degrees F (about -59 C), which was off the scale of most thermometers, and down on the frozen river, only 30 feet (9 m) below us, it was another ten degrees colder! No one went out when it was this cold unless they had to and sick people seemed just too ill to come to the clinic. In some cases a hastily written note was delivered to us by a half-frozen youngster to ask for a home visit and a specific medication.

Getting up in the morning was much harder in the wintertime. It was somewhere between coffee time and lunch time when the sky would lighten in the south, and, if the weather was good, we might see a pink glow in the sky. When the sun showed itself momentarily over the southern horizon early in January, someone, usually one of the teachers, organized a "sun-returning party," but everyone reluctantly acknowledged that we had another four and a half months of snow and ice ahead of us. But hope was both seen and felt with that brief glimpse of sunlight because we could all look forward to rapidly increasing daylight.

With the return of the sun, the countryside began to come back to life, and there were unmistakable signs that many life forms had survived the winter's cold temperatures. The trees began to absorb the sun's heat, and over a period of time the snow would recede from around their trunks, leaving large holes that seemed to be there to trap the unwary dogsledder travelling with a loaded toboggan. The toboggan would tip, causing the musher to hurl abuse at his dogs, and the dogs in turn would look around pathetically at their added work before heaving forward to pull the toboggan out of the hole.

In the early springtime when the bright sun shone warmly, a red algae sometimes appeared on the snow, looking as though cayenne pepper had been sprinkled over the surface; we saw miles of this peculiar phenomenon. And about the same time that it appeared we would see small mosquito-like insects crawling over the snowy surface. They were very slow and sluggish and I could not see them getting anything to eat. A few foolhardy spiders would venture out, maybe to eat these "mosquitoes," and I wondered how they would survive as the nighttime temperatures were still going down to at least minus 20 F (-28 C) or so.

When I moved some boxes from an outside shed, I found a big bumblebee in one corner and brought it inside to examine it. I put it on the kitchen table while I did some minor chore, and when I came back, it was moving around so I transferred it to a jar. After a few hours, the bee became quite active, so I put it outside where the temperature still hovered around minus 20 F (-28 C). Like the sensible insect that it was, it went back to sleep again. The next day I repeated the experiment and watched the same performance by the bee. This time when it went to sleep again, I put it into some loose dirt in a protected place in the shed. I had probably shortened its expected life span, but I was amazed how these small creatures could adapt to such extremes of temperature.

12

As soon as the flurry of activity that accompanied the Christmas season was over, it was a relief to sit down at coffee time and talk to the staff about their lives. William was always willing to share stories with us, but our nursing station housemaid, Maria Itsi, a very quiet and as yet unmarried young lady in her early twenties, was quite different. She kept the "business end" of the clinic clean and tidy, prepared and served meals for any in-patients and did some baking when it was required. She did her work well and never complained when mountains of washing or dirty dishes confronted her on a Monday morning after we had experienced a very busy weekend or a birth during the night. (Disposable diapers were only available at the clinic for newborn babies. The stores had not yet caught on to the idea, but anything disposable was expensive because of the high cost of freighting.)

"It's okay," Maria would say with a big grin and a toss of her long black hair whenever we apologized for an unusual work load, and she would don a white cotton apron over her colourful blouse and black pants and work steadily until everything was finished.

Then one morning Maria came to work late without giving us any reason, and she was even quieter than usual. As she very rarely came late, we did not say anything to her about it, knowing that sooner or later we would hear what had happened if it was at all relevant. However, at coffee time William came in and looked surprised when he saw Maria there. Instead of taking off his moccasin rubbers at the door, he beckoned me to come outside where I joined him on the clinic steps. He whispered, "I thought Maria was getting married today. Why is she here?"

This was the first I had heard about any wedding. "I'll find out," I told him. "But maybe I'll just see Don first so that I don't embarrass Maria." Don Wootten was the Anglican minister for the village and, if anyone was going to get married on this or any other day, he would know about it because he would be the one to perform the ceremony.

When I asked Don if Maria was getting married, he told me that he had been asked to perform the ceremony, which was scheduled for mid-afternoon, although no one had confirmed it with him yet. "But," he added, "I'm going ahead as though there will be a wedding."

After conferring with Muriel, I asked Maria if it was true that she was supposed to get married that afternoon.

She looked rather shy and answered, "I dunno... I guess so!"

"Well, what time is the wedding? How come you are at work? You must have a lot to do."

"Oh, I was going to ask you if I could have the afternoon off," she replied.

I really did not know how to react. I just could not understand her way of thinking. I wanted to congratulate her on her coming marriage and I also wanted to ask her why she had not mentioned it earlier. Instead, I said, "Well, congratulations! Perhaps you'd better go now and get ready. How long will you be away? Are you going to have a honeymoon?"

"No, I'll be here tomorrow," she said, looking surprised that I would even ask such a question.

That afternoon, only about an hour after the time originally given to the minister, Maria was married in a long white wedding gown and posed for photographs with her husband, Neil, outside the little white church. It made me wonder why we take months to prepare for such an occasion when this one went off just as well on such short notice.

Maria stayed working at the nursing station for about a year after her marriage, then shortly after visiting Muriel for a pregnancy check-up, she announced that she was going to quit her job at the end of the month. We did not see very much of her until she delivered her baby in the nursing station several months later. The baby was born prematurely with hyaline membrane disease and died shortly after birth before we could get him to the hospital in Inuvik. Maria was distraught and we were shattered, this being one of the problems that we faced in having to care for people who were all becoming our friends.

Some time later, Maria had another baby, a breech presentation, which I delivered during one of Muriel's rare absences from the nursing station. Apart from acute anxiety on my part, everyone—Maria, the baby and the baby's father—did very well, and Maria was discharged from the nursing station three days later with her new daughter. That summer she moved out to her husband's fish camp where she cleaned and dried the fish that were to be used for food for themselves and their dogs during the coming winter. Then one day some natives living in the next camp came rushing into the village to report to the police that Maria had fallen out of a canoe and was missing. We all waited for the police to return from dragging the river near the camp, hoping that all would be well but fearing the worst because we knew that Maria could not swim and that the river was very cold even in mid-summer.

Twenty-four hours later, the police freighter canoe pulled into the small dock below the village, and they carried Maria's body up to the nursing station where it was carefully placed in one of our outbuildings. With heavy hearts, Muriel and I laid out the discoloured drowning victim. We tried to make her look as presentable as possible with the aid of cosmetics and new clothes though we had never been trained to do these things, but we knew we were expected to fill the position of undertaker along with all our other birth-to-death

The old Anglican church in Fort McPherson has a graveyard full of memories.

responsibilities. Rather than feeling that it was an onerous job, we felt that it was a privilege to be able to ease the suffering of Maria's family and friends.

When we had finished, we let the community know that anyone could come by to see her, and all afternoon people filed in to pay their last respects. The quiet grief that the Gwich'in people showed was very difficult for us to deal with along with our own private grief, so with aching throats and tears in our eyes we stepped outside until the last person had left. We then placed her body in the casket that her relatives had made, and the RCMP brought down their truck and took her on her last ride to the church. After a service conducted by Don, Maria was buried in the permafrost in the little graveyard.

13

FLEMING HALL, FORT McPHERSON'S residential school hostel, was unique. Unlike the situation in other community residential schools, the children only lived there while their parents were out hunting or trapping or when some social need arose, such as sick parents or a mother going out of the community to have a baby. The hostel, which provided beds, clothes, meals and any other necessities, was administered by Al Jackson. A quiet-spoken man, he sometimes appeared nervous because of a slight hesitance in his speech, but he knew every boy and girl in the school by name and they all respected him.

The hostel had originally been run by the Anglican Church, though like all residential schools it had been taken over by the federal government in the early 1960s. The staff had all remained when the change took place, and I don't think anyone in the community really noticed the difference in who was now responsible for running the institution.

The children from the hostel went across the road to Peter Warren Dease School, and it was the school's principal, Otto Tucker, who introduced us to school showers. The majority of Gwich'in homes did not have running water, and water for drinking, washing, and cooking was carried in pails from water stand-pipes spaced around the village wherever the utilador system was located. This meant that people living away from the central part of the village either carried

School children line up for immunizations in the nursing station waiting room.

their water a long distance or went down to the river to get it just as they had done at their camps before Fort McPherson with its "modern conveniences" had been established. However, in spite of the shortage of easily obtained water, long lines of washing could be seen hanging out on clothes lines throughout the village. Even when it was below freezing, the washing was still hung out, and on the first day the clothes waved stiffly in the breeze as though rigor mortis had affected them, but the severe dry cold evaporated the moisture and a day later the clothes would be brought inside smelling fresh and feeling wonderfully soft.

The school age children, on the other hand, like children the world over, seemed to avoid washing, especially behind their ears, their armpits and other sweaty places. Consequently, when the school classroom was full of sweaty young bodies, there was a no-ticeable aroma that permeated the hallowed halls of the school. In a school meeting one evening, this unsavoury topic was raised by one of the teachers of the smaller children who asked if the school could do anything about the problem. Al Jackson said that there should not be any problems with the children from the hostel because they had to shower daily and were given clean clothes, but he recognized that the majority of children came to school from the village. But he offered the hostel showers if there was someone who could supervise the children to prevent accidents. Of course, everyone was in favour of the children going to the hostel for showers as long as the parents were agreeable, but as there would be some children left in the classroom, the teacher would have to stay with them. All eyes in the meeting room turned to Muriel and me, who had been sitting there listening and agreeing that the children should have an opportunity to keep clean. "It would be an opportunity to see that the children were well looked after and had no blemishes, and it is fortunate that we have a married couple for nurses," Otto said to us. "Keith could look after the boys and Muriel the girls. Excellent!" His mind was made up and I could not think of an excuse that would take him or the group away from the course of action toward which they were pointing us. So by the end of the meeting, it was agreed that Muriel and I would supervise the children in the showers for a couple of hours one afternoon a week.

It became an afternoon that I detested. My glasses would steam up in the humid shower room and my shirt would be soaked. Trying to keep a dozen squealing boys from throwing wet facecloths at each other or playfully turning off the hot water on their partner's faucet was not my idea of fun. Getting the boys to dry themselves thoroughly before they dressed in their clean clothes was often futile, though as they ran back to the school, they looked clean and healthy and their black hair shone. I am sure that Muriel had the same problems with the girls, and we were both exhausted when we staggered over to the school for afternoon coffee. By this time I was so hot that I worried the teachers would think that I should go home for a shower and a change of clothes too!

Periodically in the wintertime there would be an outbreak of head lice and children would be sent down to the clinic with their mothers so that confirmation of the infestation could be made and treatment instituted. The poor unfortunates would return to school with the unmistakable odour of head lice oil wafting from their heads. During inspections at the school, Muriel and I went from child to child as they sat at their desks and we combed their hair with the fine-toothed combs that capture the head lice. When we found any, we would tap the comb onto a piece of paper tissue on the desktop. Some children provided quite a collection. One little boy was delighted at the number we had found in his hair, and as I tapped the comb onto the paper, he quickly picked one of the lice up and threw it onto the head of the child in front of him! With that sort of co-operation it was no wonder that the infestations were sometimes rampant. Another source of cross-infection was the fur trim on the parka hoods. When it was cold, all the children had their hoods pulled up and then, as soon as they came into the school, they hung the parkas up by the hood on the hooks provided, thus assuring that any lice on one child's fur trim could easily migrate to the next.

In the nursing station we were always conscious of the possibility of catching something ourselves—lice or disease—and we were always very careful to keep eating utensils and clothes separate from the clinical end of the nursing station. Later when we had children of our own, we constructed a gate to keep the children at the residence end, and we always wore white coats when we went into the patient area.

When little children had to stay in the clinic as in-patients for treatment or while waiting for a plane to take them to hospital, they were put into cribs or we had a parent or relative stay with them because we never knew when both of us would be called out for a medical emergency, and we could never leave a patient alone. When we admitted elderly patients, we sometimes had someone come in to watch them because our hospital beds were quite high, and these elderly people were, in general, quite small, and we didn't want any of them falling out of bed and getting hurt. But it was surprising just how strong some of the old people were, and their appearance fooled us more than once.

Harriet Stewart filleting whitefish at her fishcamp.

Old Harriet was 91 years old and had what appeared to be Parkinsonism, but she looked after herself at home and we often saw her walking about the village. One day she came to the clinic with an interpreter who told us that she had complained that her head felt heavy and she was feeling dizzy. We checked her over and found that her blood pressure was very good and no other findings indicated what was wrong with her.

"How long have you been feeling like this, Harriet?" I asked.

"Just today," she answered herself without the aid of the interpreter.

"Can you walk in a straight line or do you get dizzy now?"

The interpreter spoke. "Just this morning she nearly fell. We were down on the river collecting driftwood for the fire and packing it home and she went right over!"

We wondered if this was a rare event for a 91-year-old driftwood-packing lady!

14

THERE WAS ALWAYS SO much to do to provide a good health service to the people of Fort McPherson. Besides clinics every day for diagnosis and treatment, we held special well-baby clinics when we immunized infants and toddlers and dispensed nutrition and healthy baby information whenever the opportunity arose. We scheduled tests for the community water supply, checked the state of the garbage dump, inspected the cafe and the residential school, and taught first aid to volunteer firemen. We also tried to fit in home visits to the old people and the chronically sick. Planning these and all our other responsibilities was very wearing so we thought that it would be a good time to have some friends round for a social evening and put the work aside for awhile. But unknown to us, at the same time that we were relaxing and enjoying company in the nursing station, a tragedy was occurring out in the bush.

Bella Vitsik was at her bush cabin 15 miles north (24 km) of the village on a branch of the Peel River. Her husband, Joe, had gone with a friend to hunt caribou in the Richardson Mountains and expected to be gone for about a week or ten days. He had taken the good dog team with him, leaving Bella with a couple of old dogs in case she needed them to haul a bit more wood or a heavy pail of water from the hole in the river ice that Joe had cut when they moved to the camp. Bella was not worried about wood or water, but she did worry about her youngest child who had been feverish and did not want to nurse. She put him into the suspended blanket swing and as she cooked some meat and bannock for her other two children she would give this improvised swing a gentle push. Later she put her older children to bed and tried unsuccessfully to feed her infant again, but the fever in his body and his pale face caused her a great deal of concern. She knew that he was very ill.

In the nursing station, warmed by an oil furnace, we were not aware of Bella's plight. The music and laughter continued as we took turns telling tall stories of our experiences and listening to the radio station from Inuvik. The area outside the station was well lit and everything inside was cozy. At midnight we went to bed after first checking the temperature outside; as it had gone down nearly ten degrees from -25 F (-32 C) to -35 F (-38 C) and was getting colder, I turned up the thermostat. Earlier, William had come around to do a last-minute check on the building and had told us, "It's going to be a cold one tonight."

By this time Bella had made up her mind what she was going to do. She would walk the fifteen miles to the nursing station with her sick baby, using the two old sled dogs to pull her other two children on the little wooden toboggan. She said later that she felt less anxious once her decision had been made and she began fashioning a makeshift arrangement to keep the two children on the toboggan where they would be secure and well wrapped in blankets. On her back, in traditional style, was her infant son, wrapped in a baby blanket, then secured there with a big plaid blanket that she fastened in the front. An embroidered baby belt went under the baby's buttocks, around Bella's shoulders and was fastened with two moosehide straps in front.

Then, wearing an old pair of snowshoes, she started out for Fort McPherson. Behind her, the two old dogs pulled the small toboggan in which the other two children slept soundly. The moon cast an eerie glow over the frozen river but was bright enough to show the trail to the lonely woman and her dogs. Step after step, mile after mile, she walked on. When she looked up and saw the lights of Fort McPherson, she knew she had only eight miles (12 km) to go. Her spirits were momentarily raised and she slipped the baby around to her front to try to feed him again. She unwrapped his blanket a little, but immediately noticed that he felt different. He was not as hot as he had been, and she looked at her baby in the moonlight. She touched his skin and with horror realized that her baby was dead.

Bella's survival instincts, coupled with her courageous heritage, must have goaded her on because she had to care for her other children and knew that she could not leave them out in the cold much longer. She secured the dead baby to the toboggan with the baby belt while the other two young children slept on, unaware of their new passenger.

The sound of the doorbell ringing continually took me to the door in seconds and, as I pulled it open, I saw Bella standing on the doorstep holding out a small bundle of blankets toward me.

"Bella! Come in, what's wrong?" I asked.

She took a faltering step inside, keeping her arms extended as though she was offering me the bundle.

I lifted a corner of the blanket. I saw a small motionless hand and quickly uncovered the rest of the infant, and when I saw the face of the dark-haired little boy, I knew that he was past any care I could give him.

Muriel joined us in the clinic, and her soft words were obviously a comfort to Bella because the whole story came out suddenly. She told us of her growing concern for the baby, the absence of Joe, and her uncertainty of what to do. She spoke of the long gruelling walk and the heartbreak of finding her baby dead just as she reached the point where she saw the lights of the village, which at first had given her some comfort, only to have it snatched cruelly away from her again. She cried, rocking backward and forward, as she told her story, and both Muriel and I shed tears of pity for this woman.

The cold light of dawn was breaking by the time Bella left the nursing station. Her mother had come to take the other children, and already news of the death was spreading through the village. I promised to send a radio message to Joe immediately.

In their tent in the mountains, Joe and Fred had awakened early and were getting ready to go hunting. While they cooked some caribou meat for breakfast, they tuned into Inuvik radio station CHAK as usual to listen to the messages, and both were stunned to hear the announcer repeat, "We have an urgent message for Joe Vitsik at Rock River. Please return to Fort McPherson immediately. Bella is here already. Signed, Keith. Anyone hearing this message is asked to pass it along as soon as possible." They knew something serious had happened, and after throwing their sleeping bags and a few supplies into their toboggans, they hitched up their two dog teams and started out immediately for home, in their haste leaving the tent to be collected later.

The nursing station was quiet all morning. The RCMP and the coroner had been notified of the death, as were the medical personnel in Inuvik. We had seen small groups of people passing the nursing station on their way to mourn with Bella. Late in the afternoon the clinic door opened quietly.

"Keith?" a man's voice said. I looked up and saw Joe, still in his trail clothes and speckled with snow, his beaded mitts hanging from a braided string around his neck. Bella was standing discreetly behind her husband.

"I want to see the baby."

I took them to the little outbuilding where the baby was and went inside with Joe, but Bella was too upset and chose to remain by the door. I uncovered the tiny body for Joe to see. Dressed in new baby clothes, he looked like a sleeping doll. Joe bent down and stroked the black hair. The realization that the baby was dead must have torn his heart, and he brushed his sleeve across his eyes but did not say anything. My throat felt constricted and my chest ached with trying to hold my own emotions together.

"Okay, Joe," I said at last. "Let's go now. Bella needs you." A quick glance at me and then a lingering look at the baby and he turned toward the door.

"Thanks for everything, Keith," he said and walked slowly away, with Bella, in the Gwich'in tradition, a few respectful feet behind him.

I felt drained. After carefully closing the door, I went into the clinic and poured a cup of coffee. I thought about Joe and Bella and their hard life and wondered what I was doing here myself. And then I thought of what Joe had said as he was leaving. "Thanks for everything, Keith." He did not expect us to perform miracles. He accepted us along with our limitations just as he accepted life and death. We had so much to learn.

15

A PROBLEM THAT WAS common to both the native and the non-native people of Fort McPherson was the desire for alcohol. (John Firth was known to drink ink when nothing better was to be found.) But there's no doubt that it was the non-natives who introduced the natives to homebrew, and by the time we lived in Fort McPherson there were very few people who did not make a batch of brew on a weekly basis. I was surprised when I first walked into a house and saw a great pail of what looked like slops sitting on the stove top. When I inquired why they were heating this mess, it brought gales of laughter.

"That's our brew!" someone called out.

One sight of that brew put me off completely so I never tried any of it and doubt that I ever will. I have been told, however, that in Fort McPherson the brew never reached its full potency because it was made early in the day and was gone before it reached a potent stage. One study reported that when scientifically sampled some of this brew measured only two percent alcohol, but in spite of this, there were some people who acted in a very intoxicated manner after drinking it.

Late one night the police brought us one of their "customers" who had been into the brew. They reported that his wife had used the back of an axe to hit him on the nose, splitting it down the centre, and it was an awful bloody mess. Although it had stopped bleeding by the time he was brought to the nursing station, his face and chest were soaked in blood. He was a tall man, well over six feet, and he did not know that it was his wife who had assaulted him with the axe, but she must have had to stand on a chair to do it because she was a small mouse of a woman, and I doubt that she reached five feet! He kept shouting that when he found the guy that hit him, "*then* there'll be trouble!" I had to get him to sit down in the chair so that I could sew his nose together, but when I got the local anaesthetic ready, he started getting fidgety and the constable had to restrain him.

"I don't want needle!" he shouted, trying to get up.

"Listen, friend," the constable said quite firmly, "you'll get just what Keith has to give you. We can't let you go around like this because you look uglier than usual!" This last remark was said in a jocular manner, and I was glad that the patient took it that way as it was going to be hard enough to fix him up as it was.

However, even though I explained what I had to do, the patient was quite adamant. "Go ahead and sew me up," he said. "I don't mind but don't give me needle."

I did not waste his or my time trying to explain that, one way or another, I was going to have to stick some kind of a needle into him in order to sew him up, so instead, I prepared the necessary material and cleaned his wound. After refusing to let me put any sterile towels around the wound because it prevented him from seeing me, he sat there like a statue. Feeling a little nervous about what his reaction might be when I put the first suture in, I was very careful and all ready to jump back, but while he did not move his head at all, his eyes followed that needle everywhere, and the policeman and I were in stitches ourselves by the time I was halfway through. His eyes would cross as he watched the needle go into the skin and out the other side, and as I pulled the 18 inches (45 cm) of nylon tight, his eyes swept up and out, never straying from the needle. Down came the needle and into the skin again, and down swooped his eyes, crossing again as they tried to focus on it. By the time I had put nine small stitches down his nose, I had trouble keeping my hand steady, and the policeman was turning red and leaning against the sink in an apoplectic fit of laughter. Through all of this, the patient kept a very straight face, which made the whole thing seem even more comical.

I was getting a dressing ready to put over the wound when I was nudged by the patient. "Don't put any of that stuff on it." It was not a request, it was an order, the kind that you instinctively know it is no use arguing with.

"I have to put something on it, otherwise it may get infected," I told him, beginning to feel in control of myself again.

"Put some of that paint on it." He pointed to the Mercurochrome that sat in a bottle on the dressing tray.

"But that's bright red!" I told him with a laugh. He was a big man with a nose that could be described as "Roman," and when he sobered up, I didn't want him to feel that I had made him look like a clown.

"I don't care, but don't put that cloth on it," pointing to the gauze.

I looked at the policeman and he just shrugged and said, "If it isn't going to harm him, may as well use it. It's his request!"

Getting a small piece of cotton and the Mercurochrome, I painted all around the wound, then stood back to admire my work. It would never get me through an exam, but the customer was satisfied, and he stood up and admired it in the mirror. "Bring him back tomorrow," I told the constable, "and I'll see how he feels about it then." So the officer escorted my colourful patient out of the clinic. I was thankful that the Mercurochrome was not fluorescent; it could have started a whole new fad!

ONE SUNNY AFTERNOON I was called to a patient who had severe burns. The events surrounding his injuries were quite obscure though we were able to piece together something of the history. It seems that, as the sun was very hot, a group of people had been sitting around on the riverbank or on firewood logs outside their houses, smoking or gossiping the hours away. After a time three of the men had decided to have a drink and then, because it was hot, to have another and then another, and so on.

Joe, our patient-to-be, was one of the three men in the drinking party. He was from Aklavik, and we hadn't met him before the day the RCMP introduced him to us. He had been sitting on the ground with a bottle that was supposedly filled with rum, holding it between his legs and occasionally raising it to his lips or passing it to his friends, but always making sure that it was returned to him. The more he drank, the more uncoordinated he became, and he splashed some of the bottle's contents down his shirt front. At that point, apparently feeling the urge for some different stimulant, he fumbled with his cigarette papers and rolled himself a smoke. Then he located his matches and struck one.

What happened next was a little vague. Apparently, as soon as Joe struck the match, there was a flash and he staggered upright, his clothes on fire. He yelled out and leaned against a nearby shed wall with his hands held above his head. A smell of burning material and flesh pervaded the area. Someone—we don't know who—saw what was happening, ran into a nearby cabin and grabbed a blanket. They rolled Joe in the blanket, putting out the fire, although his clothes still smouldered. Someone else called the RCMP and they in turn sent for us.

I arrived breathless minutes after the police, expecting to see a house on fire but there was no smoke at all. Instead, I saw Joe writhing around on the ground. I quickly checked him over. He was conscious and groaning, but I couldn't make out what he was saying, both because of his groans and because he was drunk. We lifted him into the RCMP truck and took him to the nursing station. But before we left the scene, I asked what had happened. Someone gave me his name but no one offered any more information. Maybe the corporal's presence inhibited them or maybe they just didn't know.

As soon as we had Joe in the nursing station, we began to cut away his clothing to find the extent of the burns, a job made difficult by his writhing around and the fact that he was holding his hands together between his legs. "Joe!" I tried to sound as authoritarian as I could. "Joe, move your hands out of the way so that we can help you."

He mumbled something but I did not recognize any of the words. But as he moved, I saw that he was holding something in his blackened hands. I looked closely and thought that he was holding something like a dirty white glove. I rolled him onto his back, so that I could see better.

"Just look at this!" I whispered to Muriel, who was getting dressings and medication ready.

Joe was not clutching gloves. He was clutching the skin that had peeled away from his hands and his fingers—just like the skin peels off a tomato that has been dipped in boiling water! It was difficult to know where to start, but we knew immediately that there was not a lot we could do for him with our limited facilities. He was going to have to go to hospital.

The corporal, who had been hovering around in the nursing station, came at once when we called him, and after we had given him a brief explanation, he went to his office to call a plane to take Joe to Inuvik. We put protective dressings over the wounds and set up an intravenous fluid drip, once again wishing we had plasma available, but we still only had dextrose solutions.

By the time Joe was ready for evacuation to hospital and had been given a shot to ease his pain, we heard the plane overhead. The corporal went to meet it and bring the doctor to the nursing station. The doctor examined Joe to make sure that he was able to make the trip while we outlined the extent of his injuries so that the doctor would not have to disturb the dressings before he was in the operating room. We were all concerned about what Joe had been drinking and how much of it because this could affect any anaesthetic or medication he was given, and we had already given him an intramuscular painkiller. When Joe reached the Inuvik hospital, the doctors decided that even their facilities were too limited, and they sent him on to Edmonton, where he could have specialist treatment.

Meanwhile, back in Fort McPherson we were trying to piece together what had happened. Someone suggested that maybe Joe had been drinking rubbing alcohol or sniffing gas, but his drinking companions, now sobered up, swore that they had only been drinking good liquor. When the police experimented by setting fire to some rum, there was very little effect as the rum they experimented with had a very low flash point. Of course, no one knew where the bottles had gone from which the group had been drinking, so no actual samples of Joe's drink could be analyzed. The RCMP then wasted quite a bit of their own good Scotch conducting experiments on the flammability of liquor, but they found that it was very hard to get a burn that could have caused such damage to our patient. They concluded that the lost bottle must have contained something that would burn easily because, although Joe did smell of liquor as did the two men who had been drinking with him, his burns were too severe and catastrophic to be caused by ordinary booze.

Joe survived but never returned to Fort McPherson. We were naturally curious about the outcome of his case, but when we inquired at the hospital, we received the usual bland reply that "Joe Blank was as comfortable as could be expected in the circumstance." But he left a legacy on the shed wall in the middle of Fort McPherson—the RCMP corporal showed us the imprint of a pair of hands on the burned shed wall. He also left imprinted on our minds the picture of a man curled up in pain as he clutched in his hands his own skin like a tattered glove.

SOMETIMES THE DRINKING led to violent acts that resulted in death, and then we were far from amused. One non-native man who was working at a nearby mineral exploration camp was overcome with a desire for alcohol and drank a quantity of anti-freeze. He was brought to the nursing station in a semi-coma, and no one would admit to knowing what was wrong with him. Both Muriel and I could smell some fluid associated with engines, but we could not identify it, and we put it down to the general oily type of smell that the oil rig workers always seemed to have on them. When his condition started to deteriorate, we were lucky to get him on a plane to Inuvik within a very short time. Later we heard that he had been flown to Edmonton where he died a few days later and that the cause had been ingestion of anti-freeze. All we could ask was "Why?" It seemed so senseless. We knew that the men who worked on the oil rigs and seismic camps did not have the social interaction that we enjoyed in the village and their entertainment seemed to be of the "macho" variety. In fact, one foolish game that we heard about was for a group of men to sit around daring each other to put out their cigarettes by quickly immersing them in a can of flammable liquid!

IN ALL OF OUR YEARS in the north, we were only faced with one murder, and that, too, was alcohol-related. In this case, after a very successful caribou hunt, a family had celebrated with a large quantity of homebrew. There had been a lot of visiting back and forth between various relatives and, as the night wore on, tempers flared. One man sat at the back of his cabin, boasting drunkenly about his strength and what a good hunter he was and that he was the best shot in town.

"I'll show you what a good shot I am." He laughed drunkenly at his sister and picked up his .308 rifle. "I'll shoot the next sucker that walks through that door!" Just then the sound of footsteps were heard in the porch, and he levelled the rifle as best he could. The door opened and he pulled the trigger. His elder brother pitched forward, bleeding profusely from the bullet wound.

Within 20 minutes the RCMP had been called, and both Muriel and I were fetched by the police. As we were driven down to the cabin, we were told what details were known. The victim had not been moved and was still alive, and the RCMP were waiting for us to examine him before they moved him or did anything else.

It was dark outside the cabin, and after hearing the circumstances under which the patient had been shot, I graciously stepped aside to let the Mountie enter the cabin first, and Muriel brought up the rear. A quick examination of the patient by flashlight did not reveal very much, except a huge amount of blood. By the way he had fallen, grasping his groin, and the large clots of blood in that area, we had to assume that he had been shot in the lower abdomen. There was no other bleeding evident, and as he needed the urgent care that could only be provided in the nursing station, we placed him on a stretcher and with the help of one of the Mounties and their truck we moved him as quickly as possible, leaving the other two Mounties to deal with the offender.

As we bumped slowly along, I could not help but think of the difficulties we worked under. Here we were, crouched down in the pitch-black interior of a truck with the back open because the long stretcher did not allow the tailgate to be closed. The fumes from the exhaust drifted in as did the snow and the cold. It was a far cry from the conditions in which we had been trained.

Once we were in the warm, lighted station, we transferred the patient to a bed that we then immediately elevated by putting the end of it on a couple of chairs. Considering the collapsed state of the man, I was surprised to be able to find a vein, and I started an intravenous infusion of dextrose water as quickly as I could. In those days we had neither blood, cross-matching capabilities, or even plasma to give. Our main goal was to replace some fluid and keep a vein open.

On the way to the station we had passed our native community health representative, Tadit Francis, a man recently trained in basic first aid and other health matters, and we had yelled out from the truck for him to come to the station as soon as he could. We now set him to work cutting the pant legs off the patient's clothing and getting the X-ray machine ready. We gave the victim a quick wash to remove the blood so that we could locate the entry site of the bullet. I found the small entry hole in the upper thigh just below the groin, and when I lifted his leg I could see an exit wound, too. We pulled the clothing from under him, and Muriel found the expended bullet, which, after passing through the leg, had gone through his "long johns" but hadn't exited through the jeans. She passed it to me and I dropped it into my pocket, not realizing that it was a crucial piece of evidence as far as the police were concerned.

The RCMP had notified the Inuvik detachment about the incident and relayed our request to the hospital for urgent medical aid and blood supplies to be sent to us as soon as possible. One of the Mounties stuck his head in the treatment room to see how we were doing and to tell us that two doctors were going to fly in immediately in the dark and bring everything we needed with them. "Oh, and Freddy Carmichael is the pilot."

I am sure the unspoken comment from each of us was "Who else?"

Freddy had said that he would have to warm up his plane, the temperature being nearly 30 below F (-34 C), and while he was doing that and loading the doctors and the supplies, a strip was to be marked out in Fort McPherson and lit by any means possible. The night was clear, and though the stars shone brightly, it was moonless, but we knew that if Freddy Carmichael said he could make it, then we could expect him within a couple of hours, moon or no moon. The RCMP quickly gathered volunteers and, with a case of toilet rolls and two drums of kerosene, they drove down to the airstrip. Maybe because there was no television reception in Fort McPherson or perhaps because people had a strong community feeling and wanted to be a part of anything exciting, there was no shortage of volunteers. There were enough people to spread out along the runway, each with a toilet roll soaked in kerosene and a box of matches. They were instructed to light the toilet roll as soon as they heard the plane approaching.

Meanwhile, in the nursing station, we had taken an X-ray and developed it, and we could see that the bullet had missed the femur but had made a mess of the muscle tissue. We now elevated the leg more and, because the wound had started to bleed again, we applied a tourniquet. We knew that surgery was required, and, as the doctors were on their way, we could only keep things going as they were. The patient kept groaning and trying to reach out to his leg, and although he recognized me, we could not get him to understand where he was or what had happened to him, either because of the shock or the homebrew—or a mixture of both.

By this time Freddy was taking off from the Inuvik airstrip with the two doctors and a planeload of supplies. As one of the doctors described it to me later, the small Cessna 185 had climbed into the dark sky and the lights of Inuvik had sparkled in the snow then grown dim as Freddy set a southwest course. The plane climbed steadily and they saw the Mackenzie Delta shining eerily in the dim starlight. Then on the horizon they saw a faint glow, and Freddy indicated that it was Fort McPherson.

Someone banged on our door. "Hey!" a woman's voice yelled. "Look at all the lights down at the airstrip! Come out and see it!"

I glanced out of the window and saw the airstrip lit up with small fires every 20 feet (6 m) or so. The flames reflected on the snow and lit up quite a large area, and I thought that whoever had come up with the idea must have been quite pleased with the results.

"Sorry," I yelled. "We can't come. We're busy, and those flares are for a plane coming in for us!"

"Eh?" said the hesitant voice on the other side of the door. I visualized the person suddenly comprehending that there was a medical emergency of some proportion for a plane to fly in during the night.

We heard the plane arrive but as much as I wanted to watch it land, we had to stay by the patient who was now trying to pull out the intravenous needle. "Try and keep still!" I yelled close to his ear, trying to break through to his foggy brain.

"Keith," he said, "what you doin' here? Help me straighten out my leg," and he reached for his leg again. I tried to get through to him but he sank back into his own world, muttering people's names and apparently having an argument with them.

Doctors Wright and McNay walked through the doorway carrying boxes and medical bags, and in behind them came Corporal Jim Simpson, equally weighed down with supplies. The doctors stripped off their parkas, and while they were recounting their unique trip, they opened up the boxes and bags, and we brought them up to date on the patient's condition. They washed their hands thoroughly, not having the time to scrub up as they would in the operating room, then donned aprons and gloves. One of the doctors mixed a plasma solution and started it through the intravenous tubing, while the other explored the bullet wound with his gloved finger. The decision was made to open the leg wound, find the major cause of bleeding and stop it, stabilize the patient, and get back to Inuvik with him as quickly as possible.

Muriel and I now relaxed considerably. The decisions were someone else's and we just had to provide assistance. My previous operating room experience helped in laying out the instruments and other paraphernalia and getting the operation site ready. We did not have time for all of the niceties of modern surgery, but we did the best we could under the circumstances. The cause of the major bleeding turned out to be the right iliac artery, which had about one and a half inches (3.8 cm) missing where the bullet had plowed through the leg. The iliac artery being the main blood vessel of the leg, the patient had lost a lot of blood rapidly, and even by the time we had reached him, his blood pressure had already plummeted.

It took about an hour for the doctors to perform the surgery, pump as much plasma and fluid as possible into him, and for us to get things ready to medivac him out. Freddy went down to the plane and warmed it up, and we moved the patient onto a stretcher and wrapped him in blankets. A bottle of intravenous fluid was left running, but once we got outside into the frigid temperature, we were not sure how long the fluid would run through the thin plastic tubing before freezing.

The short bumpy ride down to the airstrip and the loading of the plane was done speedily and mostly in silence, the fatigue and strain

Corporal Jim Simpson in red serge on court day, standing beside one of the very few vehicles in Fort McPherson.

beginning to show on us all. As soon as everything was tied down and the passengers belted in, Freddy fired up the plane, switched on his incredibly bright landing lights and taxied to the very end of the lighted airstrip. I was surprised to see most of the toilet rolls were still sputtering in the snow, giving Freddy an indication of the airstrip's limits. With a roar the little plane careened down the strip and took off, leaving us watching the small red and green wingtip lights until they disappeared amongst the myriads of stars.

As nurses used to do years ago, we went back to the station and started to clean up. It looked as though every sheet and blanket, gauze and towel had been used to wipe up blood and then dumped on the floor. We put everything we could to soak in water and cleaned the rest of the rooms up in case another accident occurred, then went to bed in the small hours of the morning.

Our patient died in hospital the next day. Secondary shock, we were told. He would be flown back for burial as soon as an autopsy had been performed. The victim's brother, who had reportedly shot him, was in custody, now charged with manslaughter. It was three days before Christmas.

The small shell that Muriel had found and that I had put into my pocket was the object that had caused the injury, and both Muriel and I had to write out statements for the RCMP detailing our every move and the movement of that small piece of lead from the time that Muriel picked it up until one day later when I handed it to the police officer. Court was held in Fort McPherson some months later, the accused pleaded guilty, and was given an 18-month sentence that was to be served in Alberta. He was sent south to a prison in St. Albert, far from home and family, in a completely strange and foreign environment with strange customs, clothing and food. He would feel that he was being severely punished but, because of homebrew and some foolishness, the real victim lay buried and preserved in the permafrost of the Fort McPherson cemetery.

16

TIME WAS USUALLY OF no significance in Fort McPherson or in any of the Delta communities in general, and things got done, by and large, when they had to get done or they waited until a more convenient time. Today, tomorrow, next week—it didn't really matter. However, three times a day everything stopped, and for 15 or 20 minutes very little happened. If we had a patient in the examining room, we lost their concentration for a short time. The occasion? Radio station CHAK's "Neighbourly News and Messages." In Fort McPherson the program was preceded by Herb Alpert's "Tijuana Taxi," a lively piece of music that to us remains synonymous with message time. The program was broadcast from Inuvik to such places as Aklavik, Tuktoyaktuk, Reindeer Station, Holman Island, Fort Good Hope, Norman Wells, Colville Lake and many campsites along the coast and throughout the whole Delta region.

Rarely did we receive messages over the radio, but we always knew someone who was either the recipient or the sender of the message, and it made us feel like one big family because we could share in the happiness or the sadness or just the simple information that was passed along. We laughed when the message was one of thanks—"Thanks for the parcel, it sure tasted good!"—and were left guessing if the parcel had contained liquid or solid refreshment, although if the message had originated from Fort McPherson, we sometimes found out by seeing the results of overindulgence in the clinic the following day.

When I was visiting hunting and trapping camps and all activity had ceased for the day, we had a last drink of tea and the candle was extinguished. I would be lying back in my sleeping bag, smelling the carpet of pine boughs underneath me, when my drifting thoughts would be suddenly pulled upright by the signature tune of the "Neighbourly News and Messages." Then, while the logs crackled in the wood stove, we would listen to the announcer telling us what was happening to the rest of the people back in the villages. When he finished, my host would turn the radio off to save the batteries. There might be a few comments from one or another occupant of the big tent and then there would be silence. The stove would lose its heat slowly and the cold would creep across the floor. I would pull my toque down over my ears, snuggle down in my thick sleeping bag and fall asleep.

For the most part, the "transients"—the non-Indian people who came north to do a specific job for a specific time—stayed in the village. Ray Hunter, the Indian agent, travelled out to the camps

The Reverend Don Wootten (left) with Keith in camp at Rat River.

whenever he could, but subsequent administrators chose to do their work from a nice warm office. The only other government employee who went anywhere was the game warden who went up and down the frozen rivers to the accessible camps in his Bombardier, a pick-up-sized vehicle equipped with skis and tracks and powered by a large V8 engine. By contrast the native people were always travelling out to the bush, and one old lady informed us that in the old days the white people were always out on the trail to visit people in the camps and to check on their welfare. We had been talking to her about how the village and the people had changed during her lifetime and resignedly she had said, "They really got to know the people and how we lived. Now they just sit in their warm houses and offices. They never go anywhere that their machines can't go."

Teachers, other government employees like the game warden, the RCMP, storekeepers and engineers, all with their families, made up the mosaic of the transient residents. Our teacher friends, Mike and Bett Wiggins, were an outgoing couple and like us were eager to learn more about the people that we were living among. Whether we were in their house or they in ours, they made a point of making us feel comfortable and very rarely did we hear them complain about anything. They were in the north by choice and expected to enjoy it and they did, and though their primary work was with the school, they did their best to get out to the camps to see how families lived so that they could better understand their students and wherever possible relate the lessons they taught to the lifestyle of the Gwich'in.

On one occasion I had been moaning about being up all night and the work being too much and grumbling that the people didn't want to learn, going on and on ad nauseum when Mike reprimanded me for complaining. However, he did it in an inoffensive way that was casual and friendly but made me sit up and take notice. He had listened patiently for a long time and then when he had heard enough simply said, "Keith, my heart bleeds for you!" It was said in such a tone that I was quite taken aback and realized what a bore I had been. It was my choice to be in that job and I didn't want anyone else's job. I could always quit and head south any time I liked, knowing that Muriel would come with me. I tried to stop complaining after that comment, not always successfully, but at least I hoped I had stopped boring my friends.

There were times when we all got on each other's nerves. The cold days and longer nights of winter seemed to blur our senses and small problems easily became large problems. There would be neighbourly feuds, petty rivalries and romantic triangles. Muriel and I felt so inexperienced that, when these problems were brought to us, we would put on knowledgeable faces and do the best we could, which usually meant listening sympathetically to the current tale of woe. I asked one of the visiting doctors for advice and he conceded that he, too, had difficulty treating the kind of depression we all saw in the north. He commented that what was really needed in all of the communities was a psychiatrist and a psychologist, and he calculated that the "medical" workload would decrease by 75 percent!

It was people like Mike and Bett who helped the village keep its sense of proportion. They would organize square dances, large or small, and many times they would host parties and suppers. And it was they who introduced us to hair cutting in the north. We had been living in Fort McPherson for a few months and my hair was getting quite long compared to the very short hairstyles that were current. Mike and Bett were coming to our house for supper and had arrived early because, Bett told Muriel with a smile, the babysitter had arrived early and they were glad to let her start early.

"I'll just cut Mike's hair while we wait," Bett said breezily. "Where's your scissors?" Mike got some old newsprint and rolled it out on the floor, and Bett went to the bathroom and came back with a towel to put around his shoulders. Both Muriel and I were quite amused and a bit surprised by the way they made themselves at home and took for granted that we wouldn't mind. We didn't, of course, but we still had the old characteristic English reserve and wouldn't ourselves have felt comfortable cutting hair while waiting for the host to cook supper! We were, however, quite happy that they felt relaxed enough to do such a thing and that we never had to search for topics of conversation when either of them were around.

Knowing that there was no barber in Fort McPherson, Muriel and I had discussed having to cut my hair but it was one of those things that we had been putting off because I wasn't too sure what the results would be. So now we looked forward to seeing Bett cutting Mike's hair so that we, or Muriel in particular, could get some pointers for the procedure. Bett started at the back of the neck and snipped her way round to one ear, at which point Mike immediately feigned the loss of his ear and then complained of sundry stabs and cuts, but finally she finished and gave his hair a last combing before standing back to admire her handiwork.

"Well, there is always one thing to remember at times like this," she said, putting the scissors on the table. "There are only a few days difference between a good and a bad haircut."

We learned later what Bett had meant when Muriel, eager to put her recent observations into practice, cut my hair. Everything seemed to be going well for a while, and then I heard her say "Oops!" I found this to be quite disconcerting because I could not see what she was doing but I have quite a vivid imagination. I sat tensely waiting for a description of the disaster. "Oh, never mind" she said casually. "Remember what Bett said the other day? You'll look fine in a few days—or maybe a week!" And she laughed, which did nothing to allay my fears, and I reached for a mirror. Fortunately, the results were not too bad for a first try. It had taken a long time to finish the job but I felt that I could still face the world. The small area of denuded scalp could be covered, and Muriel's "Oops!" area would barely show. As the weeks went by and other men in the village succumbed to their wives' tonsorial endeavours, we would compare the "steps" that we each had and remark that the barbers in Fort McPherson all gave the same style of haircut. On one of my rare trips to Edmonton, I went to a barbershop and the barber stood back and looked me over. Then he shook his head as he asked me where on earth I had my hair cut last time. The resulting conversation lasted for the entire haircut.

As I walked out, I was tempted to say that my other haircuts had been a lot cheaper than what he had charged, but I thought I may have to go back there again one day.

I never had the opportunity to cut anyone's hair, which was just as well, although when I worked in hospital I once did start to cut a young patient's hair. It was only when I was halfway through and realized that I was making a mess of it that I started to panic. Fortunately, the phone rang and there was a message for me, so someone else offered to take over and I did not get back until the haircut was finished.

Periodically patients came into the nursing station with wounds to the scalp, and then I was faced with the difficulty of sorting out the black nylon thread from the patient's coarse black hair. Sometimes I found that when I was ready to tie a knot and pulled the suture tight with the small forceps, the nylon turned out to be a stray hair, which was pulled out in the process, but the patient did not feel anything because of the local anaesthetic.

FREEZE-UP TIME WAS when a lot of the white transient males gave up using razor blades, and scruffy-looking men could be seen everywhere—scruffy that is, until there was enough hair on the chin to honestly say an individual had a beard. The members of the RCMP were not supposed to join this retinue of the unshaved because of their regulations, but one Mountie we knew did grow a beard while he was at a temporary posting at an isolated one-man detachment. Just before his commanding officer arrived after freeze-up, the constable shaved off his luxurious growth only to find his face was very pale where the beard had been!

My own beard had been in place for over five years by this time, and while everyone was talking about growing beards, I began to wonder what I looked like underneath the bristles. "Why not shave off my beard while everyone else is growing theirs?" I asked myself. I talked it over with Muriel time and time again, trying to get her to encourage me to shave, but she didn't want to be responsible for the results, so I procrastinated and lost the opportunity to do the reverse of what every other male was doing at freeze-up. I waited until I was ready to make my first trip to Arctic Red River by dog team, then talked to Muriel about it once more.

"Look," she said, as she was combing her long hair, "I've been thinking of cutting my hair short again, so while you are away why don't you shave and I'll cut my hair, and then it will be all done by the time you get back!" And all of a sudden I wasn't sure that I wanted to shave now that there was nothing stopping me.

When I arrived at Arctic Red, I told Joe Roenspiece, the corporal at the detachment, about the deal that I had made with Muriel, partly so that he would not be surprised when he saw me in the morning and partly so that it would force me into action. Joe's wife was visiting down south so I wouldn't have to put up with any teasing from her or her children, and that was something of a relief.

Joe laughed. "Go ahead and shave but just don't block the sink. I'm going to bed so we'll have an identification parade in the morning!" and with those words he retired, leaving me to my "surgery." I studied my face in the bathroom mirror. I tried holding my beard close to my face to see what its shape would be, but though I turned this way and that, I knew there was only one way to really find out. I picked up my long unused razor and inserted a new blade and started to shave off my moustache, and Ow! it really hurt. Maybe I should have tried using some lather. I didn't have any shaving cream, so I used toilet soap as a poor substitute. Was my upper lip really that big? And my nose seemed to look more of a blob than ever!

I shaved off one side-burn, and half way around my chin. I now knew that I should not have shaved. I sure hoped Muriel was going ahead with her part of the deal, otherwise I was going to be the only one to look very different! I shaved my chin and then thought I was seeing double. And I was! I had grown another chin! I couldn't stick the hair back on again so I quickly finished the job and washed my face. Even that felt strange as my hands rubbed over the fresh expanse of flesh, and when, a little while later, I was getting into bed, I had to smile when after so many years the blanket actually tickled my chin.

Joe was up and cooking breakfast as I came into the kitchen the next morning, and when he looked up at me, a big smile spread across his face. "I didn't think a beard could make that much of a difference!" He put down the eggs and stared at me.

"Thanks Joe, that makes me feel full of confidence to face the big wide world. I just caught sight of myself in the mirror and I'm sure that my head has shrunk and my face has the same shape as Charlie Brown's. Muriel's going to move out when she sees this!"

When I arrived back in Fort McPherson, I was bundled up with my parka and scarf until I reached home—I was still not prepared to reveal the real me to anyone. I went into the nursing station kitchen with my scarf around my face.

"Muriel, I'm home!"

"Did you do it?" she called out of the bedroom.

"Of course. Did you?"

In answer she stepped out of the bedroom and stood there looking at me, her hair cut short, neat and attractive. "That's not fair," she chuckled. "You've got your face covered!"

"I think I'm going to keep it that way, too! You look terrific but wait until you see this!" And I whipped off my scarf.

"Oh dear!" Muriel smiled. "Well, it didn't take you too long to grow a beard last time," she said.

Some of the people in the village didn't recognize me, and when I visited the school, the children had a lot of fun, prodding each other and giggling. The older native people didn't bat an eye. "Good afternoon, Mr. Billington," Peter Thompson said as he passed me on the street. If it had been Mike Wiggins that I had met, he would have been rolling around on the road, laughing, but that was the way people were up north.

Two weeks later things were returning to normal. I had a short beard again—or long stubble, depending upon your point of view— but I knew that never again would I willingly shave off my beard. I was not the man I used to be.

17

IT WAS COLD AND I WAS exhausted and close to panic. I was lost.

Earlier that morning I had been filled with confidence at the prospect of travelling the 38 miles (61 km) from Fort McPherson to Arctic Red River by dog team by myself. I had already made the journey twice previously with a guide when daylight was almost non-existent and when the lone trail between the two communities had looked quite straightforward. Now I was all alone, my dogs were tired and I was exhausted. I had left a dead dog on the trail some distance back and now I sat wearily on my toboggan and assessed my plight, my sense of adventure rapidly waning along with my body temperature.

This was to have been a routine visit to Arctic Red River (now called "Tsiigehtchic") to look after any sick people, immunize the children or do any of the hundred and one things that community health nurses do daily throughout the north. In the darkness of the early morning I had loaded my dog-toboggan and hitched up the team of five dogs that had been loaned to me by William Firth. After I had asked him if I would be able to handle them on my own, he had reassured me, "Don't worry, they won't take off on you and they only have two speeds—slow and stop!" And he gave a little chuckle as he told me his joke.

Mentally I ticked off the supplies that I had to take: food, flashlight, matches and kerosene; and checked that my sleeping bag, axe and snowshoes were fastened securely to the toboggan. Then grabbing the handles on the backrest, I stood on the back of the toboggan and yelled, *"All right!"* at the excited dogs. Turning to wave to Muriel, who stood shivering in the cold morning air, was nearly my undoing—or my unfooting—because the dogs instantly quietened and then, as one, they pulled the toboggan out of the yard with me hastily gripping the backrest again as we hurtled down the main road as though being chased by monsters.

The dogs soon slowed to a trot, a pace that was faster than my walk, so I jogged for a few minutes, then jumped onto the toboggan whenever I needed to catch my breath. Ahead of me the 38 miles (61 kms) of trail lay over 39 lakes and portages. By lunchtime I had reached the halfway point at a little lake called Fish Lake where the RCMP had erected a small tent-frame as a place to stay when they were on patrol. The shelter consisted of plywood walls and a ridge pole over which a canvas tent had been stretched. A tin stove stood in the middle of the dirt floor and the stove pipe went out through the roof. This was the only man-made shelter on the trail and nearly everyone who used the trail stopped here for a rest and a warm-up.

I carried a tin with some rags soaked in kerosene and very soon I had a fire going in the stove and some tea brewing. I remembered that the last time my guide and I had passed this way I had found a gallon can that I thought might have some fuel in it and proceeded to unscrew the cap off the spout. Sensing that the cap was broken, I looked down at my gloved hand and saw that a mouse had crawled up the spout, got its head stuck and had died there and I was trying to unscrew the mouse's head off the spout! I dropped the can in disgust. Even knowing that the mouse had been dead a long time and was frozen solid, I felt squeamish about trying to pull its head off!

I would have liked to rest a lot longer but I knew that it would soon be dark and the tent frame only marked the halfway point. The dogs obviously felt like a rest as well and they gave me incredulous looks as I hauled them into position. Once again I gripped the back of the toboggan. *"All right!"* I yelled. Nothing happened. I yelled again and this time the leader slowly got up and walked forward until the loose harness was taken up. *"Get to it, you miserable hounds!"* I yelled as loud as I could. The dogs turned to look at me and I am sure that just to humour me they began to walk. I rattled the toboggan to let them know I was still there and resignedly they started to trot.

I had been on the trail again for about an hour when one of the dogs suddenly stopped pulling. I halted the team and looked him over but I could not see anything wrong with him. After checking that his harness was adjusted correctly, we set off along the trail again. A few minutes later he stopped again. Not wishing to be delayed, I unhitched him and put him in the carriole (the canvas bag on the toboggan), and set off along the trail again, but he didn't like this elevated position and jumped out and was soon left far behind. I stopped and waited, then fastened him with his chain to the back of the toboggan where he could just follow along without having to pull any load. I could only guess that he was very sick but I did not know what to do about it.

It was just getting dark in the mid-afternoon when I saw a dirty pile of snow ahead. A big bulldozer had made a fresh wide road that intersected the trail I had been following. I also found that my trail turned onto this new road but in the increasing darkness it was impossible to see whether the trail that I was following turned north or south here.

I was astonished. Although I had heard that seismic crews were working in the northern MacKenzie Delta, no one had said anything about them being in this area, which is the only reason that there would be a bulldozed road. I tried to analyze the situation. If the dog-team trail followed the road, it meant that the road would lead to Arctic Red River. But which way? Arctic Red was to the east and the bulldozer road went north and south. If I turned northwards, I would find that either the trail veered eastwards and I would eventually come to Arctic Red River or the MacKenzie River. If I travelled south, the road might veer eastwards toward Arctic Red

River or I might have to travel for days not knowing if the camp—if indeed there was a seismic camp—was at the end. According to the maps, the only habitation in the south was over 1,200 miles (1,900 km) away. I turned the dogs northward. Darkness had now fallen. This is not the darkness of the south. This was an eerie dusk where the outline of small trees could be seen against the backdrop of the snow and then later, as the darkness deepened, the stars looked more intense. The frequently seen aurora borealis—the northern lights— were dormant this night and even had they been showing in glorious Technicolor, I don't think that my anxiety would have let me appreciate them.

There were a few inches of hard packed snow on the road, so I found it quite easy to jog along behind the toboggan and give the dogs an easier time. As the road headed north, sometimes it turned to the east or the west as it went around small lakes or gullies, but always it turned north again. I knew that, if it was to lead me to Arctic Red River, it would have to make a sharp turn to the east sooner or later. After jogging continuously for over two hours, I began to think that this surely must be the wrong way. I decided that, if the road did not turn within the next half hour, I would head back to where I had turned off and break a trail with my snowshoes along the old way, even if it took longer. At least I would eventually arrive at my destination instead of wandering all over the Northwest Territories.

The half hour came and went. I wanted to see what was around the next bend and the next, so on and on I jogged, not willing to accept that I was going the wrong way. Finally I stopped, exhausted and frustrated. I realized that I should have stayed with my original decision to turn around when I said I would, and now I was going to have to retrace my steps. I was angry with myself at the wasted effort.

The dogs behaved as though they were past caring, but they obediently let me turn them around and we started back. The sick dog had flopped down on the road when we stopped and was dragged for a few feet before he stumbled to his feet and trotted along looking totally dejected. I jogged on and, as the dogs went slower, I overtook them and ran ahead to encourage them, my duffle socks and moosehide mukluks cushioning my feet on the frozen road. We arrived at the intersection and I sank exhausted into the snow bank to catch my breath. I had been running for most of the past five hours, but apart from feeling thirsty and tired, I knew that I could still go on after a short rest. I sucked on some snow as my mind raced with thoughts of what to do next. Should I go back home on my clearly marked trail, or should I see if going south on the seismic road would take me to Arctic Red River? Or maybe I should try and continue on the traditional dog-team trail and see if I could find my way? I was wracked with indecision.

It was now as dark as it was going to get but I had a good flashlight with me and I decided to have something to eat and then try the traditional dog-team trail to Arctic Red River. I found my flashlight and rummaged around in the carriole for my food bag. The dogs were all sprawled out resting after having travelled over 40 miles (64 km) so far. I flashed the light over to the sick dog. He lay stretched out at the end of his rope. His eyes were open and his tongue hung grotesquely out of his open mouth. He was dead.

"Oh no!" I whispered, a feeling of dread coming over me. For some reason I did not want to touch him. I felt both revulsion and pity and my throat ached. All thought of having something to eat vanished and all I could think of was "What shall I do *now*?"

Gingerly, I unfastened the chain that attached the dead dog to the toboggan and decided to leave him where he was. I wanted to get away from the place, feeling that this was an omen of the whole trip. I put on my snowshoes and called to the remaining dogs who surprised me by immediately getting up and following me as though they too wanted to get away from this terrible place. I struck out for an opening in the trees where the dog-team trail started again.

After a while I came to a familiar-looking narrow lake and remembered that I had to cross it at a slight angle in order to find the next portage. I walked quite quickly through the dry powdery snow, my snowshoes making a soft whooshing noise as they disturbed the frozen granules. The dogs struggled to keep up behind me and I made sure I stayed far enough ahead of them so that the lead dog wouldn't stand on my snowshoes and trip me up.

I came out exactly where the portage started and I felt comforted that everything was now going to be okay. Apart from a number of small lakes that I had to cross, there was only one that I could think of down which I would have to travel the whole length, and this one, Islands Lake, was the last one before reaching Arctic Red River. It was the only lake that had a tall marked tree called a lobstick on a point of land halfway down the lake, and its 40-foot (12 m) high limbless trunk and bushy top could be seen on all but the blackest nights.

After travelling over a few lakes and portages, I felt that I must almost be at Islands Lake, and when a few minutes later I came off a portage onto a long lake I knew that this was it. The wind blew down it and the snow was hard and crusty. I wiggled my feet out of the lampwick harness of my snowshoes and stowed them on top of the toboggan. This was a good time to let my lead dog show me his true mettle! Most good lead dogs can find their way on a trail either by memory or by feeling the old trail with their feet underneath several inches of snow. My dog pulled forward confidently, but we were only 20 or 30 yards (27 m) onto the lake when he started to head off to the right. I shone my flashlight ahead and could see a faint ridge of snow, so I called the lead dog over to it.

"C'mon boy," I called encouragingly. "We'll soon be there!" He sniffed the ridge of snow and after some hesitation started down the trail. But the lake seemed to go on forever, and I strained my eyes looking for the lobstick. However, I could see some tall trees to my right and thought that the tree I was looking for was probably among them and hidden by the gloom.

Then suddenly the dogs stopped. I went up to the leader and saw that the trail had disappeared again. I yelled for the team to go ahead again, and they moved on for a few minutes and then stopped again.

I peered forward and could see the end of the lake. It was not exactly how I remembered it but, as this was Islands Lake, the portage would show up any time now.

When we reached the end of the lake, the dogs just stopped and sat down defiantly as though to say, "*You* brought us here, you find the way!" I put on my snowshoes and walked all along the end of the lake. I could now see that it was much narrower than it should be. I took out my flashlight and went back to look at the trail. With a sinking feeling I saw that the "trail" I had made the dogs follow was nothing more than a wind ridge of snow. This was not Islands Lake after all! I suddenly felt cold and very, very tired.

I sat on the toboggan and wondered once more what I should do. What would Mrs. Roscoe think about this adventurous person she had sent north? Her words came drifting back to me: "We don't want tourists." The advertising brochures had invited us to go north "for a rewarding career working in Canada's north with the Indians and Eskimo." Well, here I was, I rationalized, going to visit a native village as per government requirements, and I did not have a guide because I did not really need one. After all, I was not lost in the real sense of the word, it was just that I did not really know where I was—all I had to do was turn around and follow my trail back to Fort McPherson and I would not be lost! But pride is a terrible thing, and I knew already that I would not be turning around and going back.

As I sat there with the cold seeping through my parka, I remembered Mrs. Roscoe telling us about our northern assignment: "You will look after the health of the people who live in another village about 40 miles away and you will have to make local arrangements for travelling there. You know, it could be quite exciting..." Exciting? I was not feeling very excited as I sat on my toboggan in the dark on a lake that I did not recognize!

My thoughts turned to Muriel, back in the warm nursing station. I wondered if the Mounties had been down to tell her that I had not arrived at Arctic Red River yet? I had made the usual arrangements with the police and told them when I was leaving and when I expected to arrive, and they had radioed this information to the Arctic Red River detachment. I was long overdue by this time, and I was sure that the airwaves would be humming.

I looked at the dogs sleeping in the snow. I could not face trying to get them to go back again—they were like me, cold, stiff and tired. And just how stiff I was I found out when I tried to stand up and put my snowshoes on again. I picked up the axe from the back of the carriole and walked to the shoreline to find some dry firewood for a fire. I cut some small dry spruce trees and hauled them over to the toboggan. I pulled a little piece of cloth out of a small tin that contained kerosene, put it under the twigs, struck a match, and in a matter of moments I was sitting by a big crackling fire.

But the fire was a mixed blessing. It gave me light and warmth, but it took away my night vision and masked out all sound. Not that there was any sound before, but now I thought that maybe wolves or bears would come around and I would not be able to hear them.

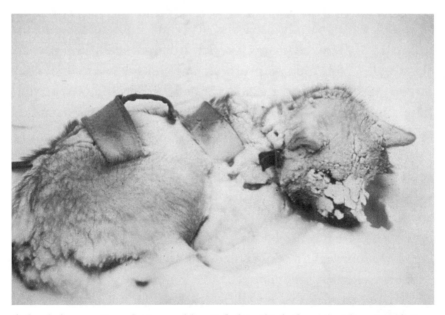

A lead dog resting during a blizzard, his thick fur providing insulation against the cold.

The shadows also had me worried, and all sorts of things came into my now irrational, tired mind. It never dawned on me that the bears were hibernating, and that the dogs, as tired as they were, would immediately stir if wolves or any other beast should come near. My fears were very real that night as I looked around, feeling as though I was being watched.

In spite of these terrors, there was one corner of my brain functioning that told me that to survive I was going to need food and rest. I found a tin of beans and put it near the fire to thaw out as I finished off my Thermos of coffee. I did not know enough then to take the dogs out of their harnesses; I just left them to sleep where they were. I also didn't realize that wearing damp clothes would prevent me from keeping warm, and I just rolled out my sleeping bag in the bottom of the toboggan and crawled in the way I was. I had read about people falling asleep in the snow and freezing to death, so I stayed awake watching the stars and thinking about home, and the next thing I knew I was awake in the pitch dark listening to the sound of a large noisy engine!

I sat up quickly and looked at my watch. It was just after one in the morning. The fire had nearly gone out and my beard was partly frozen to the sleeping bag. The noise was coming from the north and when I swung around I could see the lights of what could only have been a big diesel tractor. It was perhaps two miles (3 km) away and moving fast. It was no good trying to chase him on snowshoes through the bush, and yet how I ached to just ask him where on earth I was. This was only wishful thinking, of course, because he may just as well have been on the moon.

As I watched, the machine stopped moving and I thought of flashing my light but doubted that the driver would have seen me because of his own bright lights. After a moment or two the machine started up again and I guessed why it had stopped—my dead dog in the middle of the cat road! If the driver was headed to camp or to Arctic Red River, everyone would soon know that a collared sled dog had been found dead on the trail. There was nothing I could do now, so I threw some more wood on the fire and soon fell back asleep.

I woke up again a few hours later feeling very stiff and very cold. A full moon was shining and it looked almost as light as day. My mouth felt dry and tasted terrible so I sucked on a piece of crusty snow. I threw some wood on the fire and blew on the embers to get the fire going again to warm myself, and then to ease a growing indigestion pain, I sucked on a couple of antacid tablets. It was too cold to just sit there, so once again I crawled into my sleeping bag and slept lightly until five o'clock in the morning.

Breakfast was a tin of meat from my emergency rations—food that I had carelessly thrown into a bag because that was the thing to do, rather than considering that I might need survival rations. The dogs were plain out of luck as I had not packed food for them, but they seemed to take that as their lot in life and did not even look up when I opened the tin with my sheath knife. They just swivelled their ears around to locate the source of the sound. Afterwards I packed everything back into the toboggan and called to the dogs. They were not eager to respond but, like rebellious school children, they stretched themselves and looked at me to see if I was serious.

"Come *on!*" I yelled, and they stood up, showing me what a twisted mess they had made out of the harness. Starting with the dog next to the toboggan, the wheel dog, I worked my way forward, untangling them as I went. Next I pulled the leader around on the trail so that the team was facing up the lake in the direction from which we had come the previous night, and to my surprise they started eagerly and without any more coaxing from me. It took us 20 minutes to cross the lake that had taken us an hour to cross the night before. I stopped at the portage.

Turning to look back down the lake, I could see in the cold light of dawn that it was not Islands Lake. There was not a lobstick to be seen though I could see the stand of trees that last night had me convinced that the lobstick was among them. There were no islands and the lake was much smaller. I looked at the trail carefully. It had come onto the lake so there had to be a way off the lake. I saw a space in the willows on the shoreline about 50 yards (45 m) from where I was standing, and I felt like kicking myself. I could remember now: this was a lake that the trail barely touched; it came onto it and then almost immediately swung right, crossing a corner of the lake and then heading into the trees once again.

I turned the dogs onto the trail just at the point where my lead dog had tried to take me the night before and where, in my ignorance, I had made him go the wrong way. They pulled slowly and steadily over the unbroken trail, probably feeling the old trail under the fresh snow. Their enthusiasm surprised me, but I am sure that these uncanny dogs could sense that we were now headed for a comfortable bed and some good food! We crossed several small lakes and then, after a short portage, came out onto a long lake dotted with several islands and, off in the distance, a tall tree with a topknot that could be seen for miles—the lobstick.

At the end of Islands Lake the dogs began to pick up speed and constantly raised their heads to peer forward, their bushy tails held

Arctic Red River (Tsiigehtchic), a small Gwich'in village on the Mackenzie River, lies 40 miles east of Fort McPherson (photographed July 1967).

high, and I knew that something was ahead though I was not quite sure what. Then I saw where the snow up ahead of me had been disturbed and that someone had been to the lake to do some ice fishing, leaving a firm trail to Arctic Red River. It was now nine a.m.

By ten o'clock I was crossing the Arctic Red River and looking at the houses nestled along the bank with the Roman Catholic church dominating the scene. The houses were all belching smoke from overworked stoves so I knew that the temperature had dropped considerably during the night. I started up the road from the river and was almost run over by a dog team being driven furiously down the hill. I recognized the driver's fur hat and the yellow stripe on his pant legs. It was Corporal Don Rumpell, and I did not have to guess that he was starting out to look for me.

"Whoa!" I yelled at my dogs, and they stopped immediately and sat down. Don had more difficulty with his healthy, fresh dogs, but was able to hold them long enough for me to tell him what had happened. He yelled back that they were not really worried until a cat skinner had arrived with the news of the dead sled dog on the cat-road, and then everyone had begun to speculate on my fate.

"I'll tell you all about it when you get back." I waved as he took off down the hill, leaving a rooster tail of snow flying behind his toboggan.

Joe Masuzumi, part Japanese, part Slavey Indian, was the special constable who met me at the RCMP barracks, and I told him my story while we unfastened the dogs and tied them up. When he offered to feed them for me and told me to go on up to the corporal's house where I was expected, I did not argue, just thanked him, picked up my bedroll and went to say hello to Yvette, Don's wife, whom I had just met hurtling out of the village with his dogs. She brought me up to date with the other side of the story as soon as I had told her my tale, and as I listened, she fed me a huge breakfast of bacon and eggs, toast and coffee. As I had speculated, the message of my departure had been radioed to Arctic Red River from Fort McPherson, but when I had not arrived at a reasonable hour, the police had checked with Muriel to see if I had actually left at the hour I had said I was going to leave. When the officer expressed some concern because I had not reached my destination, Muriel told them confidently, "Oh, don't worry, he'll be all right." Later she confided that she could not imagine that I could be really lost or in trouble.

Early in the morning—this morning, I had to realize—Don had radioed Fort McPherson again to say that I still had not arrived and that a dead sled dog had been found during the night. He had decided that he should not wait any longer and set out to search for me. The temperature had gone down to minus 35 degrees F (-38 C), and if I had been injured the chances of my survival would have been small.

As Yvette finished and I was drinking my fifth cup of coffee, Don arrived back and told me that he had, in fact, set off to look for me but after meeting me so soon he had to take his dogs out for a five-mile run because they would have been impossible to turn around when they were so fresh and eager to run. We were soon discussing dog-team travel and the trail and accidents as though nothing untoward had happened. He then radioed to Fort McPherson and notified the corporal there of my arrival, and a constable went to the nursing station to tell Muriel. "See, I told you he would be okay," she said.

By the time I had washed and changed and wandered over to the store, I could tell that the moccasin telegraph had been at work. "Where did you get lost, Keith?" people asked with genuine concern. "You have to be careful on those lakes. Someone should mark the portages so that they can be seen." And someone else told me comfortingly, "I know someone who went out like that and they found him frozen stiff." I began to feel that the people almost blamed themselves for my predicament, and a few days later on my trip back I was astounded to see that, during the time I had been in Arctic Red River, someone had been out on the trail and fastened large pieces of brightly painted plywood in the trees at the beginning and end of some of the harder-to-find portages.

When I left the village after visiting the patients I had originally set out to visit, Dale Clark, a Métis, hitched up his dogs and came with me to show me where the road was and we both laughed when, with some chagrin, I found that I had been within five miles (8 km) of Arctic Red River when I had turned around and headed back! Ten hours later, travelling in the dark again but on a good, well-marked trail, I reached Fort McPherson. William Firth went up to the police barracks to report my arrival, and soon the nursing station was full of coffee drinkers listening to my story and relating escapades of their own. Yes, I thought, listening to the noise level in the living room, I think that living here is fulfilling its promise of being exciting!

18

REGULAR VISITS BY REGIONAL staff from Edmonton, though promised, did not materialize and the frequent visits by a doctor who would hold medical clinics didn't occur for months. When we arrived in Fort McPherson, Dr. Cramer had been on staff at the Inuvik hospital but he was transferred south shortly afterwards, and we were left virtually on our own. In fact, the federal government was having difficulty recruiting physicians for the north, and at one time we went for nearly 18 months without having a doctor visit the community. Then when one did materialize and we thought that at least our diagnosis of various patients' ailments would be verified, he walked into the clinic room and simply told us to "carry on" while he disinterestedly looked through some medical brochures!

The expectations of some of the doctors, who had only worked in the south, were unrealistic in isolated communities like ours. Muriel experienced this when a recently trained physician who was touring the north to gain more experience asked her during a birth where the delivery forceps were. As a trained midwife, she had delivered countless babies, always without forceps, and had only reluctantly asked this doctor if he would like to do the delivery out of politeness. She calmly told him that the last forceps she had seen were in Edmonton, 1,700 miles away (2,735 km).

Another visiting doctor welcomed an old man, Bill Charlie, into the clinic and after introductions made a cursory physical examination. He then asked a lot of relevant questions but the patient only looked a bit confused and turned to me for help. I knew, however, that the doctor wanted to get the information directly from him.

"Do you understand what I mean, Mr. Charlie?" the doctor asked.

Mr. Charlie shook his head negatively.

Doctors from outside coming to Fort McPherson usually suspected that their patients couldn't understand English very well but would assume that, if they shouted at them, the raised voice would make their words easier for the patient to translate. So now the doctor, looking a bit perplexed, shouted, "What don't you understand?"

Now it was the patient's turn to look perplexed. He hadn't said he couldn't hear. He had said he didn't understand, and there was no way that he could begin to explain that he didn't understand when he didn't understand, even if the doctor did shout. In cases like this, either Muriel or I would try to explain tactfully to the doctor that the patient could hear perfectly well and then using simple terms tell the patient what the doctor was trying to get across.

A lot of the older people of Fort McPherson had difficulty with body elimination terminology, plus they were reticent to use some of the more commonly used words. Thus, it was understandable that when one patient said quietly to the doctor, "I can't go out with water," the doctor couldn't be criticized for assuming that maybe the patient had difficulty lifting a pail of water to carry it outside. When I interpreted, "He has difficulty urinating," the doctor thought about this for a moment or two before understanding came into his eyes. He then blew the whole thing by interpreting his revelation to the patient in a loud voice in words that were supposed to show that he could communicate without medical sophistication: "Oh, you mean you can't piss?"

The patient, aware that everyone in the waiting room now knew of his secret ailment, scuffed his moccasins on the clinic floor and stared with wide eyes at his feet.

The doctor was not about to let his great discovery go unanswered. "Is that what you mean, John? Drop your pants and then bend over the table. I'm going to stick my finger in your rear end to see if I can feel what's wrong."

The patient, of course, complied, probably hoping that he would have a heart attack before he had to leave and walk back through that crowded, small waiting room.

Another visiting doctor was an avid amateur photographer and took pictures of everything he saw. This was okay when the subject was an inanimate object but he incurred the wrath of one old lady when he tried to take her photograph. Harriet Stewart had the most photogenic face in Fort McPherson. Brown and wrinkled, it spoke of hardship and yet she always had a smile for us when we visited her at home, and she would welcome us in and offer tea and a seat by the stove. As we discussed her health with her, she would nod her head and repeatedly say, "Yes, yes," though I'm not sure that she

Harriet Stewart enjoying her pipe.

understood what we were saying. But she knew we cared about her, and I think she knew we were concerned about her welfare so there was a closeness between us.

She would pull out her old briar pipe and fill it with tobacco, light it up and puff away, and I was enthralled by this little old lady, who was about as old and small as my grandmother, sitting there with a twinkle in her eye, puffing contentedly on her pipe.

It happened that when we were out for a walk with the doctor, we met old Harriet on the trail in front of the Bay manager's house and greeted one another. She was on her way to the clinic to consult with the doctor and tried to communicate this to him, but he was too busy getting his camera ready and was not really listening. He saw a wonderful opportunity for a really good "character study," and that was foremost in his mind. Ignoring Harriet's efforts to talk to him, he asked her to turn into the light. She muttered something harsh in her own language, turned abruptly around and stomped off.

Muriel and I felt acutely embarrassed by the doctor's actions and wondered what sort of repercussions this might have because an elder had been insulted. For his part, the doctor realized belatedly that he had overstepped the bounds of propriety and was quite contrite. Harriet never did come to see that doctor again but, fortunately for us, she continued to treat us with the same friendliness as before and came to the clinic regularly for us to help her with her health problems.

WHEN I VISITED A HOME, I could never bring myself to act in the manner that we had been taught, that is, to take off my coat and, turning the lining to the inside, hang it up or else fold it and, after putting some paper on a chair, place the coat on it. We were to place our medical bags on another paper, making sure that it did not come into contact with anything in the house in order to ensure that germs were not transferred from one patient to another. It was a sensible and good health practice but I was sure it would make patients feel that they were untouchable or that their houses and contents were something to be avoided at all costs. So, for better or for worse, I would go into the house and depending upon the circumstances and the health of the patient, I would sit and talk to them, even sitting on the bed if a chair was not convenient. I would drink tea if it was offered and always tried to give the impression that my time was theirs.

After going about our daily tasks we often had to get home to prepare a meal for official visitors staying at the nursing station—carpenters, sanitary engineers, the X-ray survey team, a pharmacist and many others who had work to do that was remotely associated with Medical Services facilities or the general health of the community. Sometimes we asked Al Jackson at the school hostel if he had room for people to stay, but most of the hostel's accommodation was dorm-style, and if they had a full staff complement there were no rooms available.

An ophthalmologist who was visiting was happy to stay in the nursing station and use an empty patient bed. As he prepared for bed, we jokingly told him that he would have to be turfed out if we had an emergency, never dreaming that it would really happen! At three in the morning we were aroused by a lady in labour and had to tell the doctor to vacate his bed. As he was a medical doctor, Muriel politely asked him if he would like to do the delivery. He laughed when he was asked and said that professionally he should be able to do it, "but I haven't worked on that end of a patient since I graduated!" and he gladly relinquished the task to Muriel.

One of the duties that fell to us by default was health inspections of any place that handled or stored food. This was a fairly easy task and accomplished with cooperation by the store staff, but was more complicated when we had to visit the small cafe that was operated by one of the independent store owners or "free traders" as they were known. We would take bacteriology swabs from countertops, take the temperature of refrigerators and freezers, and look for signs of vermin. Thankfully, the communities in the Delta were free of rats. (Muskrats are not the same species as *Rattus rattus*, being more like beavers in their habits and diet.) This aspect of the job was one that we least enjoyed because we had the feeling that the storekeepers felt threatened by the inspections, and if we ever thought that there was some sort of violation of the regulations, the result could cost them a lot of money to rectify. It was a problem caused by living in a very small community where everyone seemed to know everyone else's business, and if people did not know the facts they delighted in embellishing the little that they did know. Our main objective, however, was to help the native people become more health-conscious and by so doing lead longer and healthier lives.

The more we worked with the people the better we got to know them and in time we could differentiate between some of the physical family features and, even though we did not always know names, we had some idea which family each individual belonged to. Then, because we thought that it would help us to know people better if we understood the language, William Firth began teaching us a few words in the Gwich'in language. Pronouncing the Gwich'in names was quite difficult for us at first, and identifying people was equally difficult when they sometimes used their original Gwich'in family name and sometimes the name that government officials had registered them under. Because of the old bureaucracy, poor record keeping or Gwich'in family culture, the official records showed that Chief John Tetlichi had a brother called Johnny Charlie, and those were the names they were known by. Many of the native names had been anglicized—by whom and why we never did find out. It may have been traders or missionaries who could not pronounce the Gwich'in names, although most of the old traders did learn the local language. Another theory was that the natives had wished to adopt English names in the same way they had adopted European dress. William told us that in the old days names were given by the old women who, on hearing of a birth or more likely being present at the birth, would look around them and then state what the new baby's name would be. These names were eventually used as surnames when European influence again demanded that there should be both a Christian (first) name and a surname. For example, the surname Vittschik meant "his dish" but the offspring of old Colin Vittschik used his first name as their surname, and so the family became the Colin family. Similarly, the children of Robert Sindinilyan ("I want to see him") became the Robert family.

The family of Alexi were very good-looking, and yet their original name had been Ettsitishi, meaning ugly thing, and we wondered what it was that the old women had seen for them to bestow that name. But we learned that people did not take offence at such names in the old days, and they were accepted without comment. (When we had been in Fort McPherson for only a short time, we were a bit taken aback when we heard old people referred to as "that old man or woman" with the emphasis placed on the word "that" so that it seemed to have a derogative ring to it. Later, we found to the contrary—it was more a title of honour.)

One old lady named Lucy Rat had a son who had changed his name to Peters after his father's first name. Lucy's forebears had been called Ditsi Kutikhyi ("calling his grandfather"). So it went on: Litthulchud ("rotten guts") became Wilson; Sahunrakkya ("set trap before me") is now called Martin. But Koe ("treasure" or "something of value") is one of the names that remains, as does Vaneltsi ("I want to smell him") and Vittrekwa ("he has no tears or pity"). The Nerysoos (originally Neryoonoo meaning "hoping for everything") have kept their name, but the family name of Nesheh ("I want to go there") has been changed to Bonnetplume, the name of a major northern river.

THE GWICH'IN TONGUE seemed to have difficulty with my wife's name, so "Muriel" was very rarely uttered; instead she was sometimes referred to as "Mrs. Keith" or most commonly "nurse"— even at social events. On the other side of the coin, the native people had great difficulty with their description of me in my job. The word for "nurse" in Gwich'in was simply a translation of "the person who helps the people," but a male nurse gave them some difficulty (which

Lucy Rat, a blind Gwich'in lady, lived alone in her tent on the Husky Channel.

was not an unusual problem in the early 1960s when even sophisticated people down south had problems accepting a nurse in male form). The Gwich'in finally came up with a word that described me as "the person who helped the person who helped the people" but in English it was a daily education exercise to stop them calling me "doctor," simply because all the doctors they had seen had been men and the nurses had all been women.

Whatever the labels given to us, Muriel and I worked as a team. Although we tried to let the women patients consult Muriel, sometimes it was just not possible, but I think that any awkwardness was mine. As midwifery was Muriel's specialty, in all but a few instances these patients were hers exclusively; I looked after the accidents, the suturing, the dentistry, and saw the men, who appeared to be more self-conscious about their bodies than were the women.

Before we had children of our own, we took it in turns to travel to Arctic Red River, but when our family started, I made all the trips out of the village. We encouraged everyone to come to the nursing station when there was an emergency because we had a choice of equipment and supplies right there, but that was not practical for every case.

When women went into labour, they waited until the very last minute to come down to the station for delivery, and just like everywhere else in the world, the babies came when they were ready and paid no heed to the chart that told us when they were supposed to arrive. And that is exactly what happened on one very windy Saturday in the springtime when it had occurred to one of the schoolteachers to make a kite, and the idea caught on with gale force intensity. By late afternoon there were dozens of kites of every shape and size being flown, and we started a contest to see whose kite could go the highest. Rolls of string were gathered and fastened to each other, and the kites went up and up until several, including the one that Muriel and I were co-piloting, was out of sight. Leaving Muriel with it for a few minutes, I ran to the nursing station and found my binoculars but I still couldn't see those high flyers. Then just at the peak of the excitement, a woman we had seen walking down the trail tapped Muriel on the shoulder. "Nurse, the baby, it's coming!"

"Really, Alice? You're not kidding me, are you?" Muriel looked at me and then at the kite, and receiving confirmation from the expectant mother that things were indeed happening fast, we both looked around for help. A middle-aged native man who had been watching all the white people playing with their toys on the riverbank suddenly found himself the owner of a kite, and as Muriel and I hurried to catch up to our patient, we glanced back to see the new kite owner hanging onto the end of a long piece of string that went up into the heavens and had nothing to be seen on the end of it. He was standing there with his mouth open in perplexity, glancing from the string to us and back to the string again.

"Someone will show you what to do!" I called out to him and, much to our relief, one of the teachers moved closer to help him.

A while later, after the baby was born and we had cleaned up, there was a tap on the door and William stuck his head into the kitchen. "Old Amos just brought your kite down to me so that I could give it to you. He said that he had quite a time with it. He thinks you're all crazy!" And then he laughed silently behind his hand and went out, still chuckling over Amos's comments.

ANOTHER OF OUR DELIVERIES occurred very early one summer morning. The sun had risen at about three in the morning, and our alarm clock was set for seven. I awoke to a commotion on the wooden sidewalk not too far from our bedroom window. Looking out, I saw a man trying to climb the fence and calling out, "Keith, Keith, Nurse!"

"Oh no, not a drunk at this time in the morning!" I said to Muriel, who was beginning to stir with the continuing noise. (By my own choice, drunken visitors to the nursing station were my responsibility.) But when I looked out of the window again, I saw that there was a woman lying on the sidewalk.

By now the man was straddling the fence, and when he saw me at the window, he called out, "The baby's coming!" and then added, "Right now!"

Instantly wide awake, both Muriel and I threw on housecoats and dashed towards the clinic. She went to the delivery room and pulled supplies from the shelves while I hurriedly unlocked the clinic door and ran to where the woman lay. I now recognized who the couple were and asked the lady how she was doing.

"It's coming right now!" she said as she had a strong contraction.

"I'm going to pick you up, Liza," I told her and grasped her in my arms. "Try to breathe through your mouth and pant if you can." I picked her up and carried her toward the station. John, her husband, staggered along behind me, apologizing for his condition.

"She told me that it was starting last night," he explained, "so I just had a cupful until she was ready, but it took so long."

The "cupful" had been repeated many more times and he had finished the brew off before his wife decided to walk down to the nursing station. With his "help" the walk had taken longer than anticipated, and when Liza collapsed on the sidewalk, he had panicked and decided to take a shortcut for help and that's when he got hung up on the fence. Now he tried to make amends by helping me to carry his wife, and to any observers our little trip must have looked hilarious as we sashayed down the sidewalk, through the gate, and up the half dozen steps to the clinic door, which was certainly wide enough for one person to pass through but not three when one was being carried and the other was stuck like a leech to whatever piece of anatomy was available.

As soon as we were in the delivery room and even as I was putting Liza on the bed, Muriel was whipping off Liza's underclothing, and we could all see the top of the newborn's head.

John watched, fascinated. "This is the first one I've seen," he confided quietly, meaning this was the first birth he had witnessed. As the baby's head was delivered, John's eyes grew bigger and bigger, and only seconds after Liza had landed on the bed, the baby was born—much too fast, according to Muriel's professional judgment, but I was sure that, if the birth had been prolonged, John's eyes would have been delivered first! He didn't say anything for a long time, just looked at the baby and then his wife and, in spite of his happy, inebriated condition, I was sure that the birth made a profound impression on him. Although he did not change his ways immediately, in time he and Liza became outstanding examples of sobriety in the community, and their newborn son became a strong handsome young man, of whom they are very proud. And I was quite proud, too, as they gave him my name.

OF ALL THE BIRTHS that took place during our time in Fort McPherson, the most exciting were those of our own two children, Helen on December 4, 1964, and Stephen on July 2, 1966. Both children were born in Inuvik—Helen, partly because she was Muriel's first baby and we had a policy that all primiparas had to go to hospital in Inuvik for the births, and partly because it has never

been considered good practice for one family member to treat another member of the family so as to avoid direct emotional involve-
ment in the treatment and care. (We heard it said that if you treat a
member of your own family "you have a fool for a doctor and a fool
for a patient.") This second reason also decided Stephen's place of
birth.

However, the policy of sending maternity patients to Inuvik—a
policy that we followed and with which we agreed—made us see the
difficulties it caused the native people. Very few babies came on the
predicted day so that, because of the uncertainty of the weather, the
expectant mothers had to travel to Inuvik two weeks prior to their
due date and stay at the homes of friends or relatives, the school
hostel or the hospital while they waited. Meanwhile, life back home
had to continue and there were very few opportunities for the father
to travel to Inuvik and be there for this important occasion.

For our first child, Muriel flew to Inuvik in mid-November and
stayed in the hospital nurses' residence, faithfully walking downtown
and back every day in the hope that the exercise would get things
moving. At last she went into labour and sent a message to me before the scheduled plane arrived in Fort McPherson, enabling me
to fly to Inuvik before she went to the case room. Dr. Wilbush was
going to do the delivery, and he had not encouraged me to be present because Muriel and I were friends of the doctors and staff and, if
there was a crisis, my presence may have put a strain on the proceed-
ings. Instead I waited in the staff lounge and watched some slides
that Dr. Brodie Edmunds was showing, although my concentration
was not very good. After an hour the phone rang, and one of the
nurses went to answer it.

"It's for you, Keith. It's Dr. Wilbush."

Nervously I picked up the phone. "Hello, Keith here."

"Well, Keith, it's all over but I have to tell you this…" He sounded serious. "Your baby will never be able to grow a beard."

Visions of my little boy with a deformed face came into my mind,
and from the silence on my end of the line, Dr. Wilbush must have

realized I was shocked. "Don't worry, Keith! Congratulations! You have a little girl! Come on over and see Muriel and meet your new daughter!"

I hung up the phone, aware that people were looking at me. Then feeling weak-kneed but forcing a smile, I told the waiting audience what Dr. Wilbush had said and everyone laughed and called out congratulations. I headed over to the ward but when I got there, Muriel was having some personal care done, so I trotted off to the nursery to admire my offspring. Looking through the window, I saw some dark-haired babies and one with slightly lighter hair.

"That must be Helen!" I said when the nurse came and saw me looking through the nursery window, and I pointed to the baby and told her that it must be mine.

"No," she said with a smile, "that one is an Eskimo baby from Tuk. Yours is in the corner over there."

I looked at the little dark-haired baby in wonder and spent a few moments in admiration before going to see Muriel, who had done all the work. Since it was the women who made all the moccasins or "shoes" in Fort McPherson, we had been told that baby girls were announced as shoemakers and baby boys as hunters, so over radio station CHAK that evening an announcement went out:

To the people of Fort McPherson. I'm happy to say that Fort McPherson has another shoemaker. Muriel and baby are well. I'll be home tomorrow. From Keith.

Muriel and Helen came home on the scheduled flight on December 8 when the mercury stood at minus 52 degrees F (-46 C). The only vehicle that would start was the Indian agent's bulldozer, so the latest addition to the village population rode home in her mother's arms on a stoneboat pulled behind the bulldozer. She was quite oblivious to this unique welcome home.

About one month before Muriel was due to have our baby she had been forced to resign from her nursing position, there being no

Muriel demonstrates the Gwich'in style of baby-carrying using an embroidered baby belt and a McPherson tartan blanket.

such thing as maternity leave in the 1960s, and when she felt able to return to work she was re-hired—though at the beginning salary rate for nurses, in spite of her qualifications and experience. Our supervisors did not visit or show any concern that there was now a new resident in the nursing station and we assumed that they were too busy with other staffing problems or that they were just happy that we had everything under control. We hired Mary Firth as our babysitter so that Muriel was able to continue breast-feeding and we could always see Helen whenever we had a break from work. It worked out well for us, for Mary who could earn some money, for Medical Services, which did not have to recruit another nurse, and for other young mothers for whom Muriel now acted as a role model.

Helen, and later Stephen, grew very attached to Mary, as she did to our children, and she and William became their surrogate grandparents, in Gwich'in terms the "Jijuu" and "Jijii."

19

DURING THE YEARS WE spent in the north, I walked hundreds of miles on snowshoes, and in the wintertime I never went on a trip without carrying a pair with me or making sure that when I was flying to a camp I had access to a pair of snowshoes. Fortunately, all planes carried snowshoes as part of their survival gear.

On one of my regular trips to Arctic Red River by dog team during our first winter there, I had an excellent trail outward bound, but while I was there a terrific wind and snowstorm occurred, obliterating all signs of the trail. However, by this time I was confident that I could find my way home across the numerous lakes and portages, and I set out in the early morning with my dogs pulling the toboggan and my snowshoes fastened on the top of the load where they were easily accessible. After jumping through the deep snow for two miles (3.2 km), Silver, my lead dog, began to tire so I stopped the team, put my snowshoes on and strode out ahead of them. But the dogs, now having an easier trail, soon bunched up behind me, and Silver, trying to stay close to me, kept standing on my snowshoes, which caused me to stumble and generally make me irritable. I could not imagine travelling another 36 miles (58 km) under these conditions, but I had to get home and snowshoes were the only way to go.

After another 20 minutes, the dogs began to space out behind me, Silver stayed off my snowshoes, and we made slow but steady progress. I plodded on, hour after hour, until late in the afternoon, stopping once to untangle the dog harness, several times to drink tea from my Thermos, and a few more times for bathroom breaks. By the time the sun was sinking over the horizon, I was feeling quite weary. I had gone 30 (48 km) of the 38 miles (58 km) when the dogs started to surge forward again, and I saw that they were sniffing the air. There was something up ahead! I removed my snowshoes, tied them to the toboggan, then gave Silver his head to lead us to whatever was ahead.

As we rounded a small knoll some 25 yards (22 m) further on, I saw a fresh dog-team trail and a still-smoking fire. I stopped the team and looked around. There was a message written in the snow:

Dear Keith
Where are you? We waited until 4 pm.
Luv, Mike and Bett

Mike and Bett Wiggins enjoyed the outdoors and had tried everything that they could to be out there, including driving dogs. Mike owned two beautiful Malamutes and had obviously borrowed a few more animals and taken a run out on the trail for some fun. Their fresh trail headed across the lake, and with a feeling of relief I pulled out my pack, filled the tea pail with snow, and stirred the embers of my friends' fire. I relaxed on my toboggan, watching the fire and waiting for the water to boil for a cup of tea. I was sorry to have missed my friends but their trail was a real gift to me, and I knew that Silver would be able to lead me home within hours.

When after a half-hour the dogs started to get restless and I began to feel the cold, I finished my tea, collected everything together, and straightened out the dogs. I called out, *"All right!"* and the team ran down the trail with renewed energy, their heads held high. It was dark when I reached the village, but the dogs ran straight to their posts and stood still while I unharnessed them, gave them a good pat, and then unloaded the toboggan.

When I stepped inside the nursing station, Muriel told me that

Mike and Bett had called by to say that they hadn't seen any sign of me, so I sent a message by William, thanking them for breaking trail. Mike told me later that he and Bett had hoped to meet me so that we could travel back together. He knew that my dogs would be tired and maybe he wanted to be sure that I didn't get lost again!

IN MID-MARCH 1964 MIKE and Bett told us they were thinking of making a dog-team trip somewhere and suggested we take two teams and go to Aklavik for the Easter long weekend Mad Trappers Rendezvous. Aklavik is only 70 air miles north of Fort McPherson, on a branch of the Mackenzie River. Together we looked at a map of the Mackenzie Delta, a Medussa of intertwined rivers and lakes, and we rather naively figured we could easily make portages where the river snakes, and we should be able to make it to Aklavik within a couple of days if we went by way of the mouth of the Peel.

Mike and Bett arranged to get substitute teachers, and the school principal gave his permission willingly as most of the trip would be on the long weekend and would not involve too much time lost from the classroom. We were fortunate that the Bay manager's wife, Phyllis Seaton, an ex-Medical Services nurse, offered to look after any emergencies for the weekend, and we assured her we would be back in lots of time.

With the help of William Firth we collected all of the necessary equipment. We borrowed a canvas tent and a folding wood stove from the game warden, calculated how much food we would need and added some more for contingencies, and asked a number of people about the best route to take and the location of portages and trails. (Later we discovered that not too many of the older people could interpret a map very well, but when we listened to them before our trip they convinced us that it was all very clear and simple.) We were warned that we might not see many people on the trail because the route we were taking would be mostly past the summer fish camps, not the winter camps, and most if not all of the people would be back in the village for the Easter holidays.

The temperature had been averaging minus 15 degrees F (-25 C) for the week preceding our departure date, and we thought that, if the present weather held, we would have quite a comfortable trip. Alas, our hopes were shattered when on the morning of our departure I checked the mercury and saw that it was minus 51 degrees F (-46 C). Being slaves to times and dates, we had either to carry on with our plans or to cancel them altogether, but Mike and Bett were impatient like us and after some long discussions it was decided that we would set off and hope that the weather would improve.

We loaded our toboggan and hitched up the dogs. Muriel climbed into the heavy down sleeping bag, and I made her as snug as possible in the toboggan. She was able to lean back against the lazy-back and she had two hot-water bottles with her for extra warmth and comfort. I called to the dogs and jumped onto the back of the toboggan. We were off! I did not dare let go of the lazy-back handles to wave to William who had appeared early to make sure that we got away without any accidents, and in what seemed like seconds we were down on the river and heading north.

The cold was intense and I had to keep covering my face with my big wolf-fur mitts to prevent my nose from freezing. Muriel kept wiggling her toes to keep them warm, but the dogs, oblivious to the cold, pulled heartily along the trail as though they were out on a summer day. A shout behind me alerted me that Mike and his dogs were behind me with Bett wrapped up in a sleeping bag on their toboggan just like Muriel, and everybody was shielding their faces from the penetrating wind.

The dogs travelled steadily and without encouragement, only stopping when one of them had to relieve itself. They were trained to pull off the trail when they defecated, so when the urge came upon them, they stopped pulling forwards and pulled to the side into the deep snow. As soon as I saw this happening, I kicked down the small claw brake on the back of the toboggan and tramped it into the snow, effectively halting the team. When the dog had finished, he would jump back onto the trail and start pulling at the harness with renewed vigour, and the other dogs, who had used the short break to eat some snow and mark their territory, started barking, eager to be off again.

After two hours of travelling, we pulled in toward the riverbank to make a fire and heat water for tea. Muriel and Bett jumped up and down to restore their circulation although they insisted they were not really cold, just stiff from sitting in a cramped position for so long. As soon as we had finished the tea and eaten some fruit cake, we headed down the river again. Whenever I began to feel cold, I jumped off the toboggan and half-ran, half-walked, while maintaining my grip on the lazy-back. When I felt warmer or out of breath, I jumped back on to the toboggan.

In mid-afternoon, seeing a cabin on the riverbank, we headed toward it so that we could eat our lunch there out of the wind. But as we approached, we could see smoke coming from the chimney—a very cheering sight. Soon we saw other cabins, which had been hidden from view by the bushes, scattered along the riverbank, and we knew we had arrived at the mouth of the Peel.

When I knocked, a man came to the door of the cabin and looked inquiringly at us, not knowing, with our parka hoods up, who we were. "Hello, Jimmy!" I hollered at him. "You surprised to see us?"

Recognition lit his face, and he gave a big grin. "Oh hello, Mr. Billington, Mrs. Billington. I sure wondered who was coming. Come on in, come on in." Jimmy Thompson, one of the elders from Fort McPherson, was always formal in his greetings and polite in his conversation. Mike and Bett pulled up behind us and Jimmy told us all to come in for a cup of tea. The kettle was already singing on the stove when we went in, and after a shy greeting from Mrs. Thompson, she put a few more sticks on the fire and brought the kettle to a full boil.

"I've just made some bannock, maybe you'd like some?" Even as she asked the question, she pulled out a pan containing a golden brown bannock and began cutting it into pieces.

We sat in silence and ate hot buttered bannock and drank sweet tea, as warmth and drowsiness crept over us. The small log cabin was furnished with old but well-cared-for furniture, and cushions made the chairs comfortable. Photographs were stuck on the log walls with thumbtacks, and a religious calendar was used to mark off the days of the month. A black felt pen nearby showed that it was a daily habit. Like most cabins, a Coleman gas lamp hung over the table, and unlit candles were stuck onto tin lids and spaced around the room. These were probably used more often to conserve the precious white gas.

Jimmy broke the silence. "You going to stay the night?" he asked casually. I am sure that he would have not been put out had we decided to stay, and his wife would have soon found places for us to sleep, either in their cabin or one of the adjacent empty ones.

"No thanks, we've got to push on and try to get as far as we can, but I'm going to give the dogs a little lunch first." Mike and I got up reluctantly and, putting on our parkas, went out into the cold afternoon air.

Normally the dogs were not given a midday meal because they would not work so well after it. Instead they had their one and only food ration at the end of the day when the work was all finished. But after travelling many times with a dog team, I saw dogs that were just too tired to eat at the end of the day, and the food I had ladled out was still there the next morning, frozen to the ground. But the dogs would get up and bark excitedly as the team was harnessed and still put in a good day's work, and it never ceased to amaze me how such a small amount of food sustained these hard-working animals. But today because it was so cold, we had been told to give each dog half a pound of "beef tallow" to help them retain their energy. The dogs certainly didn't object and gobbled the fat down in seconds and they were not fussy if a piece of the wax paper was still frozen to the fat—it was all swallowed fast.

A thermometer outside the cabin showed that the temperature had moderated a little, and now was only minus 30 degrees F (-34 C), but as cold as it was, we wanted to be on our way, so we went in to say goodbye to our hosts and to tell Muriel and Bett that we were ready to go. The drowsiness that had started to overcome us in the warm cabin was dispelled once we were packed up and ready to go again.

When we left the Thompsons' cabin, we turned up the Peel Channel toward Aklavik. The trail was very indistinct, having been made by the game warden's Bombardier several weeks previously, but although we could barely see it amid the snow, the dogs were able to follow it quite well. The river trail was not very exciting—it was flat and twisted and turned—and we looked forward to some new vista to be revealed around the next bend. Whenever we saw a cabin or old tent frame, it gave us a moment of excitement and, I suppose, a sense of security to know that human beings had existed in this inhospitable place before us. It was getting dark when we spotted a small cabin high on the riverbank, and even though we had a tent and a stove with us, we decided that it would be better to sleep in the cabin and not have to bother putting up the tent. Mike put on his snowshoes and made a trail up the bank to the cabin, and Bett jumped out of the toboggan and drove Mike's team after him. We followed suit.

The cabin was very small, the furniture consisting of a single wire-frame bed, a rickety table with some old chairs but, more importantly, a barrel-type wood stove. There was no firewood, so I went outside to see if there was any standing dry wood in the area. I saw a big tree standing alone amongst some willow bushes, walked over to it on my snowshoes, and cut it down with my axe. It never occurred to me that it was unusual for a good dry tree to be left untouched so close to a native campsite. To me it was standing dry, and that is what William had told me to look for. However, when I started to cut it up, I found some wire attached to the top of it. I pulled the wire and saw that it went over toward the cabin. I had chopped down the tree that held the radio aerial! Oh well, too late now. I continued to cut up the tree and found the work exhausted me. By the time I had collected sufficient wood, it was dark and the others had unpacked the toboggans and tied up the dogs. Mike had found some bits and pieces of wood lying around the floor and started a small fire, but it was still cold in the cabin, and we sat with our parkas on, waiting for the newly cut wood to burn and throw off some heat. We waited a long time.

We tossed a coin for the bed and Mike and Bett won, which was fortunate for us because they were thin individuals and barely fitted on the narrow frame. Muriel and I put our sleeping bags together—one inside the other—and slept very uncomfortably on the floor until 5:30 in the morning, when I got up and started trying to coax some heat from the stove once again. Mike got up to help me, but all we succeeded in doing was filling the cabin with acrid smoke. We were running around in our "long johns" underwear, determined to get some heat from the fire, and it was only after two and a half hours that we conceded defeat, got dressed, and had a cup of luke-warm tea and some sandwiches for breakfast. It was almost a relief to pack up and be on our way, but it was 9:30 before we were on the river trail again.

The day continued to be as frustrating as it had started out. We could not find the portage trails and went up one blind creek after another, and we now saw that all our studying and marking of the map had been in vain. One or the other of us had not asked the right questions or had misunderstood the answers. We knew that we were taking too much time investigating all of the hoped-for portages so we finally decided to simply follow the river, although it would add another 50 or so miles (80 km) to our journey. At least we would get there.

We stopped, as planned, every two hours for tea and had a longer break for lunch, but by the time it got dark again we still had not made as many miles as we had hoped. We kept wishing for a good cabin to stay in and were caught between not wanting to put up the tent and not wanting to experience a second night in a cold cabin.

Then on a narrow, difficult part of the trail that wound along the top of the riverbank and at a time when we were all feeling tired, Muriel jumped out of the toboggan so that the dogs could get through a snowdrift more easily. She walked behind the team on her snowshoes, and Mike's team soon caught up with her. For some reason, his second-to-lead dog suddenly made a lunge forward and sank his teeth into Muriel's calf. She fell to the ground with tears of anger, pain and frustration. Mike ran forward and kicked the offending dog while I struggled to stop my team and tie the toboggan to a stout tree. The incident made us stop and rest, and Bett helped Muriel to wash and dress the wound. Afterwards, we travelled on into the dark night until, at nine o'clock, a big bright moon came over the horizon and gave us excellent light. We were tired, the dogs were tired, but like automatons we continued step after weary step along the river. Several hours later we saw what looked like a big log house with some outbuildings high on the bank but no smoke or lights showed. I was sorry that it looked so deserted but happy that some kind of shelter had appeared.

"Whatever it's like, let's stay here." Muriel's voice came to me out of her frost-encrusted parka. I looked around at Mike and pointed to the cabin. He waved in acknowledgment. It was obvious that we were all feeling the same way, and the four of us had soon scaled the steep bank. The tired dogs immediately slumped onto their bellies in the snow, and we had no fear that they were going to move on without us. We snowshoed over to the dark cabin and peered inside first and then walked in through the unlocked door. The cabin had apparently been deserted after a flood, and debris was strewn all over the lower floor, but upstairs it was relatively clean and that is where we prepared to stay. There was an old but useable wood stove in what was apparently the living room, and it was soon putting out some very welcome heat.

We heaved the bag of food up the bank and into the house so the two women could prepare supper. Because there were no trees or bushes down on the river, Mike and I hauled the dogs up the steep bank one by one and tied them up around the cabin. Next we dragged the contents of the toboggans up the bank, leaving the toboggans turned upside down on the river ice. Just as I reached the top of the bank, I dropped a hot-water bottle and it slithered partway down again and fell into a crack. I couldn't be bothered trying to retrieve it so just left it there until morning. It took us over an hour to complete these tasks and we were physically worn out when we finished, but, even so, we mixed the dogs' feed with hot water and fed each dog before going in to eat our own supper. It was now 1:30 in the morning.

Later that morning we were wakened by the cold, and after making a fire, I retreated to bed until the house had warmed. After breakfast, curiosity soon made us investigate our surroundings. We could tell from old photographs and some letters that had been left by the flood waters that the place had been a commercial mink farm and that some people called Harrison had lived there. Old clothes and furniture, which had been of good quality until the muddy river had spoiled them, were scattered around the downstairs rooms. The high water mark was halfway up the living room wall, meaning that the river had risen over 35 feet (10.6 m) from its present level. The very thought of that awesome amount of water was quite frightening, and I was glad that it was now winter.

We investigated the outbuildings and saw where the mink pens had been, and found a small cabin with dozens of pelt stretcher boards stacked away. A tall cache with a ladder leading up to it caught our attention, and Mike and I climbed up to see what was in it. Boxes of ammunition, reloading equipment and several very old rifles lay on the floor along with boxes containing unlabelled jars of various powders. Cyanide came to mind for some reason but I was not about to investigate further in that regard. Our curiosity was now really aroused, and it was quite frustrating not having anyone to ask if the recent occupants had drowned or just moved away. However, we knew that we would find out when we got to Aklavik because nothing happened in the Delta that the natives did not get to know about.

The dogs were reluctant to get up and remained lying down until we unfastened them and lowered them down the riverbank, but once in harness they started to bark again in their customary excited way. I found where I had dropped the hot water bottle, but it was frozen into a very difficult shape and refused to come out of its resting place, so there it stayed. We loaded everything else aboard and set off up the river once more.

When we left Harrison's old mink farm, as we now called it, the weather was clear and sunny but as the day wore on, the weather wore out. First the sky became covered by high overcast and then darker clouds moved in. Within an hour we were travelling in light snow that covered everything, and when we stopped, the dogs shook themselves vigorously while we wiped the snow off our parkas and even our eyelashes. Visibility was reduced to about 100 yards (91 m), and so it was with some surprise that shortly after lunch we heard dogs barking in the distance.

Our dogs immediately smartened up. Heads perked up, as did tails, and the dogs all pulled as though they had just started out.

Johnny Lenny's cabin was out of a picture book. Made of logs, it was quite low but had a deep drift of snow against it on the leeward side. Trappers' furnishings were hung on its walls and a neat pile of pine wood was stacked close to the door. A powerful team of dogs were tethered in a row, each with a little doghouse of its own. A dog toboggan that stood near the dogs was immaculate, with laced moosehide carriole sides. We later learned that Johnny ironed wax onto the toboggan bottom to give it more glide and speed.

Johnny Lenny introduced himself and invited us all into the cabin, where we met his wife and two children. The smell of freshly baked bread assailed us, and once again we nodded enthusiastically in response to the invitation: "Would you like to have some freshly baked bread with your coffee? I'm sorry I only have some cheddar cheese to go with it." The memory of those thick slices of bread with butter and cheese have tantalized my taste buds for years because it was one of the nicest meals I have ever had. Freshly perked coffee followed every mouthful of bread and cheese, and once again we felt our energy sagging as the heat from the wood stove engulfed us.

I was falling asleep at the table during a lull in the conversation, and all I could hear was some drama on the radio and the crackling of the wood fire. "Did you hear about the big earthquake in Alaska?" Johnny motioned with his head toward the radio. "That's the Red

Cross messages on right now."

"We felt the tremors right here. We could hardly stand up," his wife continued and she gave us a brief description of what she had heard on the radio.

"And you never felt anything?" Johnny asked incredulously.

"We were too tired to feel anything, and if we had done, I would have just thought it was Keith snoring!" Mike laughed, and we all turned our attention to the radio that was now broadcasting messages to the Alaskan public from the Red Cross about who was where, and messages were being sent out to the bush to advise worried relatives that such and such a family was safe or asking if someone would please contact someone else about some family's welfare, and so on. Alaska was only 400 miles to the west, and Johnny said that we would see evidence of the earthquake once we left the cabin and followed his trail to the home of his nearest neighbours, the Carmichaels, about two and a half hours away. The continuing news flashes confirmed that it had been an earthquake of huge proportions, measuring 7.5 on the Richter scale. It had been felt so close to us and yet we had been too exhausted to notice. We were rather glad that we had not known anything about it.

"Talking about disasters," Mike said, "what happened to that cabin high on the bank upriver? It looks as though people just up and left and never went back. There are traps and furniture and papers all over the place."

"Oh, you must mean the Harrisons' old mink farm. Yes, they were flooded out last spring when the ice jammed just below them. They were lucky to get out. Yes," he continued thoughtfully, "they haven't come back yet. They'll probably wait until spring, but that house is getting closer and closer to the bank every year. I bet it'll fall in maybe next year or the year after that."

The general consensus was that we should move on while we were still awake and before we got too comfortable in the cabin. It was with some reluctance that we collected our things together and went out to the equally reluctant dogs. We felt that we were really letting our hosts down because they tried so hard to get us to stay with them, but they understood that we were already behind schedule and did not want anyone to have to come looking for us. Johnny gave us directions for the trail to Aklavik, and we left them standing waving to us as we entered the trees and now followed a very well-marked trail.

When we came off the portage onto a big lake, we saw the first evidence of the Alaskan earthquake. Pieces of ice weighing several tons had been pushed up and onto the surrounding ice, making the usually smooth surface of the lake look like a major river at breakup time. As we travelled on into the dusk, we thought of the warm cabin we had left behind and the bread and cheese that had been so tasty and became aware of our increasing hunger, but when we saw the lights of another cabin ahead, the dogs picked up their pace again and at seven o'clock we pulled into the Carmichaels' yard. Our two weary dog teams lay down with hardly a glance around them.

The Carmichaels had seen or heard us coming and by the time we went into their cabin, they had caribou steaks and potatoes cooking for us. "Of course, you'll be staying the night with us," Mr. Carmichael said by way of greeting. "If your dogs are friendly, I'll tie them up and give them something to eat. Just go right in and make yourself at home." We were almost speechless. This man had greeted us, did not know who we were or where we had come from, but without any hesitation he and his wife had prepared food for us and were quite happy to keep us under their roof for the night.

Mike spoke hesitatingly. "Uh-h… Mr. Carmichael, we really will have to go into Aklavik tonight or else the game warden or the police will come looking for us because we're late arriving from Fort McPherson." And he gave him a brief outline of our trip and our difficulties.

"We'll talk about it inside afterwards." Mr. Carmichael went off to get some dog feed, leaving us feeling as though we had been scolded by a parent. Obediently we went inside the cabin and breathed in the aroma of cooked steaks.

After feeding the dogs some fish, Mr. Carmichael returned to the cabin, and in between mouthfuls of steak and potatoes we answered his questions about the trail. We shook our heads in unison when he asked us if we had been scared by the earthquake. (We didn't tell him that we would have been scared if we had known about it.) He pointed out that at the speed we were travelling it would take us another four or five hours to get to Aklavik and that our dogs were played out. Although he made us feel thoroughly guilty, the thoughts of a search party kept us to our objective, and when we finally convinced him that we would not stay, he went outside and gave each of the dogs a piece of beef fat to give them the energy to get us to town. Then once again we put on our outdoor clothes and went reluctantly from the warm cabin out into the cold night air.

Now as we travelled, we relied entirely on the dogs to follow the trail because we could hardly see anything ourselves for, although it was a clear starry night, the snow did not seem to reflect anything to light us on our way. Muriel, from her vantage point in the sled, saw a red light low in the sky and tried to bring our attention to it by shouting and pointing. We stopped the dogs when she shouted, but at first we could not see her outstretched arm. After we understood and had seen the light, we decided that it was a radio antenna in Aklavik, so we must be very close. But this decision caused us some frustration because, after travelling along the winding river for more than an hour, the antenna's light was no closer. We tried not to look at it and just kept going along the trail so that we would have no expectation and therefore no disappointment, but we couldn't help but glance at it periodically.

I don't know whether it was the hot fatty food inside the dogs or the knowledge that we were nearly at our destination, but after a time we noticed that the dogs were trotting along nicely without any encouragement from us. Then on what turned out to be the last stretch of river before arriving at Aklavik, I glanced behind me and saw the most spectacular display of northern lights I had ever seen. The vivid hues of pulsating light stretched out across the river and it seemed as though they were close enough to touch. The shimmering colours changed from ruby red to green, blue, yellow and back to red, and the shapes stretched as they danced in an arc that moved northward over us. The dogs stopped and lay down and we just stared in awe and listened intently for any indication that the aurora made any noise, but all we could hear was the panting of the dogs and our own heavy breathing.

When the cold began to eat through our parkas, we called to the dogs again. They stood up immediately and started off for Aklavik, and we arrived a short time later. It was 11:45 pm, March 27, 1964. We drove the dogs down the deserted main street until we saw someone come out of a house "Hey!" Mike shouted. "Do you know where the RCMP are?"

"No," came the brief reply and the person shot off between two houses.

"So much for the hospitality here!" I said to no one in particular, but when I thought about the sight that we must have presented—two frost-bearded men asking for the police—it was no wonder that no one wanted to get involved with us!

Almost immediately after this encounter, we saw a sign pointing to the RCMP barracks and pulled up outside. They had made arrangements for our accommodation, and we were told where the best place would be to tie up the dogs. We were not long in getting everything together, our supplies put away from marauders—both the two- and four-legged variety—and our sleeping bags and personal gear hauled up to the house that we were to stay in. Then finally we fed the dogs who had worked so well for such inexperienced masters. Hot baths, warm drinks and tall tales kept us all going into the small hours, and when we finally went to bed, we were surprised to find that it was too warm in the house with sheets and blankets over us, so we got up and opened the window to let in some fresh air.

We stayed for a day in Aklavik and attended the Rendezvous games, which included tea and bannock-making where the contestants had to split wood, make a fire and then do the cooking, as well as more physical activities such as snowshoe and dog-team races, and it all ended with a tug-of-war, men against the women. And yes, you guessed right—the women won! We then decided that, because we had taken so long to reach the village, it could easily take us as long to go back, so Muriel and Bett would fly back to Fort McPherson, and Mike and I would drive the dog teams and maybe make quicker time with lighter loads, and we would return by a different channel that should take us directly to the Peel River.

On the following morning Muriel and Bett bought tickets to fly back home on the scheduled Pacific Western Airways plane, while Mike and I prepared the toboggans and harnesses and loaded up our food and other supplies. We were ready before the plane came so we said goodbye to our wives and headed back along the trail. The sun shone out of a cold, clear blue sky. As the trail followed the river, we decided to climb into the carriole and have a short snooze while the dogs did all the work. We would do our share when we came to the portages.

We heard the sound of the PWA Otter taking off and saw it head in the direction of Fort McPherson, a mere half-hour's flight away. We were on the ground and three days' journey away from home, but I wouldn't have had it any other way. The sun felt hot and the motion of the toboggan on the undulating snow soon lulled us to sleep. We both woke up when our teams suddenly stopped, and when we looked around, neither of us recognized where we were. But a man stood in the bushes looking at us, and when we walked over to him, we saw that he was living in what could only be described as a snow cave. A big drift of snow in the trees had been hollowed out, and spruce branches put on the floor. His bedding was pushed up into a corner.

"We seem to have come the wrong way," Mike called to the man, who was dressed in quite ragged clothes. "We're looking for the trail to Carmichael's."

"You'll have to go back about three miles where the trail turns off to your right. You must have seen it when you came by."

"Okay, thanks," Mike answered, and smiling he turned to me and said, "We might have seen it if we'd been awake!"

We waved to the man, turned the dogs around, and headed back toward Aklavik, feeling annoyed with ourselves that we had wasted so much time and given the dogs that much more unnecessary work. (After we had reached home, Muriel and Bett said that they had seen two teams from the air but had concluded that it couldn't have been us because the teams were obviously going too far down the river.) We had lunch at Carmichael's and he gave us instructions that would take us towards home on a slightly different route but would lead us to the portages, instead of following the winding river. Feeling we could trust this man's knowledge and information, we took his advice.

One piece of information that he gave us, which we remembered very well, was that if we stopped by Knute Laing's place, we should not accept an invitation to eat there.

"Why not?" I asked out of curiosity.

"Well, old Ed Rydstedt lives there alone now ever since Knute passed away, and Ed used to look after things. And he still does but he's a bit different. Been out there on his own too long. You'll see his harness all laid out and he'll tell you that he's leaving tomorrow to go caribou hunting, but he's been saying this for about four years, I think, and he's never been anywhere yet. Someone either takes some grub out for him or he still uses the supplies that Knute had when he ran a little store." He paused and then said, "Oh, and they say that Ed raises pups and eats them."

We resolved not to eat anything at the cabin if there was anyone there. Later that day, after we had been travelling for three or four hours and were beginning to think of supper, we pulled around a bend in the river and heard a dog bark in the distance. Overlooking the river we saw a cluster of small cabins and knew that we had reached Laing's place.

"Remember the pups!" Mike said and flashed me an evil grin.

We urged our dogs up the bank toward the cabins, and after tying the lead dogs and the toboggans, went to see if anyone was around. Passing a small log storehouse, our eyes were drawn to the eaves. Staring down at us was the frozen head of a dog. A spiny skeleton jutted grotesquely from the head. Mike and I both recoiled in shock.

"Look at that!" I whispered to Mike, who was doing just that and not looking very happy while he was about it.

"There's some dead pups up there too," Mike said, peering over the logs.

Just as we were recovering from this discovery an old man dressed in patched clothes came out of the largest cabin, squinting at us as his eyes adjusted to the brilliant sunshine. "Come on in," he said with a broad grin. "I'll put the kettle on." He did not look at all surprised to see us, and he turned around and went back into the cabin without another word, leaving us to follow him inside.

We introduced ourselves and shook hands, and Ed settled in, all ready to talk. The cabin was furnished with old store-bought furniture, and as our eyes adjusted to the dark interior, we noticed that it looked reasonably clean and tidy, apart from the old wood stove that stood in the centre of the room. Bits of wood shavings and bark were scattered around it and, as Ed talked, he made an attempt to sweep around the stove with his foot.

"Don't get many visitors these days," he said, picking up a few sticks of firewood. "People just go on by, just not friendly these days. I don't care, anyway. I'm going after some caribou tomorrow. Did you see my harness out there? I would have gone today but I lost some dogs the other day." He put the firewood into the stove and shut the door. "I don't know what's the matter with them," he muttered more to himself than to us. We did not want to venture any guesses of what had become of them, but the vision of the dog's head flashed into my mind.

We were silent as Ed stepped outside and came back with a handful of dry firewood. He talked about caribou, the weather and dogs. He opened the stove door and put the wood inside and then blew hard on the embers. We saw a few flames as he quickly shut the stove door then moved the kettle to the middle of the stove, where he watched it, talking to us all the time. The last stick must have burned up just as the kettle boiled, and he scooped some loose tea out of a battered old can and dropped it into a big old teapot and poured some water over the leaves. He let it stand a minute and then poured us each a cupful of the strongest looking tea I'd ever seen.

"You know, this pot just doesn't hold enough." He put the teapot back on the stove. "I make several pots of it every day. I don't understand it." (Later that year when an RCMP dog-team patrol came by, we learned what had been wrong with the teapot. Ed used a scoop of tea every time he made a pot, but he never emptied any out—just kept adding more tea! There was only enough room for about three cups of water in that two-quart teapot!)

"I've got lots of room here if you want somewhere to stay," Ed told us, "and there's lots of grub, too."

"Thanks anyway, but John Lenny is expecting us, in fact, we should be leaving very soon." I didn't want to sound ungrateful for his hospitality, but the thought of staying at this camp did not fill me with enthusiasm, and I knew Mike would feel the same way.

Ed peered out the window. "Nice dogs you've got out there."

We nodded and looked at each other with the sort of look that said, "Yes and we'd like to keep them that way, too."

"How about some cold meat and fried potatoes?" Ed asked. "You may as well let the dogs have a rest."

We argued that we had no time, but he persisted and then, without waiting for another word, went outside. Mike and I had a hurried consultation. "This is a bit awkward," Mike said, "but let's wait and see what he's got, and if we don't recognize it, we'll just have to refuse."

I agreed. "Good idea, but I've lost my appetite already."

To our relief Ed returned with a few potatoes and a tin of Spam luncheon meat. He put a whole piece of wood on the stove this time, and started to fry the potatoes in some beef fat, which we watched him take out of the package, because being suspicious, we watched his every move. Then he sliced the Spam and fried it, too.

We ate while he continued talking. "Don't worry about me. I've got some meat left over from yesterday and I'll have that," he said. "I'm leaving to go hunting pretty soon and I don't want a lot of leftovers."

We told him that we really would have to be on our way and thanked him for his hospitality. He did not come out to see us off. We went on our way harbouring peculiar emotions—a mixture of pity, awe, horror and sadness—and we did not feel comfortable again until we saw the lights of the Lennys' cabin and told them of our experience. Mrs. Lenny said, "We check on him from time to time. He doesn't bother anyone and he lives in his own world. They say that he has been getting a pension cheque for years but he won't cash them. Doesn't want anything from the government. He's just thoroughly bushed."

It took Mike and I another day and a half to reach Fort McPherson, the last day spent travelling up the Peel River in a blizzard. But I had one good laugh that afternoon when Mike stopped to relieve himself. He had been travelling behind me, and when he stopped, he pulled down his wind pants and unfastened the zipper on his wool pants. He had just got comfortable when his dogs decided they didn't want to get left behind and took off after me. I heard a yell and a curse behind me and when I turned, through the blizzard I saw the fuzzy outline of a man trying to run with his pants down. He was holding onto the long headline rope to the toboggan while his dogs trotted on without a care in the world! I was laughing so hard I couldn't find my camera fast enough. I stopped the dogs until Mike caught up with his team and readjusted his clothing. He couldn't help laughing at himself and yelled, "Just you wait, Billington! You'll get yours one of these days!"

20

SPRINGTIME MEANT THE return of the great caribou herds as they headed north along the Richardson Mountains to the calving grounds, just as they had done for thousands of years. The Gwich'in people depended upon these animals for their annual supply of meat, and they used the hides with the hair left on for blankets, placing them under their sleeping bags because the hollow hairs are the best natural insulators from the cold ground. The sinews would also be dried and used like thread to make or mend moccasin slippers and mukluks.

Whole families, except for the school-aged children, would head up past the headwaters of Stoney Creek to Rock River in anticipation of the hunt, prepared to stay a month or more to make dry meat to last them until the following spring. Each family would have several dog teams, and typically the father would go on ahead with all the camping gear and equipment on his toboggan, and the mother would come along second with the kitchen, the food and the bedding, among which would ride the babies and toddlers. Teenagers or young adults would take the extra bedding and pots and many of the other items that would be needed. At one camp where I stayed, the people used metal cutlery, crockery cups and plates, and even carried a piece of linoleum that they placed on the floor by the stove to use as a table. All of this came out of a huge wooden box that would have taken up a third of the toboggan space.

I recall a new doctor examining a patient who had come to our clinic complaining of a sore back. He advised the patient to sleep on a hard surface and perhaps put a piece of plywood under his mattress. I tried to explain to the doctor that the man did not have a mattress; he did not even have a bed; he just put his sleeping blanket down on the floor, and I was sure that you could not get a firmer bed than that, but I could see that the doctor just could not comprehend such a lifestyle. The patient, forever polite (as the Gwich'in always are) just nodded in agreement and thanked the doctor for his help.

When people left to go to their bush camps and cabins, many of them stopped at the clinic to pick up first aid supplies and have their babies immunized. In winter they would stay away from the village for weeks and sometimes months trapping, and in the fall they would be away putting up dry "stick fish." These were "crooked-backs," a bony whitefish with a hump on the spine, that were caught in nets placed across river eddies. Ten at a time, they were strung through their gills on willow sticks and hung on a wooden frame to freeze. They were used almost exclusively for dog feed.

But it was in spring when the large Porcupine caribou herd was sighted moving northward, that the hunters prepared to set out. It took them many days to move up, but they went at their own pace. No one was in a hurry. William Vittrekwa said that the people knew where the caribou would be and there was "lots of time" to get there. He told me that white men were always in a hurry and always looked at their watches. "But me, I know. My stomach, it tell me when I'm hungry, no need watch!"

After the people had been away for a few weeks, the village was very quiet. Periodically a hunter would return for more supplies and bring in a toboggan load of meat for the people who could not travel away, and it was in March 1965 that one of these visitors brought a message asking if I would like to visit George Vittrekwa (William Vittrekwa's brother) at his meat camp at Rock River. Muriel and I had established from the beginning that the best way that we could serve the people who still lived this traditional lifestyle was by visiting them where they lived, and over the years we travelled to camps for work-related reasons as well as to spend our holidays. So now I sent a message back saying I would be up there in a few days' time, and for people to keep an eye open for me. I knew that William Vittrekwa was camped at Road River, which was on the way to Rock River, and I hoped to visit him, too.

I engaged Peter Thompson to guide me to my destination and back. As Peter was very patient and his dogs were old and slow, he could manage them without exhausting himself. I thought that was not too bad for a man in his sixties. Then Don Wootten, the Anglican minister, heard I was going to the camps and asked if he could come along with his own team. We packed our toboggans with just ten days' supply of food for the dogs and ourselves in the knowledge that we would be able to supplement this ration with caribou meat when we reached the camps. All my preparations were overseen by William Firth, who hovered over me like a father. When our final arrangements were complete, we sent out a radio message to William and George to tell them when we were leaving.

It being March, the days were long and for the most part sunny. Temperatures were about minus 20 F (-28 C) with another ten degrees of frost during the night. The bright spring sunshine could cause sunburn and snow blindness very quickly so we always carried good sunglasses with us. The strength and heat of the sun can be very deceiving in the north. I once drove my dogs back from Arctic Red River in early April, and though the snow was thawing out in the direct sun's rays, the temperature hovered around zero for most of the day. I had been jogging behind my dogs for several hours because they were tired, having run the 38 miles (61 km) from Fort McPherson the day before, and in record time too—five and one half hours. After reaching halfway, I couldn't stand having a shirt on because I was sweating so much, so off it came, leaving me running behind the toboggan in my undershirt and trousers. The afternoon sun seemed even stronger, so I thought to heck with it, there was no one around, and off came my undershirt, exposing my white skin to the arctic air. It felt so good as long as I was running, but as soon as I stopped, the goose bumps stood at attention all over me, and I couldn't wait to get my shirt back on again. Some hours after I reached home, my back began to burn, and when Muriel checked it out, she discovered I had a minor sunburn. After that experience I took more care, but I still often burned my face and forearms while driving dogs on long trips in the spring sun.

Don Wootten and I followed Peter south up the Peel River until we came to Eighteen Mile where a tent was set up close to the riverbank. Smoke was coming from the stovepipe, and the owner's dogs started to howl as soon as they caught our scent. Bertha Francis came to the tent door and waved and when we were closer, she said something to Peter in the Gwich'in language while beckoning us towards her tent. Peter said that we had been invited to lunch, which was very welcome news to us. If the dogs could have understood, I'm sure that they would have agreed because, although they wouldn't get any feed yet, they would at least have a good rest.

After some hot tea, bannock and dry meat, we said goodbye to our hosts and set off up the river again. It was quiet, the only sounds coming from the tinkling of the dog harness bells and the creak of the toboggan boards on the dry snow. My thoughts were far away when Peter suddenly stopped his dogs and grabbed his snowshoes and then his rifle. His eyes stayed on the far riverbank. I strained my eyes to see what had caught his attention.

"See that moose?" Peter said, putting his snowshoes on without even bending down.

Don and I strained our eyes before we saw something black moving in the trees on the other side of the river. When it moved higher up the bank, Peter took aim and fired. He fired again and then waited, still holding his gun to his shoulder. The moose stopped and then moved higher still. Once more Peter fired but the moose made it to the top of a small hill overlooking the river and disappeared over the top.

Peter walked nonchalantly over to the toboggan and put his

snowshoes on top of the load. "My rifle, it's getting old now, not as good as it used to be," he said and showed it to me. It was well used and the stock shiny. I didn't know very much about guns, but although this one was well-oiled and looked clean, I could see why it "wasn't as good as it used to be"—the screw holding the barrel to the stock was missing, and in its place were several turns of black electrical tape. When I held the rifle up, the stock felt loose, so I surmised that when Peter fired the rifle, in all probability the shot went wide. In spite of this handicap, Peter did get several caribou a few days later, so whether this was just an off day for Peter or his rifle, I will never know.

We travelled 50 miles (80 km) that day, which is a fair day's travel with a load of supplies. We stopped at a vacant cabin and, although someone owned it, Peter said we should stay there and they wouldn't mind. Very few people locked their cabins. There were not that many people in the whole territory so, if something went missing, it wouldn't take long for it to show up somewhere, and the local people had an uncanny knack for recognizing other people's belongings. Once, having borrowed a nondescript team of dogs, I arrived at a camp where someone casually remarked that the team I was driving of old Johnnie's was a really good team. It was just as if he had recognized a well-known Porsche.

The following morning we all felt uncomfortably hot in the cabin even after we had put out the fire, and Peter informed us that we were in a chinook. Warm air had blown in from the west and brought up the temperature dramatically. It could have gone above freezing, but fortunately it stayed cold enough for us to travel, and Peter told us that chinooks in the MacKenzie Delta rarely lasted for more than 48 hours.

We had a tough day in the unaccustomed warmth, and even though the dogs pulled well, the toboggans dragged over the surface and did not slide as they had done previously. We left the Peel River where the Road River enters it, and it was here that Chief John Tetlichi had his cabin. He and his wife invited us in for tea and then, as Peter said that we still had a long way to go, we bade John and his wife goodbye and headed west up some hills behind the cabin. Now we had to push the toboggans in order to help the dogs pull them through the soft wet snow.

LATER IN THE AFTERNOON we smelled wood smoke and heard dogs barking, and as we were tired out, Don and I hoped that we had at last reached a camp where we could stay for the night. But when we came around a bend in the small creek we were now travelling up, we saw a team of dogs tied up and their driver, John Edward Snowshoe, having tea by the side of a roaring fire. He had a big load of meat on his toboggan and was heading for the village. As we sipped scalding tea from his kettle, he told us the camp was still another four hours' travel away. Peter just nodded and said, "Aha, aha." We also nodded and accepted that we were going to be a lot more tired by the end of the day.

We continued our journey in the dusk and then in the star-lit dark, the dogs following the well-used trail without any difficulty. As the evening drew on, the temperature went down, making travelling easier, and when the moon appeared over the mountains, it cast quite a brilliant light, turning the scenery around us into a surreal painting. The steam rising from the panting dogs hung over us, catching the moons' rays and making it look much colder than it really was.

It was after nine when we next heard dogs barking and saw several lights in the trees where tents were pitched. The soft light that came through the canvas tents looked very welcoming, but instead of feeling tired, I became wide awake and full of energy.

William Vittrekwa appeared on the trail and called me over. "You stay my place, okay?" It certainly was okay and he led my team over to his tent, while Peter and Don went to the next big tent and said they would stay there. I was not sure but thought that since Don was a minister and Peter a church deacon, they would be staying with someone who was either a deacon or who would at least conduct himself appropriately.

George Vittrekwa III performs a whip dance at his grandfather's camp.

William helped me to unhitch the dogs, and we chained them to some trees a short distance from the tent. I made a small bed of spruce boughs for each one, fondled their ears and told them what good dogs they were, and they sank onto their beds and proceeded to chew and lick the ice and snow from their paws. I washed my hands with snow and went into the tent where Mary, William's wife, had some hot tea ready for me and some meat and bannock cooking on the stove.

I had finished eating when William came in and said he had fed my dogs a big piece of meat each that would make them really strong. As usual, the radio was put on for the "Neighbourly News and Messages" from CHAK in Inuvik, and while William and his wife had a late-night snack of roast caribou, we all had another cup of tea. I unrolled my sleeping bag in a corner of the tent and crawled in. The smell of the pine-branch flooring and the crackling of the wood in the stove had its usual hypnotic effect on me, and I was soon asleep.

Something slapped me and interfered with my dreams. I rolled over, but the slapping continued and woke me. In the dim light I saw that I had rolled up against the side of the tent and pushed the canvas free and it was flapping in a strong wind. As the tea from the previous night had already been through my kidneys, I thought that this was as good a time as any to get up and get rid of it and fix the tent wall at the same time. When I went outside, a warm wind greeted me and the snow felt quite wet. The chinook was blowing in stronger and warmer. We would not be able to travel anywhere if it stayed like that. I relieved myself, fixed up the tent wall and went back to bed.

I woke much later to the sound of the fire being lit and saw William putting a big pot full of snow on the stove. As the air in the tent warmed, I lay in my sleeping bag and looked around my accommodation. The tent was quite large, about 18 by 20 feet (5 by 6 m), and because it was set up at close to the same height as the surrounding snow level with the interior being at ground level, there was a lot of headroom. An interior framework of peeled poles had been set up, not to hold up the tent, but to serve as drying racks for meat. There were large pieces of finely cut meat hanging from them, and later on I saw Mary feeling each one. If it was deemed firm and dry and could be stored without any danger of it rotting, she removed it and other pieces were adjusted so that they could continue the drying process. There was a definite aroma of raw meat in the tent but it was something that I soon got used to.

After a breakfast of oatmeal and fried meat, we sat around and talked. We would have to stay in camp for a day and wait for the chinook to pass, but there was lots to do and Mary told me that quite a few people in the camp wanted to see me for various ailments. I was glad I had brought a good selection of medical supplies. I harboured a secret worry that, if people knew I was coming to hold a clinic, they might delay bringing someone into the village who was seriously sick, but in all the years that we provided health care in Fort McPherson that did not happen, and I think the directors of the Health Service didn't always give the people credit for making rational decisions where their health was involved.

That morning I listened to chests, took blood pressures and temperatures, listened to complaints of sore backs and sprained muscles, and dispensed some analgesics, one bottle of infants' antibiotic and lots of advice. I found the people were all relatively healthy, and the ailments they did have were mostly associated with their rigorous outdoor lifestyle. (I think I ached as much as any of the patients I saw that day, and I knew why, too.)

While I was using their tent as a clinic, William went out to cut firewood and Mary put on her snowshoes and went slushing through the wet snow to cut some more brush for the tent floor. As soon as I had finished the clinic, she came into the tent with an armload of fresh pine branches and kneeling down deftly laid the new flooring. As the pine needles warmed, the tent started to give off a strong pine aroma, which I found to be very pleasant.

IN THE LATE AFTERNOON we were just settling down to some tea and bannock when someone tapped on the canvas flap of the tent and in walked a young woman. I was not too sure who she was, but I did recognize her features. Mary said, "Effie, she's got real bad tooth and she can't sleep. It bother her too much, but she's scared."

I told Effie to sit down and let me just take a look. I promised I would not hurt her. She knelt on the pine boughs and obligingly opened her mouth. I could immediately see by the light of my flashlight which tooth was causing her pain. A molar—or more precisely the remains of a molar—was surrounded by angry-looking tissue. I had to think of the best thing to do in the circumstances, but I didn't want the patient to see I was in a dilemma, so I continued looking at her other teeth and went back periodically to the offending one to see if it would give me any inspiration. Had this young woman been in the village, I would have given her an antibiotic and something for the pain and then, when the infection had gone, removed the remains of the tooth. But we were at least two long days' travel away from the village.

"I think that I should pull out the tooth," I said at last.

I was surprised that she looked almost relieved, and she nodded in agreement.

"That's what she want," Mary said. Effie gave a wan smile.

I had noticed that, when women came to the clinic to see either Muriel or me, they rarely came alone, and the "escort" frequently spoke for the patient even though they were equal in understanding English. I had the feeling they had discussed the ailment, decided on the treatment and were only guiding me politely to what they had wanted in the first place.

I asked Mary to help, thinking this was going to be a Medical Services first: in a tent, no hygienic surroundings, no running water, no chair, not even a white lab coat to put on. Oh, well! I had pulled teeth in a cabin, but by comparison that seemed a sterile environment. I washed my hands in the bowl of warm water that Mary provided for me and then laid out my equipment on a clean towel, trying to keep them out of the patient's direct view. Then turning my back on her, I withdrew a syringe and local anaesthetic from the insulated bag I carried and filled up the syringe.

Mary helped to brace Effie's back, but I noticed that she turned slightly away as the syringe came into view. It is very difficult to anaesthetize a tooth when the gum is all inflamed, but I managed to give the area a nerve block while Effie stayed very still. When I withdrew the needle, she just rubbed her jaw and I saw that she was perspiring a bit, though not as much as I was.

In a few minutes she started touching her lip and I asked her if it felt funny. She nodded and told me it felt big. I told her this was good and she wouldn't feel a thing, sounding more confident than I felt. I asked her to open her mouth and tested her feeling around the tooth by pressing a small instrument against the gum. As she didn't respond to the pressure, I used an instrument to loosen the gum margin from the tooth. If it had not been frozen, she would certainly have let me know by this stage, but I asked again if it hurt and she indicated it was fine. So far so good. I picked up the appropriate instrument and weighed it in my hand thoughtfully. When I was being trained to do emergency extractions, I had asked how I was to know which instrument to use. The dentist had said the best way was to pick up what looked like the right instrument and see if it would fit onto the tooth that was to be pulled. If the tooth was on the upper left side, the instrument would be curved appropriately, and the head of the instrument would tell me if it was made for grasping the tooth, and so it went for all the areas of the mouth. He also said it was not brute strength that removed the tooth, but the action of the wrist and arm which would lever the tooth out. I don't think the dentist had in mind practising dentistry in a tent in the mountains, but that is where I was and I had to make the best of it for the patient's sake.

The extractor, which I called a cow-horn because of its two curved pincers, slipped neatly between the roots and popped the tooth out quickly and easily without breaking it. I was quite relieved, and when

I showed the tooth to Effie, she looked relieved, too, though she was quite startled.

"It's out?"

I smiled and nodded.

With her hand held over her mouth, she stood up. "Oh, thank you, Keith. I was so scared!"

I finished off my work by giving her a piece of gauze to bite on for a while, then gave her a course of antibiotics to take over the next week and a couple of painkillers for when the freezing came out later in the day. I also told her to keep out of the cold for a while. It seemed silly to say that, considering where we were, but it slipped out without my thinking about it at the time. Afterwards I borrowed another pan from Mary, and washed everything in soapy water, then in the good old-fashioned way of sterilizing equipment, I boiled it all in clean melted snow water.

Effie went back to her tent clutching the old rotten tooth to show to her family. Exit another satisfied customer!

As soon as it was light the next morning, in the renewed cold weather we loaded up our toboggans and hitched up the dogs. Just as William had told me, the meat seemed to have filled them with energy, and the day of rest made them behave like pop bottles that had been shaken and half-opened.

Some of the men who had been camped around us were going on to hunt that morning so there were twelve dog teams on the trail. Sixty or more dogs and 12 toboggans made a long procession. Two miles (3.2 km) from camp we came to overflow on the creek. The water was being forced out over the ice and in places was over a foot (.30 m) deep. The dogs were very reluctant to go into the water, but with loud shouts from us and a few cracks of our whips in the air they went in and then they couldn't wait to get out on the other side. The toboggans, being heavy with camp supplies, rode well through the water and fortunately were not in it long enough to soak through the canvas or moosehide carrioles, but when we stopped on the other side, we had to bang the ice off the sides and bottom of the toboggans so they would not be too heavy or drag too much. We remained quite dry ourselves because, as soon as the toboggans entered the water, we rode on top of our loads until the dogs pulled us to firm ice.

We followed this creek to its source and then climbed even higher to the pass that goes over the Richardson Mountains. There is a large lake up there that empties into a canyon and the start of Rock River. In the summer time this is a fast flowing river but on this occasion it was a frozen waterslide with the windswept ice showing blue and green in the morning sun.

William Vittrekwa told me that many years earlier he had been a guide for a man travelling up this river and that at the start the man had wanted to bring too many supplies along. When he had insisted that all of it was necessary, William made him go through it and tell him what each thing was for because, as William would be doing most of the work, he didn't intend to carry anything that was not absolutely essential. When they came to a whole case of toilet rolls, William asked incredulously what it was for—not that he didn't know what toilet paper was for, but a whole case? And out in the bush?

"But what am I to do without any toilet paper?" the man wailed.

And here William, in telling the tale, would start to laugh. "I said to him, 'Use stick!'" and William laughed loudly as he remembered the incident.

On this March day just as we entered the canyon, one of the men pointed up to the mountains and shouted, "Caribou!"

At first I couldn't see anything and then suddenly I was aware that the whole mountainside was a seething mass of moving animals. There were hundreds, if not thousands, of them and they were all moving northward like slow-moving ants over an ant hill. They were about a mile away from us and must have been aware of us, but the instinct to move on was too strong and they continued to push forward.

It was impossible to control the toboggans as they careened down the frozen river. Several times I thought I was going to tip over. I was standing on the metal brake with all of my weight and the sound of it raking across the ice screeched against the canyon walls and made me think of fingernails scratching down a school blackboard. Then as the river grade lessened, we came through some snowdrifts that gave us some control over our descent.

George Vittrekwa's camp was only a few miles further down Rock River so we were soon enjoying Gwich'in hospitality again. Peter went to stay with some of the other men who had come down from the last camp with us. They all worked at putting up a tent and before an hour had gone by, smoke was pouring from its stove-pipe. Don, William and I stayed in George's tent, which was huge in comparison to William's. Besides the three of us new arrivals, the tent accommodated George and his wife, their adult daughter and her young daughter, but the tent was so big that our sleeping bags only took up one-third of the floor area when they were laid out at night. A large wood heater stood in the centre and, as in William's tent, there was a wooden framework of poles with racks of drying meat.

Late in the afternoon the men from the other tents began to filter into George's big tent to sit around drinking tea and smoking. But after everyone had arrived, it became obvious that this was not just a social gathering but a planning meeting. No one chaired it as they would have in a formal meeting, but it was plain that William and George Vittrekwa were the men who were about to share their knowledge of the area and decide on the strategy for the big hunt the next day. I looked around at the men. They all looked excited at the prospect of a good hunt, but mostly they sat in respectful silence, listening to William and George tell them how they should proceed, only interrupting to have some detail explained. They spoke in their native language, and though I couldn't understand everything, I had some idea of the gist of the meeting, a phenomenon I had noticed before and one I was to experience many times in the future.

Of course, the subject in this case was the caribou hunt so I had something to go on as I tried to interpret all of the talk, but both William and George used their hands to describe going around the mountains to the right or the left, and then with a quick flick of the wrists one of them would describe a canyon or a gully and which side of it to climb. One hand would be held in mid-air, showing where the hunters would be, and the other hand would draw an arc in the air to show the path of the oncoming caribou.

William would hold his hands as though he was holding a rifle but continue speaking in his own language, and then he would flick both of his fingers, indicating he had fired several times. Then holding his arms straight out again, he would twist both wrists over and, with a loud exclamation indicate he had shot two caribou. He was very much in his element when telling the younger men what to do, but I think he was even more enthusiastic in the telling of his tales because he had two white men for an audience and he could see that we were hanging on to his every word.

However, if we had thought we were going to be in the main hunting party, we were wrong. William had planned something else for us, something more fitting for an old hunter like him and a couple of inexperienced, unfit men such as Don and I. He told us that we were going to go in a different direction to the others and we would see lots of caribou, and that is all he would tell us. But we both trusted him, and when I crawled into my sleeping bag that night, I wondered if I would be able to go to sleep. However, it wasn't long before I woke, and feeling the cold night air around my ears, I found my toque, pulled it over my ears, snuggled down and drifted off to sleep again.

It was almost light when I was awakened by the creak of the metal stove door being opened and the sound of a firestick and kindling being put into the stove. I heard a match being struck and soon shadows were dancing around the tent. The stove door was shut and the wood crackled in the stove and one by one the people in the tent stirred, sat up, stretching and yawning and scratching. The two women gathered up the dishes they would need to prepare breakfast and then, while the snow melted in the kettle, they washed their hands and faces and combed their long black hair. I was impressed that they made the effort to be clean because, when I had stayed in the camps with only men, they hadn't been very fastidious about hygiene although most did wash with a handful of snow when they went outside. Following the women's example, I got up and washed my hands and face and ran a comb through my hair, but though this made me feel better, I know that instead of having uncombed messy hair, I now had combed messy hair.

For breakfast we had hot cereal, with bannock and strawberry jam. William poured some melted fat onto his cereal, saying that this would keep the cold out. Mention of the temperature made me aware that it did feel cooler in the tent even with the stove blazing away, and I realized that since the chinook a few days ago, the temperature had been falling steadily. I had brought a small thermometer with me and, when I checked it outside later, I saw that it was 35 below F (-38 C).

The dogs were to stay in camp so that they would not disturb the caribou. George Vittrekwa and his family were also going to stay in camp because they had meat to cut up, bones to render down, bannock to make, firewood to get, and all the numerous jobs that have to be done when you stay in camp for any length of time. A big pile of freshly cleaned bones were on a snow shelf just inside the tent door, and George and his wife set to pulverizing them with an axe. Mrs. Vittrekwa then put them in a big pan on the stove and boiled them all day. When all the fat and marrow had been rendered down, the pot was put outside to cool and the next morning the solidified fat was removed and put into cans. This, George informed me, was what they used for butter when they stayed out in the bush for a long time. It was also mixed with beaten, dried meat along with some flour and sugar and rolled into balls—what the old voyagers had called pemmican but the natives called "itsoo cho" or big meat balls. They were very sustaining when travelling on a cold day when

William Vittrekwa crushes caribou bones before boiling them to extract the fat and marrow, which is eaten with bannock.

fat was what the body craved, and when I was on the trail I really liked them. I took some home with me, but when I ate it after being at home for a few days on my regular diet, I found it had quite a different taste and I couldn't eat more than a small amount of it; my body didn't need the extra fat when I lived at home.

William waited until all the others had set off in the direction he had indicated to them, and then motioning to Don and me, he set off with his rifle and snowshoes. We followed a small creek until we came to an icefall about 20 feet (6 m) high, and this we had to climb in our mukluks. William went first and made it look very difficult because I was filming him with my 8mm-movie camera. I never met a native man who was such a ham actor, but he loved it all, and I guess he knew I was going to invite him to the nursing station for a private showing when we got back.

For over an hour we walked and climbed upward and then, following William's lead, we sat down for a rest. The mountains and rivers all lay below us but everything seemed to have lost its colour. It was a grey day to begin with and now the windswept mountains appeared grey and white, and in the distance the evergreens nestling in all the sheltered spots looked more black than green. At our feet, clinging to the rocks and growing in thick patches all around us, we could see the greyish-green lichen that was the staple food of the caribou. As we sat there, William explained what he had in mind. He had sent the men around to the other side of the mountain that faced us. He said the caribou would be on the other side, too, and he had instructed the hunters to approach very carefully downwind of the animals, which would be feeding. They were to spread themselves out along the brow of the mountain above the caribou, and then fire into the herd from there. He said that when surprised, the caribou would first run to higher ground and then try to find a way from the disturbance. They would then continue north on their migratory trek.

He pointed ahead to a draw between two knolls. "They going to come down there, so we go down and wait where they cross." He was quite sure the caribou would do exactly as he predicted. I decided to withhold judgment until I had seen what would happen but it seemed a lot to expect, even hearing William say it so confidently. But we sat on the wind-blown grey rocks and watched and waited. After a half-hour I was cold and stiff, but William just sat there and talked to us about hunting and trapping. Suddenly he stopped talking and cocked his head to one side. Rifle fire! Echoing around the mountains as it did, it was impossible for us to determine exactly where the shots were coming from but to William that didn't matter. Getting up, he told us to follow him. While the rifle fire continued sporadically for the next five or ten minutes, we went partway down the mountain and stopped on a ridge overlooking a pass. Now everything was silent except for the wind sighing between the rocks. To concentrate my hearing, I would take a breath and hold it, but then the thudding of my heart would sound too loud. Don and I couldn't keep our eyes from the place where William had said the caribou would appear. William just watched the mountains.

When the caribou came, they didn't come at a full gallop as I had expected. They plodded slowly along, the fright of half an hour earlier gone from their minds. But they poured over the hill between the knolls exactly as William had predicted and came down in a continuing stream toward us. The leader was slightly ahead of the herd and obviously on the lookout for trouble. His ears flicked this way and that, but whether his nose was up in an effort to pick up a scent I was not sure because of the way caribou walk as though they are concentrating on balancing the huge rack of antlers on their heads. This leader had antlers but they were not very big, although the body size indicated that it was probably male. I had heard or read that the caribou is the only species of ungulates where the females also have antlers, so I found it very hard to differentiate between the young males and the females.

Then the leading caribou stopped suddenly and veered to the side, leading the herd along the hill away from us. Keeping just below the brow of a small hill, they went west where we caught glimpses of them as they steered clear of us. Thinking about it later, I wondered if the animal heard the sound of the spring unwinding in my movie camera because, when it was unwinding in the cold, it gasped and creaked. As I was used to the noise it made, I hadn't noticed anything at all. Or it could have been that the caribou caught our scent. (I know I certainly did, and thoughts of a shower or bath flashed through my mind more than once during the trip.)

I couldn't count how many caribou there were, but we sat and watched the herd for twenty minutes before we got up and followed William down the mountain. "No use to worry," he said philosophically as we descended. "The boys, he get lots of meat. They give us some, and poor ones we give to dogs." As he had shared his knowledge with the younger men, he knew that he would not be left out when the meat was shared out.

Complaining about bad luck was not William's way. He accepted whatever happened. He didn't blame us or anyone or anything for the fickleness of the animals; it was just the way it was. For my part, I was thrilled that the caribou had behaved just as William had said and I was not disappointed in not having participated in the actual kill. I was sure that I would have lots of opportunity to take film of that in the future.

We made our way back to camp and spent the rest of the day checking the dog harness, drinking tea and talking. We were having supper before the hunters started coming back. They would have had to gut the animals that had been killed and prop them up to drain and freeze, ready to be hauled in with the dog teams the following day. Some of the men brought some fresh meat down with them, and most of us had fresh caribou liver and some heart cooked in bacon fat for a snack while the others ate their supper. It tasted better than anything I had eaten for days. The cold day, the mountain air, the exercise and no lunch had made me quite hungry. After the meal the men came once more into George's tent and each told his hunting story amidst laughs, groans and comments in English, such as "Hey, Joe, don't lie!" so I gathered the stories were told just as they are in any other part of the world, some truth, some wishful thinking and some downright lies, but all in good fun.

The next morning the men who had shot caribou went up into the mountains to bring the carcasses back, and they were coming and going all day. The few others who stayed in camp skinned the animals and cut up the meat into quarters. I knew that the head was considered a delicacy but I didn't know how it was prepared or consumed. I was interested to see that some of the heads were placed in the embers of a fire that had been burning outside for some hours. The hair immediately singed and yet the heads were left in the cooler ashes for some time. Then one of the older men scraped as much of the burned hair off as he could with a sharp knife. He told me the old people really liked the head and they would put it into the cookstove oven all day to roast it and then eat everything—eyes, tongue, lips, brains, nose—the works. I thought that was good as long as they didn't offer me any, so imagine my consternation when I went in to George's tent and saw that his daughter, Mary, had a skinned caribou head hanging by its lips on a wire from one of the poles across the roof. The wire was long enough for the head to hang at the same level as the wood stove. She told me this was going to be supper. Oh dear! The head spun slowly around on the wire as it started to cook. Now and again there was a gurgling noise like water going down the bathtub drain, and then a thick liquid would pour out of the neck end of the head and splash into a bowl on the floor.

"What's that stuff?" I asked Mary as I pointed to the bowl. I didn't really want to know but having more than a good idea what the answer was, I had a morbid desire to hear her confirm it.

She did. "Brains," she said, then seeing the look on my face, she laughed and added, "It's really nice, but mostly it's the old people that eat it. You don't have to have any."

I thanked her for her understanding. She probably thought I was silly because to her it was like refusing candy. It was dark outside by the time supper was ready, and it had all been prepared by the light of the gas lantern. George lifted down the head and his wife started to cut it up using an axe and a large sharp knife.

Being an honoured guest has its hazards because you are offered what is considered the delicacies, and I am sorry to say that my appetite didn't run to nose or tongue, especially when the tongue was cut out and put on a plate where it sat looking like an old boot made out of blackish-tinged elephant hide. I suggested that perhaps the older men might like these morsels, because they had worked so hard and deserved it. William nodded in agreement and took possession of a good hunk of tongue. George did the same and Don and I ignored the piece that was left, hoping Mrs. Vittrekwa herself would desire it. However, she pushed it aside and continued to cut up the head. I knew I was going to have to accept something, so when she asked me if I would like the jaw, I accepted because I thought I might be able to find some meat on it to sustain me, and taking it would make me look like a thankful guest instead of an ungrateful one. I picked up the jaw. Actually it was half the jaw—the left side, I think. There was some good roast meat on it and part of the cheek, but as I picked it up to chew the meat off it as if it was some giant sparerib, I couldn't help noticing that the teeth were still in place and the lower part of the tongue was attached along the gum line. It was not too long since I had done some dental work, and I could remember all the saliva and mess and I didn't relish chewing something that had been used already for the same purpose. Besides all this, I noticed that the caribou had a bad case of plaque on its teeth and I couldn't help but wonder why. I tried to look as though I was enjoying it, but I was sure I didn't fool my hosts any more than children can fool their parents when they don't like something on their plates and play around with it or chew the same piece for fifteen minutes. My hosts were very good about it and didn't make any comments, and I suppose we were all being diplomatic about the whole thing.

Finally Mrs. Vittrekwa put a big bucket partly out of view behind the stove and instructed everyone to put their leftovers and bones into the bucket for dog feed. I put my big piece of leftovers into the bucket although I realized that it still had enough sustenance on it to feed another person. Mary passed me a large piece of freshly baked bannock and this was closely followed by tinned creamery butter and strawberry jam. This was a real luxury when you considered that it was brought all this way by dog team. I certainly appreciated it because it settled any thoughts I had about going to bed hungry.

When we stepped out of the tent the next morning, we found it was snowing heavily and already there was a good six inches (15 cm) of the light, fluffy stuff covering the ground. As we were going to be returning to William Vittrekwa's camp that day, he was quite glad to see the snow because it would give the dogs something to grip as they pulled the meat-laden toboggans back up Rock River.

After we had travelled for nearly 20 miles (32 km), the snow stopped falling and we were able to make better time. Fortunately, the overflow creek had frozen over again, there was no sign of any water, and all the ice was covered with the new snow. Though it remained cold, the sun came out, the snow glistened, and we had to dig out our sunglasses to prevent snow blindness. When we reached the Road River camp, everyone was very excited to hear about the caribou and said they would move down to Rock River in the next day or so.

WE WERE GOING TO BE leaving for Fort McPherson the following day, but we still had to unload the meat and put it up into a cache or risk having a loose dog come along and chew a hole in the side of the carriole to get at the meat. Most nights one or two dogs got free and whoever owned them had to get up and chain them again. Most of us knew our own dogs' voices, so if we heard them barking, we would relax because they wouldn't bark if they were loose, but I was fooled several times just because of the cacophony of so many dogs barking. Chasing a loose dog around when that animal is enjoying his freedom, and you are out there in overshoes, long johns and a t-shirt, and the temperature is 30 below F (-35 C) is enough to make you want to convert the whole team into a snowmobile.

Early next morning we loaded the toboggans, hitched up the

dogs and called out our farewells and thanks to William and his wife. Then Don, Peter and I took off down the trail toward home, hauling a good load of meat for the people there. We made good time on the trail. The dogs were working well after their feed of meat and the short rest at George's camp but, even so, it was dark by the time we reached what had been our first camp. The moon was full so we had a well-lighted trail and no difficulty as we unloaded and then fastened up the dogs. Once we had the gas lamp lit inside the tent, our night vision was spoiled but by then it didn't matter. After some hot tea and bannock and caribou meat, we unrolled our sleeping bags and collapsed thankfully into them. The dogs howled at the moon, making me feel very happy on this the last night of our adventure.

The last 50 miles (80 km) were long and cold and the wind seemed to blow right through all the layers of my clothing. I was more than thankful to see the smoke of the settlement, and the dogs, knowing that we were close to home, picked up their gait. We all helped them by running behind the toboggans, and it also helped us to get warm, and an hour or so later, after a hot bath and big supper of macaroni and cheese, all the memories of hardship disappeared and only the good memories remained.

21

THE POPULATION OF THE Northwest Territories is not large, but possibly due to the hardships that people endured and the isolation and cold climate of the north, there seemed to be more than the usual quota of interesting characters living there. One of these was Louis Cardinal, and whenever I went to Arctic Red River, I visited with him and his wife, Carolyn, as soon as my work was done. They lived in a neat little cabin overlooking the great Mackenzie River; both enjoyed having visitors, and I loved hearing the stories that Louis told me about the north. When the weather was good, he would sit outside the cabin and contentedly puff on his pipe while he gazed out over the countryside that he knew so well.

He was born in 1877 in what is now Edmonton, but he told me it was nothing more than a trail through the trees the last time he saw it. When he was 20 years old, he joined the North West Mounted Police and took his basic training in Regina. A year later he was among the members of the first contingent of police to be sent to the Yukon to keep the peace amongst the gold rush hordes. Assigned to guard the Chilcoot Pass, Louis was told to be prepared to hold off the notorious Soapy Smith and his gang, even though the police had inadequate ammunition and supplies. Fortunately for Louis—or Soapy—the gangster never made it to the Pass.

Posted next to Dawson City, he found it to be a busy metropolis, but he did not have to hang around it for long because he was assigned to make dog-team patrols to Fort McPherson on a regular basis. On some of these patrols he was expected to prolong his stay in Fort McPherson and then act as a guide on patrols to Herschel Island and as far north and east as Paulatuk on the Beaufort Sea. Several times his hunting skills saved a patrol from disaster. On one springtime trip the patrol was delayed by wet snow and patches of open water and very soon ran out of food. Even the dried fish that they carried for the dogs was going rancid, not that the dogs minded, but it was unpalatable for the men. So Louis got up early one morning and walked through the slush to a marshy piece of ground where the grasses were beginning to show through the rapidly melting snow. As he was just out looking to see if there was any game, he hadn't brought along his gun, but to his surprise there were a few snow geese on the flat, feeding in the early morning light. By using some low willow bushes for cover, he inched his way forward and picked up a dry piece of driftwood. His movement made the geese uneasy and they started to walk out towards the still frozen river. Not wanting to lose his opportunity, Louis suddenly dashed out from behind his cover and threw the stick with uncanny accuracy at the nearest goose that, along with the others, was slipping and sliding over the icy marsh ground. The missile struck the luckless goose's wing and it couldn't take off. Instead, it skittered away and Louis ran after it, pounced on it, and before many minutes it was slung over its captor's back and, with mud and snow covering him, Louis walked back to the camp. The other policemen, who had begun to wonder where he had got to and were talking of breaking camp as soon as he came back, immediately cancelled all plans to leave and very soon the savoury smell of roasting goose permeated the damp air.

Louis was a great storyteller, and even a casual conversation about the weather could cause a faraway look to come into his eyes, and he would say, "Ah, yes, you can never tell with the weather. I can remember being on Travaillent Lake and caught in a strong wind, and it just blew down with nothing to stop it, and I knew if I didn't find shelter..." and he would reminisce about his adventure, reliving every moment. After a while he would stop, relight his pipe, take a few puffs of the aromatic smoke, then sit back in his chair and stare at the smoke before he started talking again. I would sit in silence watching him, worried that any noise I might make would destroy the spell of the moment.

He would finish his tale and chuckle over it as though it had just happened. Then, invariably, he would take a few more puffs on his pipe before looking over at Carolyn, who would ask if I would like some tea and bannock. When this happened, I knew that Louis was not too tired and that he was going to tell me more, and it was a pure delight to sit there in the light of the lamp, eating bannock and strawberry jam, drinking hot tea and waiting for the next episode. Sipping his tea, Louis would exclaim "Aaaah," wipe his mouth and say, "Did I tell you about that time when…"

Once when Louis had been guiding a patrol across the mountains from Dawson City, as often happened in the mountains a howling gale forced the patrol to make camp where they were virtually trapped for days by the shrieking wind and blowing snow. The fierce winds threatened to blow down the tents and visibility was cut to almost zero. Their food was all but gone, and they discussed what it would be like to eat their dogs if it became a matter of survival. But as hungry as they were on the short rations, they could not bring themselves to even think about eating their faithful dogs, though at the back of every man's mind was the thought that, if it came to starvation, he might change his mind!

As soon as the wind died down enough, Louis ventured out, shielding his eyes from the shale that was blowing off the exposed cliffs around the camp. Putting on his snowshoes, he walked up the river to where he knew there were small islands covered with the sort of willow bushes that moose liked to shelter in because it gave them something to eat as they waited out the storm. This same cover gave Louis an advantage, too, because he could hide in it, and walking upwind quietly on his snowshoes, he hoped to surprise one of the animals. Either great luck or excellent bushcraft led Louis to fresh tracks on one small island, and circling around he came suddenly face to face with a moose. It reared up in surprise as it saw Louis, but before all of its feet were on the ground again it had been hit by two of his bullets. He cleaned the animal where it lay, cut out the tongue and liver, put them into his bag, and then walked back to the camp. Without a word he stoked up the stove and put the fresh meat into the frying pan. His patrol companions just stared and finally one asked him how he had managed to get the meat. Louis shrugged. "It was just standing there," he said. And with that Louis Cardinal looked at me and laughed gently. He took another pull on his pipe and held up his cup for Caroline to refill it with tea.

Louis Cardinal retired from the NWMP in 1907 and lived for many years in Fort McPherson; then in 1927 he and his wife moved to a house on the Mackenzie River, close to Arctic Red River, where they lived off the land. In 1962 they moved into the small frame house in Arctic Red River where I knew him. From there he could sit in the sun and watch the boats coming and going on the river, and whenever he had an opportunity, he would light up his pipe and reminisce with other old-timers or tell stories to the visiting nurse.

Louis never went south again. He said that there was nothing to go for as all of his brothers and sisters had died before him, and things would have changed so much that he thought he wouldn't recognize anything. The year before he died he was a guest of the government of the Northwest Territories at the NWT Centennial Celebrations in Fort McPherson, and the commanding officer of "G" Division flew in from Inuvik to Arctic Red River to escort Louis there in style. He was by then 93 years old and unused to bright lights and throngs of people. The new buildings and modern conveniences were strange, but he faced it all with courage, standing on the stage and acknowledging his reception. The RCMP commanding officer towered over Louis, and stood with one arm supporting him, which under the circumstances was quite apt. After all, Louis had spent many years supporting the force.

These days, travellers on the Dempster Highway have to cross the Mackenzie River at Arctic Red River, and it is the ferry *Louis Cardinal* that continues the task of its namesake in ensuring that people reach their destination.

22

TRAVELLING BY DOG TEAM is relatively slow but very satisfying because it gives the traveller a good opportunity to not only see the land but to feel it, too. For Muriel and me it was a unique way to travel, but it was not always the most convenient method if a medical emergency arose far out in the bush and we were asked to attend. We soon found out why bush pilots were held in such high regard in the north.

To me, flying defies logic but I accept it, and I trusted every pilot I flew with to get their planes up and—even more important-ly—down safely. (One pilot told me that getting a plane up in the air is easy and getting it down is the difficult part. He added that all planes will come down eventually but your life depends on how they come down.) For years Muriel and I flew in small aircraft and were in close contact with the pilot, nearly always sitting in the co-pilot's seat where we had a much better view of the country and saw many wonderful sights. On one of her earliest medivacs from Fort McPherson, Muriel went as the escort in a Cessna 185. The pilot had removed the passenger seats to make room for the stretcher, and Muriel sat on a sleeping bag beside the patient and just hung on to the seat belt that was still attached to the floor. As the plane was taking off, the passenger door flew open and banged around, and Muriel caught a quick glimpse of the ground racing by below her. She gripped both the seat belt and the patient tightly until they were

Freddy Carmichael's Cessna 185 was ready to go day or night for urgent medivacs.

airborne, and then the pilot casually leaned over and shut the door. "It's always doing that!" he shouted over the engine's roar and turned nonchalantly back to his instruments.

On another occasion when she was returning from a medivac to Road River, after they were ready for take-off, the pilot just headed out across the snow on the lake behind the Road River cabins. Although the trees were coming up very fast, the pilot kept the plane thundering across the lake and then at the last minute, just when Muriel thought he was on a suicide mission, he brought the nose of the plane up. They were so close to the tops of the pine trees that she could see the cones on some of them.

On a New Year's Day flight to Inuvik I was kept very busy attending my patient who'd had a stroke. It was a very windy day but it didn't bother me too much, but when we arrived in Inuvik the pilot turned off the engine and, wiping his brow, turned to me. "Wow, Keith," he said, "that was a close call!" He had been fighting the strong crosswinds and downdraft all the way, and it was one of those times when I thought, "Ignorance is truly bliss."

On another trip to Arctic Red River in late spring, I was not ignorant of what was happening, and was genuinely scared. I had side-chartered the single-engined Otter from its regular schedule so that I could get in a last trip there to hold a clinic before breakup. The weather was quite warm although there was still snow and ice on the ground, and the plane was to land on the river ice. We were close to the village when we flew into freezing rain, which instantly froze on the windshield. The pilot, Keith Nordstrom, couldn't see anything, but what disturbed me most (I was sitting on Keith's right side) was that I couldn't see anything either. The ice buildup on the windshield was nearly a half-inch thick, and Keith could only see out of the side windows, which we had opened, and endure the icy blast of cold air.

He flew around the village once to make sure he had his bearings, then flew over the airstrip with the plane at such an angle and altitude that he could see it clearly. Then, looking very sombre, he brought the plane in for a landing by looking out of the small side window, keeping the nose high and the engine revs up as we touched down. The landing was as smooth as velvet.

Keith exhaled quite audibly when we had taxied to the end of the strip, and I didn't waste my breath asking him how he felt. When we had deplaned, he told me that it was not only the lack of vision that had bothered him. He said that, if that much ice was on the windshield, he knew that there was at least as much on the leading edge of the wings, and that could have brought our flight to an abrupt end when the wings lost their lift capacity. The plane stayed in Arctic Red for more than an hour until the weather cleared, and Keith spent most of that time scraping the ice off its windows and wings.

From then on I always thanked pilots for a safe trip because they were all truly great, and in those days they didn't have the assistance of satellite weather reports, Loran stations, Global Positioning Systems and good runways, which all came much later. They flew by "the seat of their pants" just to provide a much-needed service to the isolated communities.

WHEN I HAD TO FLY unexpectedly into the bush, it seemed that there was always something to make me apprehensive, and on a trip to Snake River—an hour's flight south of Fort McPherson—it was deep snow that caused a problem for Freddy Carmichael. And if it was a problem for the pilot, it was a problem for me, too. I had gone to check out a patient who was in the last stages of pregnancy and who had adamantly refused to come to the village throughout the entire nine months. The only transportation that she and her husband had was a dog team and with the deep snow that had fallen it would take them many days to move both adults and their other two young children to the village.

We arrived over Snake River and soon found where the family was living by the pale blue smoke that wafted up through the trees from the cabin site. Freddy flew around several times and then, when he had selected where there was a decent enough place to land, he came in close over the river and the plane settled down into the virgin snow. Down, down, down we went, and the snow flew everywhere, whisked by the propeller and the forward momentum of the plane. We could not see anything and hoped that there was not a log or piece of ice sticking up under all that white stuff, waiting to snag us.

But Freddy's worst fears were realized when he got out of the plane and found there was about eight inches of overflow on the river, and that, unless he acted fast, the plane's cold skis would freeze to the ice. He began to shovel away the snow while I scrabbled around in the plane for my medical bag. Meanwhile, William Snowshoe had walked down to the plane from his cabin. He was wearing snowshoes and, of course, I was not, and when I looked up to him as I struggled through the deep snow, I figured my nose was level with his knees. I half-waded and half-swam to the riverbank where there was a firm trail leading down to a water hole, and where thankfully

I could pull myself up onto the firm snow and follow him to the cabin.

William's wife, Bella, was very pregnant but would not listen to any of my pleadings to return with me on the plane and have her baby in the village. Her rationale for staying a bit longer was that she was not sick, was not due for another week, she had her other children to think about, and the trapping was very good right then. I was not reassured but there was nothing else I could do. Her other children were healthy and mischievous and didn't seem to be deprived by living so far away in the bush. She let me examine her and I found the baby was in a good position and appeared healthy, as was the mother. In fact, apart from the possible complications of childbirth, she was doing fine and seemed well-prepared. I left a pre-sterilized delivery pack with her and instructions for William—who had never witnessed a birth—just in case of an early delivery and told them that they really should start out for the village immediately—it would take them two or three days by dog team—if she would not fly back with me. Then I packed my things and prepared to leave.

Freddy had not been idle down at the plane. He had pulled out his emergency snowshoes and, after clearing the snow from around the plane, had put some brush under the skis to prevent them from freezing down. He had then flattened out the snow for quite a distance in front of the plane, so that we could take off easily. When we were ready to go, he revved up the engine and then, using the tail flaps, made the plane bang up and down a bit to release it from any remaining ice. Then we were on our way with the snow flying, though it was only the change in the engine's sound that told me when we were airborne. I sighed with relief!

Six or seven days later William and Bella Snowshoe arrived at the nursing station, and while Muriel examined Bella, William told me they had done really well at trapping that winter and had come back to town with the dogs without any trouble, Bella bringing in her own team. We were relieved she had made it safely and that nothing had gone wrong. It was hard to accept that as adults, these people had to take responsibility for their decisions, and it was immaterial whether we approved or not. Since it was Medical Services policy to send mothers to hospital for their fourth delivery, we sent Bella to Inuvik and she did not make any fuss about going. She was only there for four days before delivering a healthy baby boy.

WHILE TRAVELLING BY small chartered airplanes was unique, the best and most exciting way to travel was by helicopter—although, if we were evacuating a patient, we didn't always have the chance to appreciate it at the time. In the 1960s increasing interest in oil exploration in the Mackenzie Delta had brought several helicopters to Fort McPherson for the use of the geological scouts. We watched them coming and going and always hoped to get a ride, but we were too shy to just walk up and ask, and we couldn't really afford to charter one. In those days a helicopter chartered from $100 to $500 per hour, and though that is cheap by today's standards, it must be remembered that we were earning a good salary of $3,200 each per year. Thus a one-hour charter would have cost us up to two months' salary.

Most of our subsequent rides, therefore, were for medivacs, but one opportunity arose for a quick non-medivac ride when I was visiting Arctic Red River by boat in June 1966. I'd had trouble with my kicker (outboard motor) and I knew I was going to have to send it out for repairs. In the meantime, I asked Corporal Don Rumpel at the Arctic Red River RCMP barracks to keep the boat and motor under surveillance. While I was making these arrangements, Don asked if I would like to stay for supper, which was going to consist of large barbecued moose steaks. Not being able to think of a good reason to turn down such an offer—and not trying too hard to think of one—I stayed for supper, and we then chose to rest and recuperate by having a nap on the lawn. We both slept until long after the sun had gone down and were awakened suddenly by a thunderous noise and flashing lights overhead.

We were convinced that it was a plane in trouble, and as there was no landing strip there, it really would have been in trouble if the pilot had tried to land. Then as things came into focus, we realized it was a helicopter. Don got his policeman's large flashlight and signalled to the helicopter pilot by waving the light, getting him to move to the far end of the property where there were no antennas or aerials in the way. The pilot turned on his extremely bright landing light, and then very slowly the helicopter descended and, to our relief, settled on the grass without incident.

After waiting for the engine to cool, the pilot heaved himself out and introduced himself. He said he had been in Inuvik and heading to an oil rig to the south and didn't fancy staying in Inuvik where he didn't know anyone. He had heard that Don was at Arctic Red River and wondered if he might know him so, even though it was already dusk, he had whisked off and what the heck! Would we like a beer?

We went to bed about three in the morning, and the pilot said he would be delighted to give me a ride over to Fort McPherson for the price of a Kodak 35mm film, which he wanted and had forgotten to pick up when passing through Inuvik. It didn't take us very long to reach McPherson, and, as we were landing, the pilot asked if I had any family. I nodded in the affirmative.

"Would they like a quick spin?"

I nodded again enthusiastically, and the pilot spoke to me through his mike. "If you hurry, while you are getting the film, bring them back too, and we'll have a quick flight. But hurry so I won't have to switch off."

Muriel had been watching from the nursing station window as the helicopter landed and was surprised and a bit apprehensive when she saw me open the helicopter door and run toward the station. She thought there must be something seriously wrong for me to arrive in this fashion after leaving a few days ago by boat. As I grabbed the film, I told her quickly what had happened and of the pilot's offer to give us all a quick ride. Muriel, Helen and I rushed out to the helicopter and were soon strapped into our seats. I held Helen on my knees and she looked around in excitement as the engine screamed and began to vibrate. Suddenly we were taking off, and the pilot whipped the helicopter right up over the high riverbank. Muriel gasped, and Helen responded by emptying her bladder on me!

We were only in the air for five minutes, but it gave us the opportunity to take some photographs of the village as for a short moment we hovered over it like a bird of prey, surveying everything below us, aware of people like specks coming out of buildings. We saw out of the corners of our eyes some machinery moving by the garbage dump and, looking south, we could see the clearing where Eight Mile camp was. Then down we came, landing in a cloud of dust on the riverbank outside the station. We got out, closed the doors and waved goodbye, and our friendly pilot was off again, heading toward his southern destination. I went indoors and changed my pants.

23

As SPRING PROGRESSED, the snow melted rapidly, and as the ice heaved up, the meltwater ran on either side of the river ice. Then to cross the river it became necessary to wade through this water, then climb onto the ice, walk across the ice and jump down into the knee-deep water again.

About mid-April in the first spring we had spent in Fort McPherson, Muriel and I had wanted to go for a last walk along Mary Firth's trapline trail before breakup and, if possible, take a look at a beaver house on one of the lakes. We had been told that the beaver sometimes came out of their houses and could be seen sunning themselves on the ice. I hoped to film them with my 8mm movie camera. We crossed the river ice safely, stepping carefully, not fully trusting the ice. We climbed the bank on the other side of the river, then walked along the trail portage, which fortunately was quite dry, and crossed several small lakes before coming to the beaver lodge lake. We could see their house of branches on the shore across the lake and in front of it, on the ice, were two black blobs that could only have been the beaver.

We walked slowly and carefully toward them, staying close to a spit of land that stuck out into the lake and gave us some cover. We got within 75 yards (68 m) when Muriel cried out and fell through the ice into the shallow water. I glanced at her standing up to her knees in the water and whispered, "Hush, you'll scare the beaver away!" Then as the beaver disappeared under the ice, I felt ashamed of myself for thinking of the beaver before I helped Muriel. We went to the shore and dried out her socks while we enjoyed the spring sunshine then wandered over to examine the beaver tracks around the hole in the ice. At least we had seen the beaver from a distance!

ONE OF THE MORE spectacular spring breakup sights occurs on the Mackenzie River near the village of Arctic Red River, which lies on the southern shore of the Mackenzie on the downriver or northern end of the Lower Ramparts. The Mackenzie River ice, five feet (1.5 m) or more thick, begins to break up and, as the flood waters from thousands of miles away to the south and west causes pressure under the ice and raises it, it is freed from the shore and forced slowly northward. And then as the tremendous force of ice and water pushes it inexorably on, it picks up speed.

At this point the Mackenzie has had a 20-mile (32 km) straight stretch to gather momentum to force the ice down the narrow gauntlet that is the Ramparts, and the force is so great that huge pieces of ice are forced upwards until they fall back on themselves, causing a frightening, grinding, crushing monster of ice. To add to the nightmare, the Mackenzie makes a sharp right turn here to head north again, and as it grinds itself around the turn, it is joined by the ice and floodwaters of the Arctic Red River. It is hard to imagine anything that man could make that could equal such awesome power, and there is something fascinating about it.

One spring after the Peel River ice had gone out, and the boats that had been patched and painted or newly built during the winter began buzzing up and down the river, word came that the Mackenzie was partly clear of ice but that it had jammed below the Ramparts at Arctic Red. But one of the local men, Fred, said he would take me down to the mouth of the Peel if I wanted to visit the people there. The mosquitoes were still to come, and the opportunity to travel in the warm spring air appealed to me. I purchased gas for the "kicker" engine and Fred looked after everything else. I checked the medical charts of the people living at the mouth of the Peel, packed some supplies, said goodbye to Muriel, and Fred and I were away by mid-morning.

The "warm spring air" was decidedly cold travelling in an open riverboat, and I was glad I had thrown my parka in the boat and wore it instead of my life jacket. Travelling fast with the swirling, muddy current, it did not take long to reach the mouth of the Peel, Fred skilfully manoeuvring the riverboat around the trees that had been torn from the riverbank. On one tight corner he took the boat toward a huge whirlpool and, to my consternation, did not slacken power but took the boat over the lip. Then, as we began to circle the outer ring, he gunned the motor, and the boat shot over the far side and we continued our way down river. I was tense but exhilarated, and Fred never flinched but kept his eyes ahead like the good helmsman he was.

Jimmy Thompson came down to meet us as the boat pulled up quite close to his cabin, and then while Fred tied up the boat and refuelled, I visited the people in their cabins. Now that the snow had gone, every cabin had been spring-cleaned, and even the area around them had been raked and set on fire, leaving little piles of wood chips and sawdust smouldering away, which contributed a not unpleasant acrid smoke to the air. And it was nice to find that everyone was healthy, not a sniffle or cough or toothache.

When Fred joined us, we had tea and during conversation Jimmy said that the Mackenzie was jammed about six miles (9.6 km) south of the Peel and suggested that I go and look at it before heading for home. Willing to look at anything new, I asked Fred if he minded and he agreed that we should go. We swung out from Jimmy's place and turned south to where the Peel River emptied into the Mackenzie. Normally, for a boat to travel south, one had to cross to the other side of the Mackenzie to miss a large sandbar that had formed from the sediment brought down the Peel. At this time of year, however, the sandbar was far below the water level, so we were able to stay fairly close to the west bank. On the southern horizon, a shimmering white wall stretched from shore to shore, and we sped towards it, the noise of the kicker engine roaring in our ears. When we were close enough to see the huge blocks of ice clearly, Fred slowed the motor enough to keep the boat from being swept back by the current.

I had never seen a log jam, but had read about them and how there is a key log that has to be moved by some daredevil logger in order to get the logs moving. Now I looked at the mass of ice wondering which one was the key block. At last Fred let the boat turn in the current and we began drifting downriver. But when we were about a mile and a half below the ice jam, there was an ear-splitting CRACK! and a grinding noise that was so loud it could be heard above the roar of the kicker.

Fred and I both turned and saw that the ice jam had broken and was moving toward us at an incredible speed. He pulled the throttle full out and we seemed to skim across the water, but when I turned again, I saw that the ice was catching up, and on the sides of the river the trees and bushes were being ripped out by the ice blocks. I sat leaning forward, willing the boat onward, and Fred leaned forward in the stern with the same thought, as he told me later. The noise of the ice was terrible to hear, and as we raced for the mouth of the Peel, I felt as though there was a monster after us, ready to swallow us at the first opportunity. If anything happened to the kicker now…

By the time we turned in at the mouth of the Peel, the ice was less than a quarter of a mile (.4 km) behind us and, when Fred turned off the kicker, we realized the noise had increased tenfold. With the Mackenzie ice now blocking the Peels' mouth and the Peel starting to back up, the water in front of Jimmy's cabin was rising rapidly. Some stray pans of ice swirled around, and Fred said we should head for home in case his boat became trapped in the ice. We said goodbye to Jimmy and the other people there and headed up the Peel, making much slower time with the boat running against the current. Fred watched carefully for any half-submerged trees, which shot along like torpedoes, because if one were to strike us it would sink us in seconds. I pulled my life jacket closer around me. A few hours later we pulled up to the riverbank in front of the nursing station, and with some relief I unloaded my stuff and carried it up. Fred joined me for coffee and we relived the adventure again for Muriel and William.

AS SOON AS THE ICE had melted enough and the mud flats showed along the Peel River, ducks and geese by the thousands arrived, some to stay, others heading further north to their nesting grounds. No one was legally allowed to hunt migratory fowl in the springtime, a fact which I know angered some native people who had been living on caribou and moose all winter with only a little fish or other meat to eat occasionally. By the time hunting season opened in the fall, most of the birds had gone south, so it was seen as a law to benefit white hunters down south. As a result, the people who lived in the bush treated the law with disdain, and who was to know if they varied their diet with some different meat in the spring? I have visited camps in the spring and seen a lot of feathers in a pile. One old man I was visiting saw me looking at them. He pointed at the feathers and said with a twinkle in his eye, "That fox, he bring goose into camp and eat it right here, but he come at night, and no one see him. Just those feathers in the morning!" And we both laughed. When the game warden visited camps, there was some effort to cover up any evidence, but the wardens that we knew were understanding and seemed to have an unwritten rule: "If you don't tell me, I won't ask!" It was nice to see that there were sensible people working in the bureaucracy.

Herb Firth took Mike, Bett, Muriel and me for a ride up the Peel River one Saturday, and as Herb sat in the rear of the boat at the helm, the rest of us sat in the bottom of the boat with our parkas on and a tarp over our legs to keep warm. Flocks of ducks had gathered along the shoreline, and I began thinking how easy it would be to get a few ducks for supper. I started to voice my thoughts and had just said, "With all these ducks around, it's a pity no one brought…"

when BOOM! a shotgun blast drowned out my words, deafening everyone, and a flying duck suddenly dropped out of the sky! We hadn't seen Herb bring his rifle into the boat, but because of the time of the year he would not have wanted to advertise his intentions. By the time we got home late that afternoon, he had enough ducks for a good supper for his family, and we didn't blame him one bit.

24

VILHJALMUR STEFANSSON was one of the first explorers to travel and live with the Eskimo and to eat entirely what they ate, forsaking the white man's food. He found that as long as he ate substantial amounts of fat along with the fresh raw meat, he stayed healthy and did not suffer from scurvy as did so many explorers. This made sense because the Eskimo stayed healthy as long as they had enough to eat. And it was this Eskimo diet that gave me another opportunity to travel, this time to the High Arctic, that area far above the tree line that I had longed to see after reading the tales of adventure, hardship and even death that had occurred there.

Dr. John Rookes, the director of Medical Services' Inuvik Zone, put some spice into my life one beautiful, cold, clear day when the sun was beginning to make its presence felt by staying in the sky for nearly three hours a day. He phoned to ask if I would be prepared to travel to Cape Parry to immunize the Eskimo children before spring break because there was an apparent high risk of disease in that community. Normally the people there received their medical care on an annual basis when the Canadian Coast Guard icebreaker *Charles Camsell* called at the village with the year's supply of foods and fuel. But the past year the wind had held the ice inshore and the ship had been unable to make its scheduled visit. Consequently, the village was very short of supplies and medical attention.

Cape Parry is situated at the most northern point of Parry Peninsula, which separates Franklin Bay in the west from Darnley Bay to the east. The peninsula, which projects into the Beaufort Sea, was named after Captain W.E. Parry, who was a member of Franklin's 1826 expedition when he travelled by whaleboat along the northern coastline. By the end of the 19th century, Cape Parry had become the eastern limit for the American Pacific whaling fleet, and an American whaler, the *Alexander*, was wrecked on the Cape.

I would have been happy to go there even if it was only to take someone's temperature, but having a real purpose would make it really worthwhile. But when I agreed to go, Dr. Rookes admitted he was asking me because I would have to stay at the Distant Early Warning (DEW) line site, which was about three miles (4.8 km) from the Eskimo village. Apparently there were no doors on the bedrooms or bathrooms and the authorities harboured a fear that some deprived or crazed man might attack a female nurse and jeopardize the American/Canadian relationship in the Arctic!

Dr. Rookes then went on to ask me if I would do a little detective work, too. Now this was getting to be fun! "They"—I was never sure who "they" were, but by the reverent tones in which it was said I was given the impression that I could expect the death penalty if I crossed one of "them"—had received reports that the Hudson's Bay store in Cape Parry was selling sweetened condensed milk instead of evaporated milk to the Eskimo mothers, who all bottle-fed their babies. This, of course, might seem to be a petty crime, but I could see the problems that could result: overweight, pale and anaemic infants who would be very susceptible to illness. It was reported that the babies were being fed a very dilute formula of the condensed milk and, of course, they drank it hungrily because it was so sweet. The hospital staff in Inuvik had seen a number of anaemic babies and a few toddlers with incredibly bad teeth, which may have been from the sweet, sugary milk when their first teeth were erupting. Enter the Public Health Detective!

William Firth called in for coffee as usual while Muriel and I were discussing the forthcoming trip, and he was quite excited when he learned where I was going and proceeded to tell us about his trips by dog team up to the coast and almost as far as Coppermine. He said that he just could not get to sleep at night because it was so cold in the tent, and then someone he was travelling with said that he must use a piece of wood under his head and it would keep the cold out. William did this, and never had any problems after that. I could not figure out how William got to sleep with a block of wood under his head but I didn't want to spoil a good story! (As we got to know William, we were surprised to find how much he despised the Eskimo people, a general attitude that we saw and heard from time to time from other native Indians.)

I was to fly to Inuvik on the scheduled flight, pick up my supplies at the hospital, have another briefing, and then the following day take a chartered Reindeer Air Services flight to Cape Parry. Also going in on the flight was an Eskimo social worker, Billy Day, who proved to be a delightful travel companion with a great sense of humour.

It was always harder to get up in the dark of winter, and even though I was setting out on a great adventure, the morning of my flight into the High Arctic was not easy. I had flown, as planned, to Inuvik and spent the night at the hospital single men's residence. I had not slept well in the quarters because it had been too hot, and I was not used to the bed, but as bad as it was, it was better than getting up and going into the minus 40 degrees F (40 C) temperature that I had to face outside. However, after some good coffee and a hot breakfast in the hospital cafeteria, my enthusiasm for the trip began to wake up, too. The hospital driver took me down to the river airstrip where I met my pilot, Tommy Gordon, an Eskimo who worked for Freddy's Reindeer Air Services, and I had heard that he was an exceptionally good pilot. He was busy checking the gas in the Cessna 185 before he started the Herman Nelson gas heater that had been placed underneath the plane's engine to heat it. Tommy said it was usually ten degrees colder down on the river ice so the plane needed every extra bit of help they could give it, but after watching the flames roar out of the heater for 20 minutes, I was unsure if the plane's engine would operate or if it would be a mass of molten metal. Finally Tommy turned the heater off, loaded my sleeping bag and other personal and medical supplies into the plane, and with the sky turning pink on the horizon, Billy and I climbed into the still cold plane, and Tommy fired up the engine.

We headed northeast and after only a few minutes of flying, the trees—such as they were at Inuvik—disappeared, and we flew over a desolate white wilderness, truly a barren land, at least from the air. I could make out creeks and lakes but when Tommy asked if I could see the ocean, it took me a while to notice the faint outline of the shore. Blowing snow over the sea ice gave a blue-tinged marbled appearance to the surface that stretched out as far as the horizon, and there was not one drop of water to be seen nor one crack in the ice. I found this to be quite comforting, even though we were flying at 4,000 feet (1,219 m). If we were to land in an emergency, I didn't want to have the added worry of water survival!

The sun shone down on us and I found it quite hot but enjoyable, but the scenery was such that once I had looked at it for the first half hour, I had seen it all. It was nice to be able to see everything from this vantage point though it lacked some of the excitement and endurance of a ground trip, and my imagination watched explorers making their way over the sea ice with their dog teams, making camp and even using wooden blocks for pillows.

After two hours of flying, Tommy told me that we would be arriving at Cape Parry in a short time, and he would have to get clearance from the radar base. The DEW Line site was situated on a conspicuous 300-foot-high (91 m) hill, but the Eskimo village was tucked along the shoreline with very little shelter, and as a consequence the strong winds swept the snow over the houses and many of the people had to dig down through the snow to get to their front porches.

The Eskimo had not always lived at Cape Parry but had migrated there from Paulatuk to the southeast where a small outcrop of coal had been found, giving the people an unusual source of heat for the Arctic. However, the lure of jobs and white man's debris had brought them a few at a time to the Cape, followed faithfully by the Roman Catholic priest and the Hudson's Bay Company.

To the Americans in the sixties, Cape Parry was known as "Pin Main" as it was one of the main radar bases in the chain that stretched across Canada's northland. In between the main sites there were other smaller, unstaffed sites, which I understood were there to make sure no foreign objects squeezed in between the main stations. They were operated jointly by the American and Canadian governments, but the operations centre was far away in Pyramus, New Jersey, and I wondered how much control Canada actually had.

Tommy spoke into the microphone. After a few minutes he looked annoyed and spoke again. I looked down and saw the radar domes beneath us and a few scattered shacks a mile or two away from the base in a small bay. Tommy spoke into his mike again and then with a rather grim face he turned his attention to the business of landing. The flaps went down, and I felt the plane slow down and shortly we were bumping down the runway at the village, rather than that at the DEW Line site.

"Those guys up at the site," Tommy said, jerking his thumb towards the hill, "they said that they had to get permission for me to land, and they wanted to know who was on board and why." He looked annoyed again and then grinned. "I told them to come and find out and not to bother with permission. That's why I landed down here." Then he saw my worried expression. "Don't worry. By the time they've spoken to whoever in Pyramus, they'll send some-one down for you." He gave me a sly look and then added, "I hope they'll let me come back and get you or else you might be here for a long time!"

As we were unloading the plane, a truck appeared from the direction of the radar base, swung around onto the airstrip and pulled up by the plane. I went over and introduced myself to the military-looking man who was getting out of the truck. He was broad-shouldered, clean-shaven and had a military haircut. He had done his homework, too. He welcomed me to "Pin" and said I was expected—something of a relief to me after what Tommy had said—and he also said that there was a room for me at the base. While my equipment was being loaded into the truck, Billy Day had run over to one of the small buildings and engaged in an animated discussion with a man and woman. Then I saw them signing some papers that Billy put into his briefcase. He shook hands with them and ran back to the plane.

After making sure that Tommy would come and get me in three days' time, I said goodbye to both him and Billy and watched as the plane revved up and took off into the wind. I expected it would be dark before Tommy got back to Inuvik and he was flying by Visual Flight Rules (VFR). But I'm sure that it wasn't the first time Tommy had flown in the dark...

We drove the three miles to the base in what seemed like a few minutes. Not a tree in sight. While we were driving up the road I casually mentioned how bleak it looked, and the officer told me how dangerous it could be when there was a whiteout, and he advised me not to walk too far away because this phenomenon could happen very quickly and anyone outside could easily become disoriented and walk away from safety. He said it got so bad at times that they would fasten a rope from the bunkhouse to the cafeteria so that people would not get lost walking the 50 or so feet (15 m) between the buildings.

The base, which was similar to other arctic camps in the north, consisted of modular-looking, single-storey buildings with a huge radar dome overshadowing them. As we entered the gates, an American flag fluttered on one side of the road and facing it a Canadian flag kept time. I was shown around the base and told which buildings were out of bounds because of the nature of their operations. (I felt sure that the Russians probably knew as much about the base as the Canadians did!) Then pointing to my camera, this quite friendly man said I should ask any of the officials before taking photographs, but I was not too interested in taking photographs of military life. I wanted to record some Eskimo life.

After I was shown my room, I sat down and relaxed for a short time and then, letting curiosity guide me, I wandered around the units on my own, figuring that if I went to a restricted area I would soon be stopped. The complex was made up of trailer modules that formed a small, interconnected village of sleeping and living quarters, sick bay, meeting rooms, work areas and offices. To reach the radar dome, one had to leave the trailers and walk across a large yard to the perimeter of the base. The cafeteria and kitchens were in a separate group of modules, as was the movie theatre. When I went into the kitchen looking for some coffee and got talking to one of the chefs, I found that the base operated on New Jersey time, which didn't seem to have any bearing on Inuvik time, so I was quite confused as to what time of day it really was. To get into the Eskimo village I had to get a ride with the water truck early in the morning (my time), but in order to get back to the base I was told that I would be picked up just before supper, which, when I worked it out, would be 2:30 in the afternoon Inuvik time! On the positive side, the social life at the base seemed to offer everything except female company. Just having come from an isolated Indian village, I was overwhelmed by the choice of three up-to-date movies, a daily ration of beer or other alcoholic beverage (it had to be consumed that day and not saved up), and the meals were something I had only dreamed about—choices between beef roast, steaks, fish, all the fresh salad and vegetables I could eat and desserts that looked too good to eat—all served up by professional chefs. Just thinking about all of this luxury, I felt a little bit out of my depth and thought of the babies down in the village who were supposedly existing on not much more than sweet diluted milk. The next morning I made a trip to the village, met the Bay manager and the priest, both of whom lived in the Eskimo village, and received an invitation to stay in the manager's house where I could sleep on a cot in his living room. I could share his food (and he looked as though

The Hudson's Bay store and manager's residence at Cape Parry. Polar bear hides sold here for $125!

he liked eating), and I had the strong impression that he would enjoy the company. I accepted his offer and moved down later in the day, forsaking "the good life" up at the base.

There were just over one hundred people living at Cape Parry, all of them Eskimo except the Roman Catholic priest and the Bay manager. The priest was originally from France, as were most of the priests in the north. The people there called him Father Deherdivant, and his black robes underneath his parka and his huge beard made him look like one of the photographs of Oblate missionaries that can be seen in very old books. Sent first to minister to the people of Paulatuk, he had moved to Cape Parry when his tiny flock moved there. "The first year was the hardest," he told me over tea in his small house. "There was no other person who could speak either French or English, even the Hudson Bay store had not opened yet." He asked me if I would like to stay and have some lunch. "I don't have very much to offer you, but you are welcome to share it with me." As I wanted to stay and talk with him, I accepted. While he prepared lunch, I asked him how long it was before he was able to speak Inuktituk.

"Well, after the first year I had learned what various things were called, and I could make myself understood. The people tried to help me as much as they could. They didn't have a written language, so I couldn't learn from books." He put a bowl of soup in front of me "You go ahead and start. Have you ever eaten ugruk?" Then seeing my puzzled expression, he explained, "It's young seal meat."

"No, I've never had the chance to eat any, but I'd like to try some if you have enough."

He put a big piece of dark meat on my plate, and it looked a lot like stew beef. I had expected to see lots of fat on it, but thankfully there was none to be seen. He indicated for me to go on eating. "I found after the first year I began to understand a little about the language, and then it was just like a snowball and I could say more and more, though it was three years before I could speak naturally." He pressed me to have some crackers and butter with the seal meat, but I hesitated because there was only a small amount of butter left in the tin.

"Go ahead and finish it," he said. "When I first came to Paulatuk, I had nothing but the people gave me food and I ate what they did. I was very thankful for it, too." He described his first encounter with eating blubber and explained that when you eat the food of the country, and you spend a lot of time and energy fighting the cold, you begin to crave fat, and it does not make you feel ill.

"Aren't you going to have some crackers and butter, too?" I thought he had been too busy talking to eat some of the crackers.

He looked embarrassed and shook his head.

"Why not?"

He kept his eyes averted and spoke slowly, as though he was choosing his words carefully. "I don't have any more rations until the barge comes in the summertime." He looked very uncomfortable.

"Do you mean that I've just finished off the last of your food?" I was appalled that I had just left the luxury of the base cafeteria and dropped into someone's house and eaten their last morsel. "The boat won't be able to get in here for another five months!"

"That's all right. I wanted you to have it. Think nothing of it. I'm glad you visited. Please do not feel bad and anyway," he smiled slightly, "the people will make sure I'm not without. They're good people."

I said, "Thank you" and nothing more because I could think of nothing to say to this humble man who had shown me what generosity really was. The priest's only concession to civilization was a small generator that he started up at 8:55 every morning. He hadn't had it very long and only kept it on long enough to power the small transmitter and receiver that he used to give the weather reports to the station in Inuvik.

Gary, the Bay manager also spent considerable time with his radio transmitter, and once he had received the current coded fur prices and passed on various messages, he would go to the frequency of some other outpost and listen to their messages. When he had heard one side of the conversation, he turned the dials furiously to catch the other side of the conversation, and this occupied him for quite some time. If he had no visitors—which was quite often—he relaxed in a chair and read a book, and judging by the number of books he had on his shelves, he read several a week. He was from southern Canada, an almost unique situation because most of the non-native people in the north seemed to be from France, Australia, the United States or the British Isles. When discussing this phenomenon back in Fort McPherson, we had come to the conclusion that it was because the north was on the Canadian doorstep and therefore familiar, whereas for foreigners the north still held a certain mystique and excitement.

I was very conscious of my ulterior motive for visiting the community, but Gary was very open and told me about his work and showed me his stock of supplies, which wasn't very great. In fact, the store shelves were virtually empty. Just a few dry goods but food items were almost non-existent. He said he had been expecting a supply plane for weeks, and when he checked in with other stores along the coast he was told that they, too, were expecting a plane at "any time."

I saw that there were several cases of sweetened condensed milk on the shelf and asked if that was what the mothers were buying to feed their babies.

"Sure is," he said, "because that's all I've got until that plane comes in."

"What do they use normally?" I tried to make the question sound natural.

"Oh, they use Carnation most of the time but I think they give them this stuff," and he indicated the condensed milk, "when they're short of rations. I guess it goes further."

"But it's not good for the babies," I replied, thinking I had better do some health education while I was there. "They'll just get fat, be anaemic and unable to fight disease, and it will rot their teeth." Nothing like giving out everything in one shot, I thought.

"But if they say they are buying it for cooking, how am I supposed to know what they do with it? I don't keep a check on who does what with their food."

I didn't want to look as though I was blaming him and I could see his point of view. He was the storekeeper, not the nurse, and though he sold condensed milk at the moment, knowing it was going to the babies, it was probably better that they had this milk than go without milk altogether. Too bad that the mothers didn't breast-feed any more, I thought. It was obvious that there was a lot of health education needed here.

I saw boxes of traps sharing shelf space with bolts of brightly coloured material used to make parka covers. Here and there around the store were a few white fox pelts hung from nails, and sealskins were stacked on the floor with the hair side of one against the hair side of the next so that the hair did not come into direct contact with the flesh side which was white and dusty from the flour that had been rubbed on it to soak up the fat and stop the hair from discolouring. The skins had not yet been graded, which Gary said he would soon be doing and then baling them before sending them out on the plane.

At the far end of the store there was a door leading to the unheated warehouse portion of the building, and in there Gary stored items he wanted kept frozen or goods that would not be damaged by frost. It was in here that I saw my first polar bear hide. In reality I saw my first nine or ten polar bear hides, the smallest one being over eight feet (2.4 m) long. They were stacked flat on the floor, hair side to hair and flesh to flesh like the sealskins, so that the hair would not be damaged. I asked how much they were worth.

"I'll sell you one for $125," Gary said, "but it will cost you another $500 or $600 to have it tanned."

"No, I don't think so. For one thing $725 is a lot of money, and the other thing is that I don't think we've got a wall big enough to put the thing on!" (Years later I found that *if* you could get a polar bear skin, you would have to pay about $5,000 for it!)

Early the next morning I started to visit the Eskimo people. I walked from the Bay house past a team of dogs that were chained individually to a long tether chain stretched out and secured in the ice with metal bars. The dogs ignored me and stayed curled up with their backs against the wind while the fine snow drifted around them. When I came to the first house, I realized that it was made from items retrieved from the base garbage dump. Pieces of crates and old boards, lots of cardboard boxes, which had been flattened and nailed to the walls, combined with the snow on the north side of the house that had drifted almost to the roof made it completely draft-proof. Outside the house, a low cache had been built on which lay a frozen seal. I found the door, and when I knocked, it was immediately opened by a round-faced child with a smile that stretched from ear to ear. He had a pudding bowl haircut and his hair was shiny and jet black.

"Come in." He turned his ruddy-coloured face up to me and asked seriously, "What's your name?"

242

There were no trees to shelter these Cape Parry sled dogs.

As I followed him inside, ducking down so that I didn't bang my head on the low doorway, I told him my name, and then in the gloom of the house I saw that there were four children and two women in the house. They all had big smiles, and the older of the women came forward and asked me if I would like some tea. It was only a short time ago that I had finished breakfast and about four cups of coffee with Gary, but I didn't want to appear impolite so within minutes of coming into the house, I was sitting holding a big mug of tea.

The children all crowded around me and were not the least bit frightened when I explained why I was there and that I would like to give each of them a needle. Instead, they seemed more interested in my beard, and one after the other a hand would dart out and touch it, and this was followed by lots of chuckles. I finished my tea and set out the equipment on a paper towel.

The children were very curious, and when I gave them their shots, instead of looking at the injection site, they congregated around the front of the next "patient," watching his or her face to see what sort

Cape Parry Eskimo children await their immunizations.

of facial reaction they would have when they had their shots. None of them cried or made a scene or even hung back when it was their turn.

I cleaned up my equipment and got up to leave. "Thank you for coming." The two ladies got up and came with me to the door. "These kids, they will show you where the people live," one of them said, and so, like the Pied Piper of Hamelin, I went from house to house with an ever-increasing number of children following me.

When I had finished my rounds and packed up my syringes, I told the children that I was going to go back to the store. I started to walk back but stopped when I saw the masthead of a small schooner sticking out of the snow. It was on the shore of the small bay, and looked as though it was in the middle of dry land, because there was nothing to show where the land finished and the sea began. I walked over to have a closer look, followed, of course, by my retinue of giggling children.

The boat lay at an angle and was a lot smaller than the St. Roche, which had been the first ship to sail the Northwest Passage, but it served to put my imagination into gear, and I thought of the voyages that had been made up and down the coast in all sorts of terrible weather. I asked one of the older children just where the shoreline was, and as her finger outlined the shape of the bay, I could make out a shadowy difference in the colour of the snow, and then as I peered into the whiteness, I thought I could detect higher ground at the shore. As it was as light as it was going to get that day, I told the children I was going to walk across the sea ice and take a photograph of the village from the other side of the bay.

"We'll come, too!" It was not a request. It was a statement and, since the company of the children would give me more opportunity for photographs, I just nodded in reply.

We set out across the ice, which was quite uneven with some sharp pieces pushing up through the crusty snow. Walking was quite difficult but it didn't seem to bother any of the boys and girls, and they all rushed around playing a form of tag. Then periodically they would run up to me and shout, "Take my picture!" and after being only too happy to take a few photographs, I had to resort to pretence so that I would have enough film left for other subjects.

The only way I knew that we were off the sea ice was when I felt the land rising and saw some shale on a windswept knoll. I walked until I felt I had the best view of the village, which could now be seen as a few small dark specks strung along the horizon, quickly took some photographs, and then headed back to the village.

When we reached the village, a woman came out of the first house and scolded one of the children. "You know you shouldn't go out over the sea ice." She cast a glance at me and I felt scolded, too. Then suddenly I remembered about the whiteouts that could come in so suddenly, and almost at the same time I thought of all the polar bear hides that had come from this area and were now in the Bay warehouse. And I remembered that polar bears are one of the few animals that will actively hunt a human. I had been very foolhardy, especially taking the children with me. But apparently the woman expected more of the children than she did of this crazy white man. I realized I had no experience travelling on sea ice, and there could have been holes or weaknesses that any of us could have fallen through. I had let the Eskimo children put their trust in me and had led them into potential danger.

Coming to another small house I had not yet visited, I turned in towards the doorway. I had been told earlier that there were no children in the house to vaccinate, but since I was passing, I didn't want the occupants to think I didn't want to visit with them. The house was nearly covered with drift, and I could gain access only by carefully climbing up one side of the snowbank and then going down some steps cut out of the snow. The porch was low, and it gave me the impression that the Eskimo had adapted their traditional igloo design to these plywood and tarpaper shacks.

I stooped and entered the porch. Lying on a large paper sack on the floor was a recently skinned seal into which was stuck the traditional Eskimo half-moon-shaped knife called an ulu.

As my eyes were growing accustomed to the gloom of the porch's interior, the house door opened, and an old Eskimo man came out dressed in polar bear overpants and a caribou skin parka. He smiled and nodded to me, walked over to the seal, bent down and sliced a large piece of the fat off the carcass and put it into his mouth. Then with a deft flick of the wrist, he cut off a mouthful of the fat with his ulu, narrowly missing his nose. (I saw even small children cutting off pieces of meat in this manner without any sign of nervousness or injury!) The old man nodded at me again and went outside chewing the fatty morsel. I looked at the seal again and gave an involuntary shudder as I thought of the seal fat sliding down my throat.

I knocked on the door and went inside as soon as I heard a welcoming answer. The lady was middle-aged, as far as I could tell, but it was really difficult to put an age to many of the native people, male or female. She beamed from her round, wrinkled face, which was framed by shining straight black hair. Two long braids hung almost to her waist, and as she came forward, she tossed them over her shoulders. When she smiled, her eyes were surrounded by skin creases that I immediately thought must be from years of looking across the glare of snow and ice.

"Coffee?" She didn't wait for an answer but started to pour some very black coffee into a huge mug. I sat down at her table. She pushed a plate of bannock over to me and said, "I saw you go over the bay. Where did you go?"

"Oh, I just went for a walk and the kids followed me. They seemed to enjoy it."

"You have to be careful doing that here." Then she explained, "The ice is never safe. There are holes covered with snow out there." She nodded in the direction of the bay. "It's easy to get lost, too. Those children are not old enough to know where they are yet."

I nodded as I thought of my trek over the ice, unaware that my movements were being monitored by at least one pair of dark eyes straining against the glare.

"Another thing," my hostess continued, "there have been a lot of bear around this year."

I thanked her for giving me the information then asked why no one had said anything to me earlier.

"Well," she thought for a second then exclaimed, "you're a white man." As though that was self-explanatory. I found this a little perplexing.

When I reached the Bay house, I refused Gary's offer of a cup of coffee and told him of my adventures. He just smiled and said people were concerned because about a week earlier a little girl had fallen off the back of a snowmobile that was going up to the radar base and was not found to be missing until the snowmobile driver reached the base. A storm had been brewing and a search party was organized immediately. Volunteers from the base had collected long ropes and compasses and then, with a lot more courage than hope, set out to search for the missing child. They had roped themselves together as the weather closed in and visibility had gone to zero. The men in the middle had followed the road markers, and the others fanned out on each side of the road, calling the little girl's name as they walked along. It took the rescuers over an hour to locate the child who by then was bewildered, frightened and cold and suffering from frostbite. She was taken to the base medical centre for treatment and later sent south on one of the military aircraft. After hearing this story I was extremely glad that I had not had any trouble and had returned safely with all the children.

On Friday morning we awoke to blowing wind and snow and knew it would be impossible for the plane to come in and get me. Gary suggested that as soon as the weather cleared a little, we should go up to the base and, if I could speak to the right person, I might be able to phone Muriel and tell her that even though I was delayed by bad weather, everything was okay. But it was not until Sunday that the weather cleared enough for us to drive up to the base on Gary's snowmobile.

When we arrived, I went up to the communications centre and spoke to the officer in charge. He was quite willing for me to make a phone call and explained that the call I wanted to make would go to Pyramus in New Jersey first and then to Edmonton and from there to Inuvik and then to Fort McPherson via the microwave system installed a short time earlier. But after going through numerous operators, I was told there was difficulty with the line to Fort McPherson, and the call could not go through, so I phoned the CN Telecommunications office in Inuvik and sent a cablegram, which would be phoned through as soon as the line was fixed. While we were still at the base, someone came looking for us to say he had been tuned to radio station CHAK Inuvik and had heard a message from Freddy Carmichael's Reindeer Air Services for me, saying they expected to be able to pick me up sometime on Monday if the weather cleared, as it was expected to do.

Monday dawned with an overcast sky and I doubted that the plane would come, but just in case I packed my bag and rolled up my sleeping bag as I had done for the last three days. The priest couldn't get any reception from Inuvik because of a malfunction on his set, so we sat in the Bay house and read books. We were suddenly brought back to reality by the sound of a plane buzzing over the house.

"I'll bet that's Tommy!" I called out and ran to get my parka and bags. Gary helped me to carry everything down to the airstrip, and by the time we got there, the plane had landed and turned, and Tommy stood beside it waiting for us.

"We have to get away quickly because there's another storm coming from the north," he told us as he heaved the bags and boxes into the plane. "But the weather is quite clear from Inuvik until you get within a few miles of here, and I'm hoping it'll stay that way for a while longer."

I said my thank yous for the hospitality and companionship of the last few days, and after a wave of farewell, Tommy fastened the door of the plane securely, and soon we were airborne. I looked back toward the village but it was already lost in the clouds and swirling snow.

"I'm going to go through this cloud and then we'll be in the sun all the way home." Tommy indicated upward with his finger, then seeing what must have looked like consternation on my face or in my eyes, he smiled and shouted, "Don't worry. There shouldn't be any air traffic around here!"

I looked out of the window and could see through the mists only as far as the end of the wing. My eyes strained to get a view of something, but I felt blind and my equilibrium was disturbed so much I had to look at the plane's instruments to convince me I was not upside down or sideways. Tommy also kept his eyes on the instruments and, as far as I could see, it was mainly these that told him that the plane was level. I knew he was only supposed to fly by Visual Flight Rules, but I told myself that he had flown into these parts just a short time ago. He knew how far the cloud extended.

Tommy was relaxed and that meant a lot to me because I have flown with pilots who looked and acted tense, and my confidence in them had soon evaporated. I watched him speak into his microphone, glance out across the wings, then up above. He looked at me and then leaned over and shouted that we were supposed to look out for a DC6B that was in the vicinity. He laughed and said for me not to worry because they knew that we were in here. Even so, I looked extra keenly out over the wing, and several times my imagination could hear the drone of the other plane over the roar of our own engine. I sat tense and a bit uncomfortable until after several minutes we broke through the clouds into dazzling sunlight, and everything seemed okay again. Then as the heat from the engine and the sun got to me, I relaxed and fell asleep.

JUST AS THE SUN WAS setting two and a half hours later, we landed at the river base airstrip in Inuvik. I thanked Tommy sincerely for the safe trip, unloaded my bags and equipment from the plane, and reloaded them into the waiting vehicle sent down from the Inuvik General Hospital.

I spent several hours with the director, explaining about the general shortage of groceries at the Bay store in Cape Parry Bay and told him that in my estimation the milk crisis would be alleviated as soon as the supply plane could reach the village. I thought that, in the circumstances, Medical Services could help the cause by passing on to the Bay executives the urgency of the supply plane and let them know that it might be better to supply the post from Inuvik if weather was still hampering them from supplying from the east.

By noon the following day I was back in Fort McPherson, and as I walked into the nursing station, I was greeted by the phone ringing. Muriel picked it up. "This is CN calling," a female voice told her. "We have a wire here from Keith Billington in Cape Parry, which reads as follows…" and she read out my wire. I couldn't help but reflect on technology in the north, where delays, plane flights, and even a night's stopover in Inuvik still allowed me to get to my destination before the national (or in this case, international) communication system could deliver a telegram to the same place, and I hoped that it would improve before there was a nuclear attack.

25

THE MACKENZIE DELTA was a rich source of protein, and the Gwich'in usually ate a large amount of meat when it was available, but they also ate great quantities of fish that they caught both summer and winter. Whitefish, pike, inconnu, crookedbacks, losh (catfish), grayling and char could be caught in abundance, depending upon the season and the method used.

Fishing under the ice was done by digging several holes through the ice and then, using a jigger or a long pole, stringing a net under the ice. I have dug a hole in lake ice with a chainsaw and found the ice to be five feet thick so I knew that cutting a half dozen holes with an axe when a chainsaw wasn't available is no easy feat! However, there seemed to be so many fish caught in nets on the Peel River that I was tempted to throw in a line myself. Eventually I bought a rod and reel and tried my luck but in the river's murky waters I was skunked every time.

However, William Vittrekwa often told me tales about a "fish hole," a place where you could almost shovel out the Arctic char and grayling because there were so many of them, but I knew that William could tell a good story and that most fishermen are given to exaggeration. And this sounded like one of those good fish stories. So I laughed politely to let him know that I understood, but my disbelief must have shown through.

"Sure, there's lots of fish, no one knows, only me been there, and

I've seen them, but lo-o-o-ong way, only way is with helicopter. I tell you, you hire helicopter and me, I'll show you where fish hole is." William was one of the few old men who would actually say the word "helicopter." People like Peter Thompson and Andrew Kunnizzi, who were church catechists, did not like to say the "hel" part of the word and just spoke of "the plane rho" or "the plane (that goes) round."

In William's mind it was simple to get a helicopter, and it was no good telling him that it was too expensive for me to hire a chopper and go flying out to goodness knows where because to William it just meant that I had to "give cheque"—as though the mere writing of a cheque magically produced the money. I suggested going to this fish hole by dog team, but he just shook his head sadly at me and explained that when the fish went up the streams to spawn there was no snow for a dog team. "Too much nigger-head to walk," he said. "Get too wet and it take nearly five days to get there, and how you gonna haul all that fish?"

I could not argue and we let the matter drop, but periodically the subject would come up again, and it did one day when William visited us at the same time Constable Frank Dunne was there.

"I've got some maps here, William," Frank said. "Can you show us where this fish hole is?" He drew some maps out of a big brown envelope and spread them on the kitchen table.

William peered at them. "Not this one." He pushed several aside. "What's this here?"

Frank read out the name of the creek to which William's gnarled finger pointed.

"Okay, over here." William's waving hand indicated west. Frank moved the map. William's finger wavered over a small creek and he said, "Here, anywhere here, you get lots of char, but only way is with helicopter. You get helicopter and I show you."

I had a creeping suspicion that William didn't want to be too specific about his fish hole to these white men. He knew that native people had lost out too many times by being generous with their information.

William Vittrekwa mending his fishnets.

Nothing more was said about the fish hole for several months. We all carried on with our usual routines as the fall weather started to close in and we had some early frost. The oil companies, which had exploration camps in the area, had begun to ferry equipment out in preparation for freeze-up and shutdown, when one day a big helicopter landed beside the RCMP office, and our new phone rang.

Frank Dunne said, "How would you like to go to the fish hole?" He explained that the helicopter had landed there because bad weather prevented it going south to an oil rig, and when the pilot had asked Frank if he knew where there was some good fishing, Frank had immediately thought of William's fish hole.

"Where's William?" I asked. If we went without William, I would feel we were betraying a trust.

"I've already checked," Frank said, "and he's out hunting somewhere up Stoney Creek, and no one really knows where he is. You know William when he gets out into the bush—he could be back tomorrow or next month."

I had to agree and, with a mixture of disappointment but growing excitement, we agreed to pay $50 each toward the cost of the fuel and to meet at the barracks within an hour. Corporal Shane Hennan wanted to stop at Millen Creek to put up a plaque there in memory of Constable Millen who had been killed there in January 1932 by Albert Johnson, the Mad Trapper of Rat River. Albert Johnson had been illegally trapping on William Nerysoo's trapline, and after trying to get Johnson to stop, William had gone to the police. When the Mounties went to Johnson's cabin on the Rat River, Johnson shot and wounded one of the policemen through the door. They police surrounded the cabin and ended up blowing it sky high with dynamite, but Johnson had escaped while the police were attending to their comrade. He became famous for leading the posse astray by walking over the mountains with his snowshoes on backwards to evade his pursuers. He was surrounded again at Millen Creek (though obviously it wasn't called that then) and he hid by the roots of a big, windfallen spruce tree, firing volley after volley at the posse so that no one was able to move. Finally the police opened fire, then they waited until there were no returning shots from Johnson, at which time Constable Millen went down the creek bank to investigate. As he got close to the fallen tree, Johnson fired and killed him. He escaped once again in the confusion but he was eventually tracked down after Wop May, a private pilot, used his plane in the first-ever aerial manhunt to spot Johnson, and the police shot and killed him close to Old Crow in the Yukon. To this day no one knows where Johnson originated. He is buried in the cemetery in Aklavik, NWT.

THERE WERE TO BE eight of us on the trip. Along with the pilot and two RCMP officers, we were to be accompanied by two men of the cloth so to speak, Don Wootten, the Anglican minister, and Ted Haas, an evangelical missionary. George Scherer, a visiting dental hygienist, would also come, having decided that it was well worth cancelling an afternoon clinic for this trip.

Muriel and I had one small problem to overcome if we were to go with them: we had a medical doctor visiting the nursing station and he was holding a clinic that day and we would usually work alongside him. Dave Posen was the Arctic's liveliest physician. He worked hard and played hard, and he had a sincere interest in everything in the north. He had made a dog-team trip with me from Fort McPherson to Arctic Red River and travelled with us by riverboat down the Peel River and then back up the Mackenzie to Arctic Red once again. He had learned to fly a small plane and was very disappointed to lose his licence later because of a latent medical problem.

We put it to Dave. Was he willing to manage on his own and give Muriel and me this unique opportunity? We knew that we did not really have to ask but it was polite to do so, even if we knew what the answer would be. Of course, Dave was frustrated that he would be unable to go, too, but he said he would be glad to stay. We were relieved because there would be medical coverage for the village while we were away, and there was no better person to do it.

We took some plastic bags to put the anticipated catch of fish in, as well as some garbage pails to stop the fish from slipping about all over the helicopter whilst we were in flight. (We were thinking positive for this fishing trip.) It was a fantastic flight and the steady rhythmic vibrations of the engine and the noise of the rotors only added the feeling of excitement that we were all feeling as we sped northwest toward Millen Creek and the unknown fish hole.

At Millen Creek the helicopter hovered over the location of the cache where Shane wanted to place the marker, then slowly the pilot manoeuvred between the trees and landed in a place that I was quite sure was not big enough for the rotors to turn without hitting something. The pilot, however, knew his stuff and brought us safely down about 75 yards (68 m) from the cache.

Millen Creek runs into Rat River, which then empties into the Nayuck Channel and so into the Mackenzie River and finally the Beaufort Sea. Like all the other creeks in the area, it is narrow and winding with steep canyon walls, but it had gone down in history because of the Johnson manhunt where Constable Edgar Millen was fatally shot. While Shane was busy nailing the memorial plaque to the cache, I looked around with my imagination in full swing and viewed the hunt and the shooting. Even though the scenery had changed a lot over the years, I could see the roots of a tree behind which Johnson had possibly hidden, and the probable place from which the Mounties had fired.

The plaque read:

On this site Const. E. Millen, RNWMP, was fatally shot by Albert Johnson, the Mad Trapper of Rat River. January 1932."

"Are you coming, Keith?"

I came back to the present with a jump, climbed back into the helicopter and strapped myself in once again, ready to fly on to the fish hole. As we neared the creek that old William had indicated on the map to Frank Dunne, the pilot brought the helicopter down low. There were a lot of pools, and we could only guess which one would be *the* fish hole, but as we flew slowly over, we soon saw that all of the pools could be good because we could see large grey shapes scurrying about in a frenzy as the water was stirred by the downdraft from the rotors.

Our pilot found a gravel bar on which to land the helicopter, and as soon as it was safe to do so, we piled out and began to put our fishing tackle together. After warning one another to watch for bears that might also be interested in doing a bit of fishing, we wandered upstream to a likely looking spot. All around the creek grew low willow bushes and ground birch, high enough to hide a small grizzly or a sleeping big one, but the creek was not fast running or noisy, and we made sure to make enough noise ourselves to warn anything around of our presence.

We looked over the bank into the clear water and saw a few fish in the deep pool. It didn't look as exciting as we had expected but I made a cast. The lure, a small Red Devil, landed in the middle, and suddenly from every part of the pool hundreds of fish converged on it.

"Look at that!" I shouted, which is what everyone was doing, and then there was a hubbub of voices and hollering as the news was relayed to those bringing up the rear.

My line went wild and in my excitement I nearly forgot what to do. Of course, advice came in from everyone but I could hardly think straight. I could not even see my fish because there were so many other fish around, all threshing about in excitement. No one thought about being quiet, as fishermen are supposed to be, but our noise didn't make any impression on the fish at all. I reeled in my catch, and everyone gathered around to look at it.

"It's an Arctic grayling!" I don't know who identified it but we all handled it and admired its large dorsal fin.

Everyone soon had a line in the water, and no sooner had they cast than they were pulling in fish. Muriel had never fished with a line before and could not resist trying her luck. She cast out into the pool and, feeling a tug on her line right away, she started to reel in. "What have I got?" she called out after seeing something on the end of the line.

"Careful there, Muriel, just pull it in carefully and I'll get my net on it." George Scherer clambered down the bank, put his net under her catch, and with a deft movement lifted it out of the water.

"What have I got?" Muriel asked again.

George struggled up the creek bank. "You sure this is the first fish you ever caught?" he asked breathlessly, "because you've caught it by the tail!" And, sure enough, there was the hook securely anchored in the fish's tail. "What's more, its an Arctic char, and they are just beautiful eating!"

Others were now catching char, which are not as exciting to catch as grayling but were more favoured for eating. Now we spread out along the creek, and Shane, the pilot, and Don went back to the helicopter and got a net to use to get some of the fish from lower down the creek. The char were from two to ten pounds (.9 kg to 4.5 kg) and the flesh was firm from the freezing cold water.

I heard someone ask about a permit but no one answered. They were too busy fishing, and, as I looked around at the RCMP officer on one end of a net and the minister on the other, I shrugged and cast my line again. Later we lit a fire on the gravel bar and cooked a few of the char, and never had I tasted such delectable fish. Of course, the whole day was unique. Flying by helicopter, the visit to Millen Creek, the cold crisp mountain air, the anticipation and then the results that were more than a fisherman's dream were almost too much for the senses.

When we had eaten, we fished some more, carefully putting back the fish that we did not want, and then after loading the helicopter, we whirled away in the direction of home, only slowing momentarily to watch a small herd of caribou grazing on a mountain slope. When we landed back in the village, we distributed our catch and headed home. Muriel and I filled a large box with char and put it in the deep freeze for William Vittrekwa, then we called William Firth and gave him some fish for his family and for the other people who were not so fortunate as we had been in going on the trip. We kept enough char for us to have periodically throughout the winter. But that night Muriel cooked us each a beef steak for supper.

We knew that this adventure may have given us the opportunity to tell one of the best fishing stories ever, but had it not been for old William, the adventure would never have occurred.

26

MURIEL AND I OFTEN talked about our future as it pertained to Fort McPherson because neither of us had any formal training in public health, even though that was what our job there was supposed to be. In early 1966 on one of those very rare occasions when we were visited by an understanding supervisor, we brought the subject up for discussion. Merle Pottinger was from Trinidad, and it was easy to talk to her because her personality was like a warm breeze on the sands, and when we had presented our problems to her, she soon had us looking on the bright side. And when we complained of being tired of eating tinned foods from the south, she offered to cook supper and made a delicious meal from canned whole chicken, canned potatoes and canned vegetables.

On this occasion Merle asked us what we would really like to do. It so happened that Muriel was pregnant again and did not want to do any more nurses' training for the time being. We discussed my doing public health or something else but still within the health field. I had thought of dentistry but with a growing family I could not afford to spend six or seven years at university and then come out with a large debt. Finally I decided to do public health, the necessary preparations were made, and the application sent to Medical Services and to Dalhousie University in Halifax, Nova Scotia, because the program there emphasized the north and northern nursing. (And by a strange coincidence, both Muriel and I had done our general nursing training in Halifax, not Nova Scotia, but England.)

I was full of apprehension. The thought of confinement in an educational institution did not fill me with excitement, and the prospect of leaving Fort McPherson with no guarantee that we could return to the community was not appealing either. For the one year of education, I had to guarantee that I would work for the government for two years or pay a percentage of the tuition and travel expenses, the latter being very expensive. Once the decision to go had been made, we broke the news first to William and then Mary. The news soon spread through the village but people were quite philosophical about it. They had seen white people come before, stay for a few years and then leave. For us, though, our lives were suddenly in turmoil and the next few months flew by.

Everything was packed and ready to move in anticipation of the arrival of two replacement nurses who had been found. Then we had a call to say the nurses were coming early and would I consider working at the Inuvik General Hospital for a few months until I could travel to Halifax?

We were already prepared for Muriel to go to Inuvik for delivery in July, but the thought of moving twice did not appeal to us at all. Yet if we did go to Inuvik, we would still be close to Fort McPherson, and Mary Firth had agreed to come to Inuvik to look after Helen when Muriel went into labour, so we agreed.

We rearranged everything so that we could leave earlier and saw our belongings underway on the barge to Edmonton where they were to be delivered to long-suffering friends who had been looking after some of our other possessions while we were in the north. As the barge disappeared from sight, I couldn't help but wonder where it would be delivered after my stint at the university.

The community organized a farewell dance for us and we were given some beautiful moccasins as going-away presents. It was a night of mixed emotions. We were so happy to be with everyone and feel their friendship, but we were sad at leaving them all behind.

Only the fact that for a while we would be close at hand and even have Mary with us made the transition easier.

We flew to Inuvik and moved into the government-supplied housing, and I was given the position of head nurse on the pediatric ward. It was a far cry from doing public health in the Richardson Mountains, but it was a job, and one that I could do. When Muriel was due, Mary Firth came to Inuvik to stay with us and look after Helen. Stephen was born on July 2, when it was hot, dry, and dusty in Inuvik. He set out to tell the world that he objected to moving, to the dry heat, and to everything. When he was about six weeks old, we said a sorrowful farewell to Mary and flew south to Edmonton, then went on by train to Halifax in Nova Scotia. On the way Stephen relaxed with the rhythm of the train and we had four days of relative peace.

After living and working at the nursing station for three years, on call twenty-four hours a day, seven days a week, going to Dalhousie University proved to be a scary, exciting adventure but a nice change from the harsh north. We were fortunate to rent a lakeside cottage from Francis Chaplin, who was moving temporarily to Winnipeg to play the violin in the symphony orchestra there, and he was kind enough to leave his boat and motor for us to use whenever we liked. Helen and Stephen were able to live in beautiful surroundings, cared for by Muriel, who was enjoying the respite from the routine of nursing station work.

After successfully completing my course in April 1967, with no small thanks to Electa MacLennan, the director who encouraged me when things looked bleak, the day came when we received a list of vacancies available throughout the north. Two places required two nurses—Chesterfield Inlet and, to our surprise, Fort McPherson! After some research in the university library, we decided that Chesterfield Inlet looked a bit too barren for our little family, and going on the premise that "better the devil you know than the devil you don't," we wrote to Medical Services to say we would like to go back to Fort McPherson.

This time we were going back into the north prepared. I ordered new dog-team harnesses from a saddlery in Edmonton and a year's supply of dog feed from Ogilvie Mills, all to be sent on the barge along with our things from our friends' basement. We looked at and then purchased a small boat and motor from the Sears' catalogue and children's books and toys for Helen and Stephen. We told our friends that this time we were not going to put a time limit on our stay in the north. We would stay until we left!

We drove through the northern US and north to Edmonton, then with great excitement and anticipation flew via Inuvik to Fort McPherson, where we were welcomed back enthusiastically by everyone. In a short time we had settled back into our old schedule, although we decided that we would proceed carefully with all the new ideas we had brought back with us because we had changed, not the community. Even though Muriel had not taken the public health nursing course, she had read all of my textbooks and gone over my assignments with me, and we had discussed northern health programs frequently.

WORKING FOR THE FEDERAL government was at times a bit of a strain, but working for them in Fort McPherson was certainly easier because the only bureaucracy was what we made ourselves.

"Policy" is the bane of every civil servant's life, but we could all live within the bounds of governmental policy as long as the administrators could be flexible in their interpretation of the myriad rules and regulations. There were some excellent people who could keep the intent or the spirit of the law, and there were those who could see no further than the letter of the law, perhaps blinded by the power they perceived themselves to have or perhaps having been promoted beyond their competency level.

When Muriel and I first went to Fort McPherson we had been awed at the responsibility we had assumed, and we had followed the letter of the law—for a while. For instance, when a minor childhood epidemic appeared in the community, we arrogantly distributed a newsletter to parents (through the school), telling them it was better to get out of town, and there was no excuse not to go out on the traplines. I shudder to this day at such an attitude. We didn't know a thing about traplines or the difficulty of travel in the freeze-up period, and we had never been in a riverboat or on a dog toboggan. The people, however, never said a word to us and did not argue. They did what everyone should do in such circumstances: they carried on with life just as they would normally. Some left town because that is what they had already planned while others stayed in town because they didn't want to leave just yet. Fortunately, we adjusted quickly and by our second tour of duty we had learned how people did things in McPherson, and we almost though not quite "did in Rome what the Romans did."

I reacquired my dog team from William Firth who had them while we were away and had done an excellent job of training them. Now I chained the dogs up on the nursing station property, well away from the public walkway, and each dog had its own kennel. And in the spring of the year I had everything raked up and the yard looking clean and tidy. Then an innocent comment from a visitor to the community found its way down to our bosses in Edmonton and alerted them to the fact that there were dogs on government property. Government bureaucrats rarely come to tell you directly not to do something that it is obvious to all that you—and you only—are doing. Instead, a general letter is sent out that says, "It has come to our attention that at some facilities animals are being kept on Health and Welfare property, and… blah… blah… blah… poor public health… dangerous… blah… blah… blah… this practice must cease forthwith or there will be serious consequences…" It took me all of three seconds to guess who the culprit was, and I looked in the mirror to check to see if I was right. Yep, it was me all right! I could see the guilt all over one side of my face. Now what should I do about this? Consulting with my wife seemed the best thing to do, and being a man of action, I did just that. We figured that it was at least 18 months since anyone had visited us from head office, and we had not heard of an impending visit by dignitaries. So my policy was formed that day: "If in doubt about whether to carry out radical policy regulations, don't."

Nothing happened. We were not fired; the dogs stayed where they were, and frequently when people from the office down south visited, I was asked to take them for a dog-team ride! I took our children for dog-team rides after clinic hours or visited Mary's trapline and continued to travel by team to Arctic Red River on my own. ("Staff must always take a guide with them if they make any visits outside the village, but in general staff should remain in the nursing station.")

Pauline Trudell, the nurse from Aklavik, came to visit us one day that winter. She was like us—she did what she had to do to get the job done. She had been waiting for a new clinic for five years, having been promised one that many years back. Her clinic was the oldest in the Arctic, and it was the coldest, too. When we visited her in the wintertime, we had to sit in her kitchen with our parkas on, even though the oil stove was cranked to "high." When she heard that there was to be another delay in the building program, she threatened to resign if Dr. Savante, the regional director, did not come to inspect the building personally, and when she heard that he was actually going to visit, she waited until the morning he was to arrive, then turned the heat to "low" and opened all the windows and turned the bedclothes back on the bed he was to use. Just before his plane landed she recovered the bed, shut the windows and turned the stove up.

Dr. Savante just could not get warm and sat with his mitts and parka on all evening. Pauline just sat there talking to him with her blouse sleeves rolled up, telling him she was glad that it had warmed up enough for his visit! Later she told us it had been worth suffering for a few hours in the cold dressed like that because when her half-frozen boss flew out the next morning, she knew that a new clinic would be built as soon as possible in the springtime.

When the plane was due in to take Pauline back to Aklavik after her visit with us, I offered to take her down to the airstrip on the river with my dogs, and she was delighted. I had the team ready in minutes, and we took off in a flurry of snow. The plane had just settled on the strip when we arrived, and as soon as it had come to a halt and the propeller had stopped, I drove her right to the plane door. It swung open and there was the regional nursing supervisor sitting there. She smiled and waved and called out a greeting to both Pauline and me and said that she hoped to visit McPherson soon. Pauline got out of the toboggan and climbed into the plane, and with more waving, I drove the dogs away, thinking that the fat was really in the fire now. Oh well! Go home and wait for the rocket. However, in spite of the original dire threats, all that happened were separate requests from two Inuvik doctors and then a social worker to go with me to Arctic Red River by dog team, and when the next visiting physician came to Fort McPherson, he nearly fell out of the plane in his eagerness to get to the toboggan.

On the other side of the argument were the people who were our clients. They wanted government people to visit them in the bush. And they had dogs around them all the time and had a very deep respect for any loose dog or dog team that came hurtling down the trail at them. In fact, they behaved just like little children (and some adults) down south who keep out of the way of fast cars and bad drivers who are loose on the city streets and highways.

We learned to live within the acceptable limits that were placed upon us, more by common sense than by some formal written policy. For example, children were not supposed to live in the nursing station. That is, nurses were not supposed to have children if they lived in a nursing station, so that when our children came along, we were violating another policy. If the unit had been strictly a public health clinic and we lived in a separate house, then maybe that would have been acceptable. But the problem that faced the authorities when Muriel had been pregnant the first time was that the people didn't want us to leave, and they thought that it was wonderful that "their nurse" was going to have a baby! I didn't think that I should have to resign when Muriel had the baby, and there was a very great

Our son, Stephen, a typical four-year-old, has found a springtime puddle.

shortage of northern nurses at that time, especially two compatible nurses. But it was surprising how easily the authorities ignored the policy when it was convenient to do so, and we soon found out that we could stay.

All the time that we lived and worked in the north we always tried to put the people before the policies, and I think that it was this that helped to make our stay so successful.

27

THE BEST TIME OF THE year was March when the days were long and the sun seemed to shine almost every day. During the day the temperature was about minus 15 degrees F (-15 C) but at night it was much colder, sometimes going to minus 30 degrees F (-35 C).

In early March 1968 Muriel and I wrote to Health Services to ask if we could take a week off if someone could be found to come to Fort McPherson to look after the nursing station for us. A quick reply came from Inuvik to say that one of the nurses from the Inuvik Health Centre had volunteered to come down, and then the letter asked if we would like the zone office to book us a flight south. Our supervisor was rather surprised when we replied negatively and said that we were going to take our dog team and go into the Richardson Mountains to visit with some of the Gwich'in families who were camped there and that we were taking Helen and Stephen with us too!

When Lorna arrived from Inuvik, we spent the day with her, introducing her to the main characters in the village. As she was familiar with the office side of the business, we let her poke around in the cupboards to familiarize herself with where things were in case of an emergency, while we packed everything we could think of into canvas and duffle bags so that we could make an early morning start. Stephen was still in diapers and we thought this might be a problem, but we also knew that the Gwich'in mothers took their

Our family car. Muriel, Stephen and Helen in our dogsled.

babies and toddlers with them so we would manage. Although disposable diapers were just coming onto the general market, Muriel took conventional cloth diapers along for Stephen, but we soon found that in order to wash them, they had to be thawed out near the wood stove, resulting, of course, in a not-too-sweet aroma! We also discovered that it took buckets full of snow and a lot of firewood to provide enough water to wash and rinse them and then they had to be dried in the tent. Up to then we had been horrified to see young mothers spending their very limited money on these throwaway items, but now we decided that disposable diapers were really a great invention, and we never said a thing afterwards when we saw them being purchased.

We packed the toboggan with enough clothes for each of us, sleeping bags, food for us and the six dogs, axe, matches and fire starter, and then enough room was found for Muriel to sit on the sleeping bags with Stephen between her legs. Helen sat at Muriel's feet, facing her, then all were wrapped in another sleeping bag.

We had travelled short distances with the children before but had not taken a lot of camping equipment with us, so that this trip was going to give the dogs a real work out. But they were fit and eager to go, and as the sun rose in the southeast, turning the far-off mountains a dusky pink, we set off down the road from the nursing station and then north down the Peel River for a short distance before we headed for the first portage and the well-packed trail that would lead us to Husky Lake. The children seemed to enjoy the movement of the toboggan, and even though it was still early in the day Stephen soon fell asleep.

After a couple of hours on the trail we began to climb the foothills. We stopped then and I made a fire. Muriel climbed out of the toboggan to stretch her stiff legs but the children stayed aboard because if they had stepped off the trail they would have wallowed in the deep snow! After a drink of hot chocolate we repacked the children into the toboggan and Muriel put on her snowshoes. The trail had been well used but walking on it was difficult and tiring because our feet kept breaking through the crust. As a result, as I ran behind the toboggan, I put my weight mostly on the handlebars. However, as we gained height I had to help push the toboggan up the hills and on really steep parts I gave the dogs a rest every hundred yards or so. I was always amazed at their stamina as they bent their backs and strained so hard to pull us. Whenever we stopped, they pushed their heads into the soft snow at the side of the trail and lay there wagging their tails and panting, making them look as though they were all smiling for the camera! While they rested, Muriel caught up to us and stopped for a rest, too, but as soon as the terrain levelled out, she tucked her snowshoes under a rope at the front of the toboggan and climbed back in, adjusting the children, who never complained at the restrictions of the packed toboggan.

We travelled all day and then descended Charlie Rat Creek, a narrow, winding waterway with thick willows that slapped our faces as we plunged down towards its mouth, and Muriel pulled the sleeping bag over the children to protect them from injury. When at last we pulled out onto the frozen Rat River, we saw a tent pitched in a small stand of spruce trees. I had heard that it was there and that it was used by anyone who was passing on their way to town or to a mountain camp, and this is where we intended to spend the night.

Once the dogs were tied up the children were free to play around the campsite. As Muriel unloaded the sled, I split wood and started a fire in the wood stove. I then made the dogs comfortable on a small bed of boughs and fed them. It wasn't long before we were sitting in the tent eating the hot supper Muriel had cooked—"slaving away over a hot stove," she laughingly said— and then as it grew darker, the children were changed into their pajamas and snuggled down in their sleeping bags. They thought that it was funny when Muriel put their toques on them, and she had to explain that, in the middle of the night when the stove went out, their ears and heads would get very cold.

I lit four candles and stuck them into old cans that someone had nailed to peeled sticks and then stuck the ends of the sticks through our spruce-bough floor and into the snow that lay below it. By this light we read for a while but the exercise and fresh air made us drowsy. While Muriel made us a last cup of hot chocolate, I made feather sticks for the morning fire and then stoked up the stove.

It was already light when we woke, and I reluctantly dragged myself from the warm sleeping bag over to the stove. As soon as the fire was going, I climbed back into the warmth until the tent had heated up. It didn't take long, and we all got up and dressed. After eating a bowl of steaming hot porridge and some fried bacon, I started to pack while Muriel cleaned up the children and got them ready for another day on the trail. She had put Stephen's dirty diapers outside the tent door and now, of course, they were frozen solid, but we had to take them with us. We could see why the old-timers used moss, which was the first disposable diaper!

That afternoon after an uneventful day of travelling through some very picturesque country, the dogs suddenly perked up and surged ahead. Muriel said that she could hear dogs barking in the distance, and we rounded a bend in the creek and saw plumes of smoke coming from five tents that were set together. Caches that were now loaded with meat had been built close by, and the dogs tied a little way off from the tents. As we approached, we could see little children running backwards and forwards between the tents and soon adults appeared in the doorways. Jane Charlie beckoned us over and I halted the dogs. Muriel took the children to Jane's tent while her husband, Johnny, helped me tie up the dogs.

When I knocked on Jane's tent door and went in, I found it crowded with people who had come to welcome us. Sipping hot tea and telling about our trip dissipated the cold, and the hours of travel seemed insignificant in this warm reception. Helen and Stephen went outside to play with the other children. "Don't you go near those dogs!" one of the women called out after them. Some of the men excused themselves and left the tent, and Muriel and I were offered boiled caribou meat and rice for supper.

Johnny returned to the tent and said something in Gwich'in to Jane, who turned to us and said that the men had pitched a tent for us and piled it high with pine boughs to keep us warm. There was a stove lit and firewood cut ready for our use. We were overwhelmed with the hospitality shown to us, and apart from saying a very inadequate "thank you," we didn't know what to say! Where the spare tent came from we didn't know, but obviously there was one available for us.

We spent a very enjoyable five days at the camp, visiting and being visited, feasting on fresh meat, and every day there was someone bringing us newly cooked bannock. They certainly knew my weakness! Meanwhile, Jane had loaned Muriel a big pan to wash the diapers in, and we saw how much snow was needed to make enough water to wash and rinse a dozen cotton diapers. As we didn't have enough time or diapers to let them hang out in the frigid air, we had to hang them in the tent to dry. One day Johnny said that he was going down the creek for firewood so I followed him with my dog team and brought a huge pile of wood back to the campsite, but I knew that it would not last too long when the stoves were kept burning all day and part of the night.

The time came for us to leave. Jane Charlie, Annie Bonnetplume, and Caroline Kay all brought us bags of cooked meat and bannock to eat on the way, and then everyone turned out to wave us off. The dogs, well rested and fed on fresh meat, bounded off down the trail as though they were pulling an empty toboggan, and by the middle of the afternoon we were back at the tent at Charlie Rat Creek. It was too far for us to reach home that day so we made camp early with the idea of setting off at dawn the following day. As there was a wind getting up, I didn't want to get caught out in the open in one of the notorious mountain storms that we had heard about. I checked the camp to make sure that nothing would blow away and made certain that the rope holding the ridgepole was tied securely to one of the two big trees that stood behind the tent.

During the night the wind increased to gale force and I was wakened by the tent flapping in the wind. I had just told Muriel that I was going outside to fasten the tent down more securely when there was a resounding crash and the tent pulled to one side. I went to the door of the tent, which fortunately was still standing, but as I stuck my head out, I was struck with fine pellets of shale that had been picked up in the wind and were now flying everywhere like hailstones. One of the big trees that had been behind the tent was now lying right beside it, and a rope that had been tied to it was broken. I stepped back into the tent and sat beside Muriel. "This is the worst windstorm I've ever seen. We were lucky that it was the tree beside us and not the one behind us that blew over, otherwise we would have been pinned under it." Muriel pulled the still sleeping children close to her, and we crowded into the corner of the tent furthest from the still-standing spruce tree.

"Remember Sarah telling us about her husband being blown off the mountain with his dog team?" Muriel said, pulling a blanket around her shoulders, "I think she said that they didn't find him until the springtime."

"Well, we're not going to get blown off the mountain," I said, trying to sound positive. "But I am worried about that tree behind us." We lay back and let the tent rock and roll in the shrieking wind that both fascinated and scared us as it rose and fell in intensity.

TOWARDS MORNING THE wind had died sufficiently for me to venture out and I tied the tent more securely. The big tree swayed in the wind but it looked firm enough to me, but then so had the one that had come crashing down! The dogs were curled up on their beds with their noses tucked under their tails, and the only movement they made was when they heard me moving around and their ears rotated towards me like radar. We had a leisurely breakfast and then, as the wind continued to die away, I thought that we should get ready. Even though we would have a late start, the fact that this time we would be going downhill most of the way meant that we would have a quicker journey, and we didn't have to make camp at the end of the day. Meanwhile, Helen and Stephen played quietly in the tent; though aware that things were different, they were not scared of the wind, having no experience of such things.

By late morning I considered it safe enough to travel and we packed everything quickly into the toboggan. As soon as the dogs were hitched up, we set off. Muriel had put her snowshoes on so that the dogs could pull the toboggan easily up Charlie Rat Creek, and I ran behind calling out to the dogs to encourage them on. The creek had drifted over considerably but the dogs found their footing and pulled us over and through the snowdrifts.

When we reached the top of the creek, I stopped the dogs to give them a rest and to wait for Muriel, who had found it harder struggling up the uneven trail. She arrived about 10 minutes later and remarked that she was glad to join us again as it had felt lonely coming up the creek once we were out of sight. "I know it's silly at this time of the year, but I kept looking around in case any bears were about!"

The dogs pulled well, following what was left of the trail without any problems because the smell of other dogs that had passed this way still lingered on the snow and bushes. We got to the level of the Peel River just as it got dark, and as we glided through the trees and onto the last portage in the gathering dusk, I experienced some of the feeling that Muriel had expressed after coming up Charlie Rat Creek—the urge to turn around as though someone or something was following me. I was thinking of wolves, and although the dogs didn't scent anything harmful, there was still that feeling… So it was with some relief that we came out onto the Peel River and we could see the lights of the village in the distance.

Lorna came out to greet us as we were tying up the dogs, and before we had finished the job William arrived to help unload. Muriel took the children inside and they chatted away to Lorna, telling her all about the camp and the wind and the long journey they had been on. When I came in, they were still talking even though they were in the tub, and Muriel said that they must be letting it all out now because they had been so quiet all day!

Lorna left on the plane the next morning, having had a quiet time with no untoward medical problems to deal with, and she confided that she was rather disappointed that nothing had really happened.

28

ON MY MANY TRIPS TO THE mountains with the Gwich'in people, after we had made camp, we sat around and told stories. Mostly I sat and listened and then, at home again, I would write everything down.

People like Andrew Kunnizzi had fascinating backgrounds, and he told us about some of his early life when we visited him or his wife, Bella, at their home or later on in their cabin on the Peel River. On one such visit to the house to see how this elderly couple were coping with the advancing years, Muriel and I were invited in for a cup of coffee—Andrew was one of the few Gwich'in people we knew who liked coffee—and after consuming some fresh bannock, he took out a cigar and we could see that we were in for the long-haul story time! (I was very surprised when he pulled a cigar out the first time, and seeing my surprise, he casually mentioned that this was a habit he had acquired when he lived in Dawson City.) A few weeks previously, after hearing that Andrew made some really compact camp stoves, I had asked him to make one for me, and now after asking where he acquired his metal-working knowledge, he started telling us some of his life history, a straightforward story that later on was backed up by other people in the village.

In the early 1900s Andrew Kunnizzi and Ronnie Pascal had left Fort McPherson to live in Dawson City in the Yukon where they had experienced many of the advantages that the city had to offer curious and hard-working young men, and the two were soon leading a reasonably sophisticated life, wearing suits and ties, smoking cigars and, in general, looking and acting like a couple of city slickers. There was very little opportunity for formal education in Dawson City, but Andrew's quick mind absorbed the principles of engineering and mechanics simply by watching the various craftsmen working in and around the goldfields. He spent hours watching a blacksmith making tools and implements, and he also watched any carpenter who had a project underway. But in 1918 when the news arrived in Dawson City from the south that the First World War was over, Andrew and Ronnie decided that it was their responsibility to take the news to the people back home in Fort McPherson. With not much more than some dried meat, bannock, an axe and their rifles, the two men snowshoed up the Ogilvie River, then up the Blackstone River, across the headwaters of the Peel River, up the Eagle River to Road River and down again to the Peel River, eventually arriving in Fort McPherson where the two of them announced to their surprised friends and relatives that the war was over! They had made a journey of over 300 miles. But when Andrew and Ronnie came back to Fort McPherson, they found that they had become very sophisticated compared to their peers who had stayed home, and stories of the wild lives that they had lived in the Yukon city and the natural tendency of newcomers to stick together resulted in the name "The Dawson Boys" being bestowed on them and some of the others who had been members of a loose but elite group of Gwich'in Indians who had lived in Dawson.

Andrew retained his love of cigars all his life, while Ronnie was content to use ordinary tobacco. While in Dawson Andrew had learned to play billiards, went bowling, and was quite at home in businesses and entertainment facilities that were unknown in Fort McPherson, even in the sixties. Both men had become very adept and could turn their hands to anything; Ronnie became an expert at making intricately woven snowshoes that were widely used in the Delta, and Andrew learned to work with sheet metal and made camp stoves that were far superior to any that could be shipped in from the south.

However, in spite of all of the southern knowledge and behaviour that he had acquired, Andrew never lost his cultural identity as could be seen when he doffed his suit and put on his bush clothes. Equally comfortable on the streets or driving a dog team, Andrew once travelled by dog team to Mayo in the Yukon to bring his widowed sister home, a trip of over 600 miles, and then on the way home detoured to Old Crow, adding another few hundred miles to his trip. He knew the Hart River Divide, the Rock and Porcupine rivers and all the land in between because he had travelled extensively in his youth in these regions with his father, Joe Kunnizzi, and he had no difficulty adapting back into the life of a hunter and trapper when he wanted to because he was as familiar with the ways of the caribou as he was with a Dawson casino.

Andrew's character was immediately apparent to us when we found out where his house was located. It was a very typical log building, chinked with moss and daubed with mud to keep any drafts at bay, but it stood right on the road allowance. It seems that a survey had been carried out to establish the village's main street and other houses had been moved to make way for it. Then the contractors came to Andrew's house. No, he said, he was not going to let it be moved. It had been there for a long time before any roads were built, and if it was moved, it could be damaged. Everyone tried to make him change his mind but he was adamant. So finally the roadway was changed a few degrees, skirting close to his house on one side and a wooden sidewalk was built around the other side of the house. And that's where the house sat for years until Andrew agreed to live in a brand new house at the south end of the village.

Bella Kunnizzi, Andrew's wife, always had a quiet smile for everyone. She was the ideal partner for him. Hard-working and resourceful, she travelled by dog team and riverboat with her husband, and they were equally respectful to each other.

Everyone who owned a dog team in the Delta used either oak

The old village of Fort McPherson with Andrew Kunnizzi's house (centre right) on the road right-of-way.

toboggans that were shipped in from the south or they fashioned birch plank sleds with the high curve that could slice through the dry crystalline snow. These toboggans with their canvas or moose-hide wrappers could be loaded with an immense amount of freight, but Andrew felt that the toboggans themselves were too heavy, so when he heard they were selling aluminum toboggans in Dawson, he was an early customer. He hitched his dogs to his new aluminum toboggan and set off for his camp, a few days' journey away, but the toboggan was a failure. On his second day of travel the weather turned warm, and Andrew felt the snow clinging to the metal. Re-calling those days, he told me that it was the only time he had to heave and push a toboggan to get it to go *downhill*. Undaunted, he finished the trip, unpacked the toboggan and loaded his goods onto a conventional one, and took the aluminum one back to the store where he traded it for something that was more useful.

Like any young man, Andrew Kunnizzi had a reputation to keep up, and he wanted to have the fastest, best-controlled dog team in the Delta so he bred his dogs to try to reduce the natural aggressiveness of many northern dogs. When he read about the obedience of Collie dogs, he was resourceful enough to locate a Collie bitch in the south and have it shipped north, where it became the mother of a number of experimental sled dogs. He did accomplish part of his goal with this move, now having the fastest team in Fort McPherson but it also turned out to be the meanest team. But like the southern man who owns a sleek sports car and has a son, Andrew often saw his team being driven away by his son!

When the Anglican church was looking for native lay persons to train as church deacons, Andrew was one of the men chosen, and he became what the Gwich'in called a catechist, who could lead the people through their religious services. But besides learning the theological principles of the Anglican church, Andrew and another Fort McPherson man, Peter Thompson, were said to have had to learn and recite three whole books of the Bible, no easy feat for anyone. These two men remained respected church leaders throughout their lives.

29

NOT ALL OF THE TRIPS that I undertook for work or pleasure were successful and a couple that always come to mind were made in wintertime when travel was usually the best—no mosquitoes, no mud, no unpredictable river levels and no mud bars to contend with. On one attempt to visit camps in the Richardson Mountains with Peter Thompson, we travelled up Vittrekwa Creek, about 20 miles (32 km) south of Fort McPherson. This creek is well known for its winter overflow where the water flowing down the creek is forced over the ice because the ice is too thick and the river itself too shallow to let the water pass under the ice. The water, which steams and crackles as it reaches the frigid air, can be six inches (15 cm) to several feet deep and this can be a real hazard to travellers.

As it would be rare to travel up or down Vittrekwa Creek and not encounter overflow, Peter and I were prepared psychologically to go around this hazard. We had carefully packed everything that we wanted to keep perfectly dry, such as spare clothes and our sleeping bags, on top of the tins of food, the stove, and the bags of dog feed. Snowshoes were as usual fastened on top of the load along with an axe, so we were ready to break trail around any overflow.

When we came to the first steaming overflow section, Peter made a detour around it by breaking trail through some scrub willow, and after a short distance we came out onto the good river ice again. It was about this time that the unexpected struck. My stomach had started to churn some time earlier in the morning but I had put it down to some mild indigestion, but as the morning wore on, I knew that I was going to have some intestinal problems. Going to the toilet when you are out in the winter wonderland and you are wearing layer upon layer of clothes to keep warm is always a cold inconvenience as all of it needs removing or lowering when you have to bare all. Add to this the problems of deep snow, a large pair of snowshoes, an eager dog team that does not want to be left behind as the team in front continues to move ahead, and you have an extraordinary problem on your hands and other areas of your anatomy. The difficulty is compounded when you have diarrhea because of the frequency with which it occurs, and you barely have time to get warm again after one session of disrobing before it is necessary to repeat the process. Our travels were really hampered by all of this, and by the end of the day we had made little progress and we were both cold. As much as I hated to call it quits, I told Peter that it would be better if we turned around the next morning and headed for home.

Peter pitched the tent on his own while I was once again contemplating the tips of my snowshoes, and I spent an uncomfortable night in and out of the tent. As soon as it was light we packed everything up and began to retrace our steps. By the time we reached the mouth of Vittrekwa Creek on the Peel River, I noticed that, in spite of the bitter cold, the sun was shining out of a clear blue sky and my stomach had stopped churning. Another two hours and I was feeling my normal self, so that when I arrived home and explained my unusual early return to Muriel, I felt as though I must have imagined it. It made me think of the patients who had come to see us saying they had been so sick at camp that they had to return home, and we had been suspicious of their reason for leaving the hunting party or the trapline, especially if there was a party that night. Now I realized that people who were out at camp and became ill would want to come back to the village even if they only had a rustic home and minimal care waiting there for them.

ONE SPRING DR. JOHN KAY asked me if I would take him to
Arctic Red River by dogsled sometime, and we tried to work out a
schedule so that he could do a medical clinic in both villages. But such
was a doctor's life in the north that between surgeries, anaesthetics,
clinics, and visits to other communities he was not able to come
to Fort McPherson until late spring when the snow was quite wet.
However, at this time of year most of the people travelled at night
because it stayed light all night and, as the temperatures dropped
below freezing then, the wet snow froze and made an excellent trail.
I had made the trip to Arctic Red River two weeks previously and
got there in the record time of five and a half hours. However, when
John arrived, I knew that we were in for a tough time. There was
a busy clinic all day and then the temperature hovered around the
freezing mark all evening, not enough to put a crust on the snow.
I was worried about the dogs' feet because the snow balls up in the
long hair between their toes and, besides being painful for them, it
can cripple them.

I told John that we would try and make it and hoped that it
would get colder as the night wore on. Wearing moccasin rubbers over our mukluks in the hope of keeping our feet dry and
warm, we set out under a grey night sky. Looking south, we could
see the glow where the sun stayed just below the horizon even at
one in the morning. In less than a month it would stay visible for
24 hours, the last of the snow would disappear and the ice would
break up and begin to move out, grinding and crushing its way
northwards.

After the first few miles I stopped the team and turned the toboggan over to scrape the ice off the bottom. It was dragging so
much that the dogs were having difficulty pulling. While I worked
on the sled, they took the opportunity to chew the ice balls that were
forming on their feet. Then every mile for the next ten miles, John
would jump out of the toboggan and I would go through the routine
of scraping the boards. The dogs were finding it very hot and, every
time we stopped, they would try to roll in the wet slush. I would

have to give a sharp shout to prevent them getting all tangled in the harnesses.

I checked my watch and realized that, at the speed we were going, it was going to take us far too long to reach our destination. I was also aware that when John flew back to Inuvik from Arctic Red River, I would have to make the return journey in the same conditions and with some very tired dogs. "John, I'm soaked," I said. "Let's pull over at the next portage and make a fire and dry out a little." I drove the dogs over to the side of the lake where some dry spruce trees were visible and, grabbing my axe, cut enough wood to make a roaring fire. As we sat on some spruce boughs and had coffee from a Thermos bottle, we watched the dogs cavorting in the snow, taking great mouthfuls of the slush and then rolling in the snow and water. I left them to it, knowing they needed the rest and needed to cool down, too. The harness could be untangled when we were ready to move again.

John and I changed our footwear and poised our wet mukluks on a stick over the fire where they would dry quickly. They were inclined to dry stiffly, but they could soon be made supple again by rubbing them together. Meanwhile, as the dampness and the cool night air had chilled us, we soaked up the heat from the fire and watched the sky reddening as the sun rose in the south. I glanced at my watch: 2:30 a.m. We opened the lunch that Muriel had made for us, and I saw that it was my favourite trail food, slabs of roast beef and bannock. I put a pan full of slushy snow on the fire so that we could refill the Thermos with tea. The dogs had quietened down by now and were sitting watching us. They didn't like to sit in the water, but at the present time there was no alternative. Now and again one of them would lift up a paw and lick it, and I got up and examined all their paws to make sure that there were no sore spots on them. I'd had a good leader who had been in a dogfight and hurt his front paw, so I had made a leather boot for him out of a small piece of moosehide. He ran with it on for about 15 minutes, then stopped abruptly, bent down, tore it off with his teeth and ate it! He finished the trip without even limping and his wound healed quickly, so since then I hadn't been too keen on providing the dogs with edible footwear.

I was reluctant to get going again because it was pleasant sitting there in the dawn, and the more I thought about the situation we were in the more I was inclined to turn around and head for home. The problem was that I had promised John this trip and he had looked forward to it for a long time. He had been taking dozens of photographs and I think that he wanted to get a photographic record of his epic foray into the bush by dog team! I was about to voice my thoughts when a cry from John, followed by a cloud of steam and the smell of burned moosehide, made me jump up, grab a stick and fish our mukluks out of the fire. The stick holding them had given way as the fire melted the snow.

"Here you are, John," I said. "One mukluk of yours is okay, but the other is a burnt offering, I'm afraid."

"That's a nuisance," John exclaimed. "I don't have any others with me."

"Mine have got some holes burned around the ankle, but I can probably wear them." I examined the duffle socks and apart from being a bit scorched they were usable. "Well, John, that's it, I guess. We are going to have to go back. We can't go on without any spare footwear." I was almost glad that an excuse had come along.

"Aren't we halfway yet?" John sounded very disappointed.

"Far from it, I'm afraid. At the rate we've been moving, it's going to take us another day and a half to get to Arctic Red," I exaggerated. "And it's going to get worse as soon as that sun warms up."

"Well, you're the boss, but I thought that if we were halfway we could go on as easily as going back."

"Sorry, but like I said, it will just take us too long and you will end up missing the last plane before breakup, and I'll get stuck, too."

John accepted the situation and we packed up, I sorted the dogs' harnesses out, and we started off for home. Within minutes my feet were soaked again but I just kept moving, jogging as much as possible to make the load easier for the dogs. On the portages I sometimes had to jump onto the toboggan because I broke through the trail more than a few times.

By the time we pulled up in front of the nursing station, the sun had appeared over the horizon, and was putting out some heat. While John unloaded the toboggan, I tied up the dogs who immediately jumped on top of their boxes and started to clean themselves up. Muriel had got up when she heard us coming in and she commiserated with us over some fresh eggs and bacon that John had brought with him from Inuvik. He was cheered up a bit after he was clean, dry, and well-fed and his disappointment didn't last long.

"Let's go and get some early morning photographs," he said.

"You go ahead," I replied. "I think I should go and feed the dogs their last winter meal. After this they will be on summer rations."

"Good idea." He donned his still-wet overshoes, took his coat and slung his camera around his neck. "See you later. I wonder what setting I should use?" And he went out. Muriel and I just sighed.

30

THE SMALL POWER BOAT we had bought from Sears catalogue served us well for short trips up and down the river with the children, and I used it to make solo trips to Arctic Red River when the weather was good, but we found that it was too small to make the camping trips that we had planned for August when most of the people were out fishing and it was quiet in the village.

However, someone in the village had built a small wooden boat and made a plexiglass canopy for it, and after this boat was demolished on a hidden log, the canopy was put up for sale. As it was standard riverboat width, I bought it and set out to build a riverboat or "scow" to put under it. As usual, when any individual in Fort McPherson started a project, there was lots of advice given and willing hands to help. In fact, it would have been difficult to keep the willing hands away from the project, and the effect was that their enthusiasm kept it going at full speed.

After I was told exactly how many sheets of plywood I would need, I purchased it at the local trader's store along with various dimensions of lumber as well as nails, which I had been told to use as the local people did instead of screws. Last of all I looked at the limited selection of paint that was available, and in the amount I wanted there was a choice between red and red.

I cleared a space in our heated warehouse and four of us set to. The RCMP corporal marked and cut out the plywood, the game

A typical square-nosed, homebuilt scow on the Peel River.

warden measured and cut the lumber, and the Bay manager built a form on which to build the boat. There was not much room for me so I kept the coffee going and observed all of the action, and when William called around, I listened to his sage advice and the inevitable account of the many trips he had made on the Peel and the MacKenzie rivers.

"I was sent down to Fort Good Hope with John Modeste to get a load of supplies and the mail," William recounted to everyone there, shouting whenever the Skilsaw was running. "We made good time going against the strong Mackenzie River current, and because John wanted to get back to McPherson in a hurry, we loaded the boat and were ready to leave Good Hope by ten o'clock at night." William took a drink of coffee and wiped his mouth with a colourful handkerchief before he continued. "John had heard about a thing called a water sail where you put a pole down either side of the boat with a wide piece of canvas stretched between them underneath the boat. The idea of this is that the current pushes against the canvas, just like wind does in a proper sail, and you get pushed down the river in the current. It keeps you in the channel and saves gas, too!" He brought his hand up to his mouth as he remembered the incident. "The trouble was that we had never tried it out in the daylight, but I was young and would try anything! We set up the water sail and it worked real well, so we decided to catch up on our sleep and let the river do the work for us." He laughed again as he worked up to the climax of his story. "We woke up about five hours later and saw that we were almost in the same place because the river had taken us onto a sandbar. It seemed like that scow was glued to it and we worked for hours getting it off!" and William slapped his leg, threw his head back and laughed aloud.

It took us about four days to construct the boat, using long lunch breaks and evenings to work on it, and then we turned it upside down for me to paint it. Another three days and several coats of paint and it was ready to launch. We hauled it out of the warehouse and onto a stoneboat, and Roy Wright brought his old Caterpillar tractor to pull it down to the river. Once in the water I fastened the 20-horsepower motor to the stern and we all piled in to take it for a test run. It seemed a little high in the prow but, after discussing how difficult it would be to change it, I felt that I could live with it as it was, and we moored the boat just below the nursing station. The last job was to slide the canopy down the bank and into the boat and then secure it. It fit perfectly.

That Saturday afternoon Muriel and I and the children took the boat up the river as far as Eight-Mile Point and found that at last we could get out with the children and move faster than the mosquitoes! We decided there and then that we would go camping for a few days as soon as we could arrange it.

It took another ten days for us to get away as Muriel had to deliver a baby. Three days later the new mom took her new baby with her, and as no one else was expected, Phyllis Seaton, the Bay manager's wife and an ex-nurse, said that she would keep an eye on the station for us. We loaded the boat with gas and oil, tent and stove, food, a rifle, and at the last moment I decided to take my favourite wheel dog, Adaijoh, a Gwich'in word that means "whiskers." I thought that if he was tied up at our camping spot and a bear came close, he would bark and let us know.

I had travelled up the river often enough with other people to give me a fairly good idea of where the river channels were and I soon had a feel for the boat and felt confident I could "read" the river. Later that day as we approached Road River, we saw a large clearing on the west bank where we thought we would find a dry campsite. After unloading the boat, we carried everything up the crumbling riverbank. Muriel let the children play close by, with dire warnings not to go near the riverbank, and we made them keep their life jackets on, just in case of mishap.

We set up our canvas tent at the edge of the clearing and installed the stove before collecting boughs for the tent floor and laying out the bedrolls. Then realizing that it was unusual to find a clearing in the thick bush unless it was man-made, we went exploring and, finding the remains of an old cabin on the far side, concluded that someone had made a home there many, many years ago. Returning, we discovered a half-dozen long aluminum irrigation pipes close to our tent, and this baffled us because the age of the old cabin and the pristine condition of the pipes did not coincide. (We later found out that the pipes had been left at the site by a winter geological survey crew.) We had supper, then sat by the river as dusk fell to watch the many changing moods of the river current as it swirled past us. The birch tree leaves were already changing from dark green to gold and yellow, and the medley of colours was quite stunning. We were reminded of how far north we were and, though people down south were enjoying their mid-summer holidays, we could feel a touch of frost in the air as the sun went down.

I tied Adayjoe to a small tree close to the tent door, and then went inside and lit our gas lamp. The tent immediately looked as bright as day so we let the children look at their books and play with the few toys they had brought along. Before going to bed I tried to find some new stations on our battery radio but it was not strong enough to catch anything audible.

In the morning after I lit the wood stove, I went outside and was surprised to see white frost on the tent roof. Fall was certainly catching up with us! Muriel had started to make breakfast—bacon and pancakes, my favourite—and the bacon fat was sputtering onto the stovetop so that the smell of burned bacon fat wafted out of the open tent door. I watched Adayjoe stand up and raise his nose in the air and thought that he was appreciating the appetizing smell of the bacon, but as he strained at his chain and looked around the corner of the tent, still sniffing the air, I went to investigate. A grizzly bear! And it was walking towards us from the other side of the clearing! "Muriel!" I called urgently. "Quick, pass me my rifle and shells!" She knew that something was coming but, not wanting to alarm the children, she simply reached for my gun and brought it out to me where I was standing watching the bear. Adayjoe had still not barked but stood there sniffing the wind.

Not being sure what to do, I walked a short distance from the tent and yelled and waved my arms. There was no reaction to this from the bear who just kept ambling along in our direction. "Get the children into the boat and be ready to cast off as soon as you can!" Muriel rushed into the tent, took the bacon off the stove and dressed the children.

The bear was now about 75 yards (68 m) away and I could see the hump on his back swaying a little as he plodded on. He was close to a lone, large spruce tree, and as he came around it, I fired at the tree because in my experience any animal that hears a loud gunshot immediately hightails it to safety. Not this grizzly! I don't think he even glanced at the tree as my .303 bullet smacked into it, even though I could see splinters flying. I tried again. Taking careful aim, I fired again, but this time my shot either went wild or the grizzly moved unexpectedly for the next thing I saw was the bear chasing its tail round and round and round, making some frightening growls. It took off into the bush and then all was quiet. I was shaking because I knew that a wounded grizzly bear is a very dangerous bear. Had I mortally wounded it? I did not like to think that I had left an animal suffering and I was in a real quandary. We decided that the best thing to do was to pack up our camp in a hurry and have everything ready in the boat. I would keep my rifle very handy as we worked.

I got hold of two of the irrigation pipes and put them down the riverbank. Muriel went down to the boat with the children who were scared by what was going on, though they were more upset about missing breakfast than they were of the possibility of the bear attacking us. Using the pipes as a chute I sent all of the tenting equipment down to Muriel, who packed it into the boat as best she could because I had not rolled everything up tight. I emptied the stove and left it to cool, then with my rifle in one hand and holding Adayjoe on his chain by the other, I walked very carefully and very slowly towards the tree where I had last seen the grizzly. As I approached the tree and the bushes began to get closer, I remembered William Vittrekwa telling me that a wounded bear will run away and then circle back to ambush its pursuer. I reached the large spruce tree and found some drops of blood on the trampled grass. Now Adayjoe was pulling me towards the bush, but there was no way that I was going to be ambushed by a large, wounded grizzly. Feeling the hair on my head standing up, I turned back toward the campsite but kept glancing over my shoulder, my senses on full alert.

We took the boat ten miles downriver and found a campsite on the other side. There we set up camp and finally had a breakfast-lunch combination. Muriel had found the bacon that she had wrapped up back at the other camp and partially satisfied the children's hunger with some crackers, cold bacon, and orange juice. I was too wired to eat until later. That afternoon Muriel relaxed and read a book while I tried to teach the children how to fish, but the water was so muddy that if we had caught one it would only have been because a fish had accidentally bumped into the lure. While we didn't catch anything, we had a nice supper and once again sat and enjoyed the scenery until dark.

The next morning I went down to the river to get some water, and the first things I saw in the soft mud at the riverside were black bear tracks! I followed them past the camp, past the boat and they disappeared into the bush. The tracks were from a small black bear so I wasn't too worried but I mentioned it to Muriel when I got back. She was worried about the children. We couldn't keep them in the tent all day and cooking smells might attract the bear back. Why it hadn't bothered us during the night was a mystery to me, but maybe it was a bear with sinus trouble!

Discretion being the better part of valour, we packed up camp and returned home. I was still worried about the wounded grizzly and I wanted to warn any hunters going up that way to be prepared.

We enjoyed coming down the river with the current and reached home without incident. We were almost sorry to get back to the village again because we knew that it would mean back to work, but the stresses associated with the work were not as stressful as coping with unpredictable bears.

31

ONE SPRING EVENING WHEN Muriel and I had finished a very busy clinic day, we heard the sound of a helicopter approaching. The pilot set his machine down on the grassy bank outside the Bay manager's house, just south of the nursing station. The engine's whine gradually lessened, and two men emerged from the cockpit, one limping badly and assisted by the other, the pilot. I thought, "Here we go again!" and ran to give assistance. The patient was a middle-aged man whom I recognized, though now he was pale and looked exhausted. I asked the inevitable question "What happened?"

It was strange that very few people volunteered information. It made me think that people could turn up with the most horrendous injury and expect either Muriel or myself to lay hands on the site and heal it without a word spoken. Of course, on the other side of the coin, native people were quite used to white people telling them what was wrong with them and what they should do about it, so perhaps they had given up trying to be informative. Now listening first to the patient then the pilot, I found out what had happened.

Clem had been out in the bush hunting beaver from his canoe, using his old .22 calibre rifle to shoot them. He had gone ashore to build a fire and make some tea, Then, after resting a while, he had thrown his pack into the small canoe, causing it to drift from the shore. He had quickly grabbed his rifle and then, holding it by the barrel, he had hooked the canoe before it drifted away. Unfortunately, the old rifle had lost its trigger guard, and as it was cocked for instant use should a beaver show up, it fired, the bullet hitting Clem in the upper thigh. He had staggered backward, but he had the presence of mind to whip off his neckerchief and fasten it tightly round his leg as a tourniquet. He lay still for some time then tried moving. His leg hurt and he saw that it spurted blood so he tightened the tourniquet.

He spent the night on the shore without food. Finally he managed to move himself to the water's edge where he filled his cup, but the movement caused the bleeding to start again. He stayed where he was for three days, off the beaten track, a mere speck amongst the trees, bush, rivers and lakes of the Delta. On his third day, almost ready to give up, he heard the sound of a helicopter approaching and knew he had only one chance to summon help. He did not have the strength or time to collect brush for a fire. Looking around for something to signal with, he glanced at the canoe, which had miraculously stayed on the shoreline without being tied up, and there was a piece of plywood lying in the bottom of it. Half-crawling, he reached into the canoe and picked up the plywood and waved it in the air. He then fell back to the ground.

The pilot was on his way north to Fort McPherson from an exploration camp, and the flight had been without incident, though he had veered a little bit this way and a little bit that way as he looked at different lakes, rocky bluffs and even a few animals. He was beginning to descend, expecting to reach the Fort in 15 minutes or so, when he thought he saw some movement on a patch of ground over to his right. He had banked slightly and flown lower, and when he looked down, he was surprised to see someone grab a board from a canoe, wave it, then fall over backwards.

The pilot landed on the small patch of open ground and ran over to the man, who had remained on his back on the ground. Immediately he saw that the man's right pant leg was blood-soaked and that there was a blood-soaked rag tightly wrapped around the upper part of the leg. Clem was conscious but he felt dizzy. He told the pilot what had happened and said he needed to go to the nursing station right away. He was helped into the helicopter, strapped in, and within a few minutes they were airborne.

In the nursing station we cut the bloody pants away and found the bullet's entry hole. I X-rayed the leg, and after developing the film, Muriel and I could see that the bullet had missed the bone but it was still lodged in the leg. Our last patient who had been shot in the leg had died from shock, and although this was a smaller calibre bullet, we were not about to take chances.

As the planes had not yet recommenced flying since breakup, and ice was still running on the Mackenzie River, the helicopter pilot volunteered to help as he was heading for Inuvik in a short time. However, he wanted an escort for the patient because the trip would take over an hour, and if Clem passed out or started bleeding again, the pilot could not risk landing in the Delta during ice breakup. I grabbed my toothbrush and put a narcotic in my medical bag, while Muriel put a firm dressing on Clem's wound and got him ready for the flight. We were on our way as soon as the pilot was ready.

On the way Clem had severe pain and began to thrash around. I wanted to give him an intramuscular injection, but this was difficult because, by the seating pattern of this particular helicopter, the pilot sat between me and my patient. However, by leaning carefully over the pilot while he sat back as far as he was able to, I got Clem's upper arm exposed and was able to administer the drug acceptably, if not in the most professional manner. Clem relaxed and then both the pilot and I did, too.

Clem fell asleep, the pilot flew the helicopter and I watched in fascination as the mighty Mackenzie River pushed the last vestiges of ice towards the ocean and, in so doing, piled huge cakes of ice on islands and up every riverbank. I watched as a black bear walked slowly over the broken ice of a lake, and I stared in wonder as one large pack of ice seemed to break up into a million pieces, and then discovered that it was an enormous flock of snow geese starting the last leg of their journey to their barren ground nesting sites. The late afternoon sun shone on the water of a thousand lakes and reflected off the ice covering thousands more, and I felt very happy and fortunate to live and work in such a wonderful place and among such great people.

Clem was admitted to the hospital in Inuvik and underwent the usual barrage of X-rays and blood tests. When I visited him, he had intravenous fluids going to make up for the dehydration due to the blood loss and exposure. He told me that the doctor had said he would not be having surgery as they would be leaving the bullet where it was. I was both relieved and deflated—relieved that Clem would not suffer any more but deflated in case the doctor thought we were now, literally, "gun shy." However, when I spoke with the doctor, he said that we had made the right decision. Now all I had to worry about was getting back home again because the planes were not due to start flying again for another couple of weeks!

That night I stayed at the hospital's single men's quarters, and the next morning as soon as breakfast was over I started to look for some sort of transportation home. Lunch came and went and I was beginning to think that I was going to have to stay in Inuvik for the duration of breakup, when I heard my name paged over the hospital intercom. I was to call the RCMP office because they had some members going to Fort McPherson in a helicopter and they thought I might want to go home. I was at the helipad within 20 minutes, waiting impatiently as bags and parcels were loaded into the helicopter's freight compartment. Finally all was ready and we took off. We were about half an hour from Fort McPherson when Steve, one of the RCMP constables, leaned over to me and said they were going to pick up a young man who had gone berserk and would have to come out in a straightjacket. Then he added that I was not to be alarmed because everything was okay, but this guy had gone berserk in the nursing station! He repeated that everything was okay and that Muriel was shaken but unharmed.

My mind nearly exploded! We had all sat comfortably chatting, I had seen them loading a straightjacket into the helicopter, and they had not said a word to me! I was fuming but, as we neared the village, I reflected on my feelings and realized that these policemen had spared me some anguish, and there was nothing that I could have done anyway. We landed and the RCMP truck met us and took me immediately to the nursing station before the officers went on to the detachment, where their client was locked up.

Muriel was all right though I could tell by the colour in her cheeks that she had been upset, but she was able to tell me what had happened. The young man had come to the clinic for some treatment that required him to have an intramuscular injection, which Muriel gave without any problems. Then as the patient fastened his clothes, he started yelling and struck her across the face. Muriel called out for help and opened the clinic door, and a man standing in the corridor, though looking scared, pulled the clinic door closed as soon as she ran out and held it closed while she ran to the phone and dialled the detachment.

Frank Dunne had answered the phone, and Muriel just blurted out, "Frank, come down right away. I need help *now!*"

Perhaps the fear or shock in her voice passed on more than Muriel knew or perhaps Frank could hear the sounds of the patient flinging the clinic furniture and instruments around, but within minutes the RCMP truck slid to a halt in a cloud of dust, and Jim and Frank ran up the stairs of the station. It was all over in minutes. The officers hustled the patient out, and Muriel used her nervous energy to clean up the clinic. She had explained to the policemen that I was in Inuvik, but that was all. This was then passed on to the Inuvik detachment where the men would have realized that I would be more than upset to hear what had happened, especially if they did not take me back with them, and also Muriel would feel safer with me home again.

Muriel was very philosophical about it all. When she had calmed down, she said that although her face was still discoloured where the patient had hit her, it was obvious that the poor fellow was sick and needed help, and his actions had not changed her feelings for the rest of the people.

I found myself reconsidering my thoughts of the previous afternoon when I had felt very happy and fortunate to live and work in such a wonderful place and among such great people. I knew that I still felt that way but hoped there would not be any more incidents that might change my feelings.

The young man spent a few months in Inuvik where we assumed he received some counselling, although we did not follow it up. He came back to Fort McPherson but we never did see him in the clinic again, probably because he was too shy to come in. In a perfect world we would have sat down with him to talk about what had happened and maybe what had precipitated his actions and how Muriel felt about it. But we both realized that the man had been ill and neither of us held a grudge against him.

32

AFTER OUR TIME IN NOVA SCOTIA, Muriel and I knew that when we returned to Fort McPherson we would have to find a way of getting some relief from the seven-day-a-week work that the nursing station demanded. We had found out that one of the problems of living where you work was that people did not think that you needed time out and did not realize that they were not the only ones who just stopped by on the weekend for some supplies that they had forgotten about during the week.

The one way that we thought that we could accomplish some time away from the village and yet be on call to real emergencies was to build a log cabin across the Peel River from the village and have a two-way radio so we could be reached if necessary. Muriel and I discussed the pros and cons of our plans: first, the materials for a cabin were nearly all available—the logs were free for the cutting and lumber from old buildings could be purchased quite cheaply. Second, we would have to get permission of some kind to build a cabin. Last, but not least, I was very conscious that I did not have a clue how to build one. During many coffee breaks we discussed the situation with William Firth, who was very enthusiastic, probably because he was convinced we would want to settle down and live in Fort McPherson for the rest of our lives, and at that point we certainly didn't have any plans for leaving.

When William Vittrekwa heard of our building plans—though

we didn't officially consider them to be plans yet—he turned up at the back door at coffee time one day, saying he just happened to be passing and decided to drop in for a coffee, something I did not for one moment believe, but I was always glad to have a visit from such an interesting and likable old man. After finishing his first cup of coffee, he casually mentioned he had heard we might be going to build a cabin somewhere. Well, yes, we had sort of talked about it, but we hadn't done anything about it yet. He would help, he said. Start in the fall, he told us, when the ground was freezing, cut the trees as close as possible to the cabin site, and he would show me how to haul the logs with my dogs and toboggan, even though there wasn't any snow. I told him not to be in too much of a rush because we didn't know where we could build or even if we would be able to put a cabin up wherever we wanted, but at the same time I felt excited at the prospect of building a cabin with William, and I thanked him by plying him with more coffee and some fresh cinnamon buns that Mary Teya, our nursing station housekeeper, had just pulled out of the oven.

Then one day Mary Firth quietly suggested that perhaps we would like to build a cabin on her trapline on the west bank of the Peel River. This was where we had played at trapping, though Mary continued to visit it every few days and any furs she got made pocket money for her, but she was also our baby-sitter during the day when we were busy with patients in the clinic. She explained that she was allowed to have cabins on her trapline and, because she was the only one that used the line, there would be very little chance anyone would bother our things. Muriel and I accepted her offer and said we would go over and look for some sites, and then check with her if we found somewhere that we liked.

"Just build it anywhere, I don't mind!" She put her hand up to her face and smiled shyly, and I think that she was pleased that we would accept her offer to let us build on her trapping area. We couldn't help thinking how people in the south would have reacted. If we could have obtained permission from them to build, I am sure we would have been asked to pay a monthly rent or an annual lease.

I checked with the Indian agent, Les Wilderspin, about building there and he was very casual about it. He said that in that part of the world we could formally request a special-use permit to build a cabin, but it would take 20 years before the authorities got around to surveying it and longer before the application was finally processed. "There's lots of land, no one is going to do anything about it and Mary has said it's okay, so if I were you I would just go ahead. Just don't publicize it unnecessarily." Les was a very practical bureaucrat and I could see why most of the local people could get on with him. When it was necessary to use regulations, he did, but when it inconvenienced everyone and would not be harmful, he was quite prepared to overlook the rules. I could live with that sort of attitude.

Now there was nothing to prevent us from building a cabin, and Muriel and I, being reasonably familiar with Mary Firth's trapline, had some idea of where we would like to build. There was a small creek opposite the village that was only navigable by canoe during high water though quite passable by dog team all winter. A half-mile up the creek another small creek drained a tiny lake with very high banks, and it was on this lake that we decided to build. We would be about 20 minutes from the village by either boat or dog team, so in the event of an emergency we could get back quite quickly if people could get a message to us.

After looking through the catalogues, of which the nursing station had an abundance (from furniture to seeds, medical equipment to toilet rolls—you name it, we could find it in a catalogue), we found the answer to our communications problem. Acme Novelty had two-way radios that would work on either batteries or electric power, had a range of three miles, and cost $110 for two units. The corporal at the RCMP detachment volunteered to keep one unit in his office because the police were on call anyway and were usually notified if there was any rough stuff going on which might cause injuries. In dire emergencies he could come and get us with his snowmobile. "Also," he added, "maybe sometimes my wife and I could use the cabin if it was not in use."

All Muriel and I had to do now was build the cabin. Toward the end of summer when the blackflies and the mosquitoes had had their fill of human blood, we went with Albert Peterson across the river to take another look at the proposed building site. Albert, who had started to work in the nursing station when William Firth retired, had volunteered to help us select some good trees. He and Willie McDonald had cut trees in the area many years earlier when Willie had been building a new house. On the bank overlooking the small lake was a small clearing where tall grasses and berry bushes grew in profusion, and it was here that we decided to build. We staked out the floor area after removing enough of the bushes so that we didn't get impaled on the thorns, and Muriel suggested we would be able to get quite a few berries from the area later in the year. Meanwhile, Albert had marked thirty of the nearby trees with his axe, and while Muriel made some tea on a camp fire, he and I set to work clearing a trail from the stand of trees to the cabin site. At the end of the day, we could see that progress had really been made and felt both excited and satisfied.

We had decided to chink between the logs with moss, and I gathered all the dog feed gunny sacks I could find so we could have something in which to haul and store the moss. On a quiet Saturday afternoon I took the sacks over, along with my new chainsaw and a small tent in which to store everything out of the late rains or early snow.

On a cloudy afternoon a week after setting up the tent I took George Scherer, our visiting adventurous dental hygienist, to visit the site and maybe to cut down a few trees. We paddled across the fast-flowing Peel River in Mary Firth's canoe without incident and then went up the first creek. The second small creek had enough water in it because of recent heavy rains and we paddled up it rapidly, skimming around logs. Coming to the lake, I thought it would be impressive to paddle the canoe right onto the small shore so we could just hop right out onto dry ground. Now anyone knows that if a canoe is partly in the water and partly on the shore, it will tip either to the right or the left. I learned that lesson rather suddenly. One minute I was jauntily thrusting the canoe toward the shore, the next minute we were swimming in the lake, and I was thinking of that saying about pride coming before a fall. George was good-natured enough to laugh at the situation once he had pulled himself ashore, and we decided we would carry on with our objective until we felt too cold. We emptied out the canoe, rescued our soggy lunch and headed up the bank to the tent.

I should have realized by now that this was not going to be my day. The tent was flattened and the light-weight aluminum poles were bent and snapped like twigs. I was sure that some kids must have come over and vandalized it, and I picked up the shredded nylon to check if anything was missing. It was then I saw the huge claw marks in the fabric just above where it had been torn. This damage had not been done by children. It had been done by a bear. Slowly we pieced together what must have happened. The bear had caught the scent of the dog feed coming from the gunny sacks inside the tent. He had torn his way through the side of the tent, been frustrated at finding no food, become disoriented in the tent and forced his way out the other side. I tried to imagine what would have happened if the bright blue tent had wrapped itself around old bruin as he took off because, being only a pup tent, it would have looked as though he was wearing a skirt. Nothing else was damaged or missing and I was pleased to know there was wildlife in the vicinity. Having a bear for a neighbour didn't bother me because we usually made a lot of noise, especially when the chainsaw was going, so I didn't expect to see anything until the building was complete.

A few days later, Muriel came over to gather moss while I felled some trees, but there was very little moss around and she was reluctant to go too far in case the bear was in the area. Thus, we put off collecting moss, and within a few weeks we had a heavy snowfall that put paid to any plans of using moss. Instead, we went to the store and bought a pack of compressed fibreglass insulation, just like any other white man would.

William Vittrekwa visited the site with me and got me to bring my dogs and toboggan over. There was very little snow around, certainly not enough to use a dog team, but William was sure we could haul some trees out of the bush. He gathered all the brush that Albert and I had discarded when we made the trail and laid it down across the trail. Then he cut more willows and laid them down, too, so the whole trail from the trees to the cabin site had a slippery carpet of wood and snow for the toboggan to slide over. Next, he cut a six-inch-diameter (15 cm) log to the same width as the toboggan and lashed it across it one quarter of the way back. He said the idea of this was that when the thick end of the building log was cinched down to the head of the toboggan, the tail or skinny end of the tree would not drag as much, and the dogs would have an easier time pulling. I wasn't too sure that it would work until I saw the dogs in action, and I'm sure that it was this idea of William's that enabled the project to succeed.

The temperature started to drop, and it wasn't very long before the Peel River was running ice, which stopped us crossing the river. The ice pans started to form, get bigger and move sluggishly downstream. Then one morning in November William Firth came in smiling to say that the ice had stopped moving and was frozen completely over. Within 24 hours he was back to tell us that someone had crossed the river, so it must be quite strong. The weekend rolled around and I hitched up the dogs ready to go across the river. As I put a pile of boards on the toboggan and lashed them down, I estimated I would have to make about 10 trips to get all of the flooring over to the cabin. The dogs pulled the load over the river and up the creek and seemed just as fresh as when we had started. I was glad about this because I wanted to use most of the day for hauling the cabin logs.

While I was still unloading the lumber, Albert Peterson walked into view and announced he had come over to help. This was a great relief because I soon found that the logs were almost too heavy to move, and on my own I would not have got very far. We puffed and grunted and heaved and got the first log onto the toboggan and

Albert tied it on securely. The dogs waited patiently as though they knew their turn was coming. At the command "All right," the harness tightened as the dogs leaned into the traces but the log didn't move. We levered the log backward and forward and then with a sudden jerk the dogs had that first log on its way, and I was surprised to see the toboggan and dogs snake along the trail we had made as though the tree weighed hardly anything. They stopped immediately as they arrived at the clearing and I shouted, "Whoa!" After several trips the dogs knew the routine perfectly: stop at the cabin site on arrival while I got my axe, then proceed back to the fallen trees and wait while I turned them round and got the toboggan lined up against the next tree to be hauled. Then without any word from me, they sat down and waited until the tree was tied onto the toboggan. As soon as I said "Aarrright!" again, they all stood up, usually shaking themselves so that all six dogs looked as though they had severe tremors, then lunged into the harness and within seconds another tree was on its way.

Over the weekends and free evenings the pile of logs grew until finally there seemed to be enough for me to start work on the cabin. The foundation consisted of some large flat rocks with about one foot (30 cm) of the butt end of some of the trees on top of them in order to keep the sill logs and the cabin floor off the ground. Most of the houses in the village were built in a similar fashion to ours with no concrete foundations, although those constructed to government specifications were built on pilings, logs that were steam-driven into the permafrost, and some of the teachers' houses in Fort McPherson had unique foundations—45-gallon barrels filled with gravel that were half-buried in the permafrost. No one particular method seemed better than another because all the buildings seemed to shift at the corners as the temperatures changed.

Building the cabin was hard work but it was fun, and William Vittrekwa came to help me whenever he was in the village. Otherwise Albert came to help whenever he could, as did a number of other people. I didn't know enough to peel the logs, and no one ever said to do anything differently (houses in the Indian village were sometimes constructed of unpeeled logs), and with the temperature averaging minus 25 degrees F (-34 C) when we were building, peeling the frozen logs would have been very difficult.

The first few logs went up easily enough and I managed without any help. Then, as soon as I could, I laid the cabin floor. That was the most boring job of all. Each day when work was finished in the nursing station, I would change into outdoor clothes, harness the dogs up and head for the cabin in the twilight to spend three or four hours working by the light of a gas lantern. It was eerie being all alone out there in the dark, and I often made myself jump when my shadow was suddenly cast onto the floor. The dogs lay curled up all around me as I worked and they watched my every move. When I first took them over to the cabin in the evening, I left them harnessed, but one dog decided to chew up a lot of the harness to relieve his boredom, and I was as mad as blazes when I had to mend it in the dark.

At about ten o'clock when they saw me making preparations to leave, they started barking. I would hitch them up and turn out the lantern. It was pitch black then and it took quite a few minutes for my eyes to adjust, but the dogs didn't want to wait, and each night that I went over to the building site, I dreaded that trip home because the dogs were so eager and raced as fast as they could down the creeks and over lumps and bumps and past or through willow bushes. They didn't seem to care as long as they got home to their boxes and their supper. It all seemed unfair—they were fit, well rested, and eager to go home, and I was tired, couldn't see, and the trail was bumpy, and I knew from history it is quite possible to lose an eye to one of the branches that hung over the creek. So I would let the tether rope drop into the snow, grip the toboggan back tightly and shout, "All right!" to my lead dog. Without a sound and without any hesitation, the dogs went. The sled snapped around the first corner, plunged down the bank onto the lake, which we crossed in seconds, and then, entering the first creek, we began the mad dash toward the Peel River. Even my ears seemed taut, let alone my hair, as I did everything in my power to keep the toboggan upright. It was like trying to surf on a huge rolling wave in the middle of the night. I bent low to avoid the willows, but some of them still slapped my face as we careened by, and the involuntary tears streamed across my cheeks. I was often overtaken by the feeling that I was being pursued and I longed to take a look back, but if I did manage to turn my head for a split second, I couldn't see anything for the blackness of the night. The dogs ran out onto the river ice where I could see the lights of the village, and after the silent racing of the dogs, I felt damp in the middle of my back. I knew that every time I went to the cabin at night I was going to feel that strange feeling of anticipation, excitement and fear, but pride or stubbornness—or a combination of both—kept me returning. I had to remind myself that I was doing this for fun. Ten minutes after leaving the cabin, I was unharnessing the panting dogs and telling them what good dogs they were as they gobbled down their ration of feed, and I thought about how much comfort there was in the glare of the yard light.

William Vittrekwa came to show me how to make better corners in the log walls, so that the water and snow melt would not sit in the notches and rot the wood, and how to lay a log that had a bend in it. He showed me how to get logs up onto the building as it got steadily higher, and then how to flatten the top logs with little effort.

The RCMP corporal said he would come and visit when we were ready to put the main beam up, and good to his word, he arrived at just the right moment with his brawny men, and they had the beam up in minutes. Constable Al Evans had only arrived in Fort McPherson that morning and this was his first northern posting. He really must have wondered what he had got himself into because his first job was helping us put up that beam. Later on Al and I made several exciting trips together by both dog team and snowmobile, and he became my young son's idol.

As winter closed in, we roofed the cabin and fitted a door and windows. I put plywood walls on the interior to give it a more finished look. It still looked rough, but we were quite proud of it. We installed a wood stove, putting the chimney carefully up through the roof, and when it was fired up, it didn't take long to heat the inside of the cabin. It was very satisfying to sit by it, soaking up the heat on a cold day and breathing the aroma of drying spruce wood.

By spring I had made some rough furniture out of surplus plywood shelving, built a unique fire guard around the stove to stop the children from burning themselves, and even constructed an indoor toilet, one of the famous "honey buckets," which worked like a charm, and we never had any problems with the plumbing.

With Easter coming up, Muriel and I thought it would be really nice to spend the break at the cabin. We planned it all out, made arrangements with the police to keep the radio for us, and packed sleeping bags, food and spare clothes to last the weekend. I took most of our supplies over in the dog toboggan with Muriel and the two children sitting on top of it all. Before I went back for more, we put the sleeping bags on the beds, hung up the radio, and generally tidied up, storing the food high up on the shelves and the rifle and shells away from the fire and out of reach of the children.

Stephen, who was only two years old, was tired so Muriel put him down for a nap, while I turned the dogs around to go back to the village to get some of the bulkier furniture I had made in the station warehouse. Just as I was leaving, Muriel called out asking what she should use to get the fire going if it were to go out, and as I unfastened the toboggan, I told her to use the stuff that was in a can in the corner of the cabin. Then away I went, skimming down the trail, and almost knocked over a group of boy scouts who were out for a picnic.

About an hour later as the dogs and I were huffing and puffing up the creek on our way back with the awkward sled load, I noted smoke rising into the blue sky. I thought the boy scouts must be having quite a cook-out judging by the size of the fire. Then I could hear the wood crackling and it was coming from the direction of the cabin, and I was suddenly hit by a feeling of foreboding. Could it be? I left the dogs and sprinted through the deep snow, passing them as I ran up the trail, and as I came to the lake I sucked in my breath. "Oh, *no!*" The cabin was engulfed in smoke, and flames were shooting out of the windows with a roar. And there was no sign of anyone around.

I ran to the trail leading up to the cabin and virtually leapt up the bank, and there was Muriel sitting on a blanket and hugging Stephen and Helen. Tears were streaming down her face as she looked at the cabin. The glass in the cabin windows was melting down the log walls, and the rifle shells inside were exploding and whizzing through the air.

I was speechless, my mind just whirling. Seeing Muriel and the children safe made a big lump come into my throat, and all I could croak out was "Wh-wh-what happened?"

Muriel explained: Stephen had been asleep and Helen looking at a book, when Muriel began to feel cold. She had looked in the stove and saw that there was still some wood in it, but it was not burning very well. She thought about what it was I had said to use. Ah, yes, pour some stuff on the fire from the can in the corner of the cabin. But there were two cans in corners. Which one to use? She made a guess and, as she said later, it was the wrong guess. She picked up the can of white gas not the one containing kerosene, uncapped it, and poured some directly onto the fire.

Whoosh! the can set on fire in her hands, the flames shooting out of the top of it. Looking around quickly, she saw that the cabin door was still open from when she had gathered kindling, and with a quick aim she threw the can toward the door. It fell short. Gas poured out of the can, setting the floor on fire, and the flames caught some clothing on the back of the door. Within seconds the whole ceiling was on fire.

Muriel grabbed a blanket and threw it out of the door, then grabbed Stephen and literally threw him out of the door to land on the blanket. Helen, who had been watching with wide eyes, was hustled out of the door to join Stephen. Muriel then started to shovel snow on the flames but it had no effect so she ran back into the cabin

Muriel, Stephen and Helen in front of our rebuilt cabin. Some of the burned logs can be seen to the left of the door and window.

to see what she could save, grabbed a red box that was sitting by the table and rushed out. Dragging the blanket away to a safe distance, she and the children sat there watching the cabin burn.

Over the noise of the fire we could hear the sound of snowmobiles coming down the trail, and with a roar equal to that of the fire, the three RCMP officers arrived, looking very concerned, but they relaxed a little when they saw we were all safe. Frank Dunne explained that the RCMP plane had been about to land in Fort McPherson when the pilot had radioed down to the detachment and asked if they knew there was a cabin on fire across the river. Knowing we were the only people with a cabin in that area, the policemen immediately ran out and all three men had come over to the cabin or, more precisely, to what was left of the cabin. Muriel explained what had happened, and I told them that I had said to use the stuff in the can but had forgotten there was some white gas in another corner of the cabin.

We watched the fire for a few more moments, but there was

nothing anyone could do, and when the police offered to take Muriel and the children back, we accepted. Muriel put the blanket in Frank's toboggan and sat in it herself, and then the two children were put in with her.

"Do you want this red box?" Frank asked, lifting up the small box that Muriel had rescued. She managed a small smile. "May as well, it's all I could get out of the cabin."

"What's in it?"

"The lunch."

As I drove the dogs back, I kept looking over my shoulder at the smoke that still rose from the ruins, feeling that it was all a bad dream. At least none of my family was hurt. In the back of my mind a little voice kept saying, "All those hours of work!" But after the initial blow, and later the encouragement and offers of more help from everyone if we wanted to rebuild and the donations of windows and a door, can you blame us that we rebuilt the cabin? By the following fall we had moved into the new cabin and spent the first of many weekends in it, and I am happy to say it gave a lot of people a place close to the community to visit and to get away from it all.

33

WE HAD RECEIVED A MESSAGE from a hunter who had just returned from the mountains to tell us that a well-known young man had come down with a mysterious ailment that "had made his head swell up twice the size" and he could not travel back home by dog team. We doubted that the signs and symptoms described to us were accurate, but because we knew the sick man very well and also knew he would not send a message to us unless something was seriously wrong with him, we gave in to our doubts about the authenticity of the message and sat down to consult all the books available to us. Then, still feeling like a novice, I phoned the doctor in Inuvik for advice, telling him we knew the man very well. As expected, the doctor could not think what could be wrong but agreed we should go and get him if a plane could land somewhere in the mountains. Meanwhile, the patient's wife had come to see us in some distress after she heard the same message from the returned hunter or, more likely, by the time she heard the message the symptoms had probably been exaggerated even more.

We identified a small lake close to where the hunters were last reported and Freddie Carmichael said he was willing to fly into the mountains with us and try to land on the lake that, he said, was called Miracle Lake. I wondered out loud if it was called that because it would be a miracle if anyone could land on it, but Freddie said it was so called because someone had cached a big pile of Miracle Brand dog feed at the lake many years ago. A special radio message was sent to the hunters telling them that Muriel and I were coming, and we took along the hunter who had brought word to us about the patient so he could point out where the camp was situated.

Because of the sudden high winds, flying in the mountains could be very dangerous, and we flew high to get a good panoramic view and to check for any alternative landing sites. After some time in the air, Freddie pointed below and said he could see some dog teams coming down the creek from the direction of the campsite. The plane was at about 5,000 feet (1,524 m) and the dog teams looked to be no more than pencil lines, and I would have missed them altogether, but he had been flying over the tundra for a long time and soon noticed anything out of the ordinary. We had no means of direct communication with the people below, so Freddie said he would fly down to them, and even though there was no place to land, we might be able to see who was there. "Okay," I shouted, "Let's go for it!"

The little Cessna 185 corkscrewed down and, as the centrifugal force pumped the blood from my brain, I began to feel light-headed. I had an urge to giggle like a drunk, and I'm sure I had a stupid grin on my face. It reminded me of times I'd had too much to drink and had lain down and everything had started to spin. I gripped the seat tightly and let my body sink into it, and there I stayed for the few minutes it took Freddy to bring the plane closer to the ground and level out. To my surprise, Muriel just sat looking out of the window as though this was a normal occurrence!

By the time Freddy had lowered the flaps and throttled back the engine, I began to feel almost normal and strained to look out of the window. One, two, three, four, five dog teams. That was as many as there should be, including the sick man's team. The hunters waved their arms madly over their heads, but we couldn't tell if they were telling us everything was all right or that things were bad.

There was nowhere to land, so, after making three or four passes, Freddie climbed a bit higher. We saw two of the hunters leave their teams and run into the middle of the frozen creek and then, as we circled them, they wrote "OK" in the snow in 20-foot (6 m) letters. At least we knew something now.

The teams were two hours' travel time from the mouth of the creek where Brian Francis's cabin was located on the Peel River, so we decided we would go down there, see if we could land and, if so, wait in the cabin for the hunters to make sure everything really was "OK." After an uneventful landing, we went to the cabin to wait. Fortunately for us, Brian and his wife were there and they gave us tea and bannock to pass the time away.

Before long, barking dogs had us on our feet and we watched the first hunter arrive. A barrage of questions hit him as he came up to us. Yes, the sick man was with them and had managed to drive his own dogs, but everyone was keeping an eye on him. And no, he was not better yet but the swelling had gone down. The other teams arrived. While someone took care of the sick man's dogs, we quickly examined him. Pale skin, rapid pulse, slight fever, a small gash on his forehead—he said he had fallen and banged his head on the ice, and as he was known to be a non-drinker, I believed him. He had some dental cavities but no noticeable sign of swelling. Muriel dressed the gash and asked the man who had brought us the message if he was prepared to drive the dogs back if we took the patient in the plane back to Fort McPherson. He agreed to do this.

When the plane came in to land on a lake back at the Fort, there was a small crowd waiting. Our patient was a well-respected young man and people were concerned, but we had noticed in similar incidents that there was always a certain amount of morbid talk around, which inevitably drew onlookers. The patient's wife detached herself from the crowd and came closer as the plane's engine stopped, and when Freddie opened the door, the relief could be seen on her face when she saw her husband. He stepped out, and I expected they would fall into each other's arms, but no! They faced each other, put their right hands out, gripped gently and shook hands once, and then as her husband walked off with us toward the nursing station for tests, she followed a few steps behind him.

It may not have been the outward demonstration of affection I had expected, but there was something there that was beautiful to see, and I was left in no doubt at all that the couple had very strong feelings for each other. Showing affection in public is to me perfectly normal, but in Fort McPherson it was rarely seen among the people who lived there. The handshake of greeting was the gentle clasp of hands and one shake. That was all. None of this stranglehold on the other person's hand and then a vigorous pumping of the hand until their eyes started to jiggle about, or the complicated manoeuvring that some people seem to engage in, twisting around and doing a high five at the end that seems more like a dance ritual than a greeting. I found the Gwich'in way quite adequate and much more effective.

34

IN THE SUMMER OF 1969, after nearly six years in the north and countless hours of tears and laughter, Muriel and I sat down to discuss our future and what lay ahead for us and the children. Should we continue to live in Fort McPherson? Should we seek to enlarge our professional careers? Should we offer our children the experiences of the south? The daily routine of the nursing station was stifling us, but the thought of leaving the people we had grown to love was painful. We heard it said that we had worked at the nursing station far longer than nurses normally stayed—the average being two years—but we were not there to break any records. We were worried that if we stayed in Fort McPherson, our enthusiasm for the work would deteriorate to the point where we would be ineffective in the public health programs and stale in the treatment programs, and yet the longer we stayed the more entrenched we became in the way of life.

As we pondered these heavy questions together and with some close friends, word leaked out that we were thinking of leaving. It is possible that someone playing with a scanner intercepted a telecommunication from Santa Lucia saying there was a job there for us and that we were to prepare to fly to Montreal immediately, but we will never know. We had indeed sent a casual inquiry to Santa Lucia because we wanted to see what was available in the nursing field, and Santa Lucia sounded about as different a location as we could find at that moment. But when we further considered it, we realized it was no good taking our children from one isolated area to another, no matter how hot it was or how blue the sea.

One evening there was a knock at the back door, and one of the local contractors stood there. He asked if he could come in and speak to me privately. I was a little worried about what I was about to learn because this particular man had never come to visit us socially, but over a cup of coffee and some fresh doughnuts Muriel was making, I was offered the job of managing the contractor's business on a percentage basis or whatever terms I thought were fair. I couldn't believe my ears. I didn't know anything about contracting and said just that, but he told me that he wanted someone who could be relied on, could organize a business, write letters properly and, with the long promised Dempster Highway starting from Dawson in the next few years, prepare for a lucrative business in which there would not be much competition at this end.

What a temptation! I could stay in the north, make a lot of money, keep my dog team, hunt caribou and fish and… and… what about Muriel and the children? I knew I would have to say no. I was overwhelmed by the offer and tried to impress this upon our visitor, and when he finally left I think he understood, but I felt as though I had let him down. Muriel and I sat up late discussing this, and we knew then that we would be leaving Fort McPherson for sure and began to prepare ourselves mentally for the wrench we knew would come.

We advised Medical Services of our intention to leave and that, if possible, we would like to be transferred to British Columbia where we knew people, where there were mountains, lakes, schools, churches, and a few shopping centres. In too short a time we received a phone call to say that Dr. Mary Habgood, the Inuvik Zone medical director, had spoken to her counterpart in the South Mainland Zone in British Columbia, Dr. John Murie, and that he would make a position available for me there, doing special projects. Muriel would take time off to care for our children, who would be starting school and would need her to be close as they adjusted to the south, a different culture, and the major changes that it would bring to their lifestyle.

I accepted the position, and we told our good friends, William and Mary Firth that we would soon be leaving them.

"Aaaaagh," said Mary when she heard. "How am I going to manage without the children?" She had been their "Jijuu" (grandmother) since they were born, and now we were going to take them away from her!

We started to pack our possessions, feeling alternately sad and excited but always guilty, and the days sped by, bringing us always closer to our September departure. Another knock on the door. A young lady stood there. "You and nurse are to go down to the old school."

"Why?"

"I don't know. That old man told me," she said as though this explained everything in the universe.

Muriel and I went obediently to the old school, and before we got there we knew what was happening. People were coming from all directions toward the school, some carrying pots and pans and some carrying bags of what appeared to be bannock. There was going to be a feast, and as we had not been asked to donate anything and would soon be leaving, we knew who it was for. Once again we felt sad though honoured by this show of affection and esteem from the Gwich'in people.

We ate caribou stew and rice, bannock and jam and assorted other goodies that people had brought. We were literally filled to the brim, both gastrically and emotionally, as people came to shake our hands and to offer us gifts of moccasins, moosehide gloves and beadwork, all the time pushing us to eat more of this or that, until in the end we had to protest at their generosity and immediately bags were furnished for us to take home what we couldn't eat.

The floor space was cleared and George Robert, a wonderful fiddler, took his place at the end of the room. Then someone else appeared with a guitar, and after some brief tuning of instruments had taken place, a familiar musical jig tune started, and a couple started to dance in the unique style of the Gwich'in. Muriel and I were loudly encouraged to get up and dance, which we did, while people clapped, "oohed" and "aahed" and giggled at the attempts we made.

Suddenly the fiddle stopped, and old William Vittrekwa came forward. He wore a sash that went around his neck and under his arm, and he said this is what the old-timers used to wear when they danced. This was news to me, and I was glad to learn a little bit more about the old customs.

William had just finished talking when the group of people standing behind him moved away to reveal John Modeste sitting down and holding a drum. He started to beat the drum rhythmically, and as he warmed up to the beat, he started to sing. I was enthralled. Muriel and I had lived amongst these people for six years and this was the first time I had seen or even heard of a drum dance in Fort McPherson. I had always assumed that drum dancing was an Eskimo tradition, and I was delighted to find out I was wrong.

As John Modeste continued to drum and sing, several people on the floor started to dance, following the same steps as when they were dancing to the fiddle and guitar, but now they formed a large circle, and the person in front of the drummer danced more enthusiastically than the others as though giving a special performance. Then after a minute or two he moved on and the next person in line took over, and the ladies took their turns along with their menfolk.

Muriel and I were pulled to the circle and self-consciously I danced my best shuffle, while Muriel performed the very dainty female part, looking quite good, and I would have thought she was not embarrassed at all, except for the tell-tale pink spots on her cheeks. We danced for what seemed hours, and when we rested, the others continued, while the sweat poured down their faces. William Vittrekwa danced wildly, throwing his arms high like a highland dancer and calling out *Heyyy!* and *Wheeee!* as he danced wildly in front of John Modeste, waving his large, coloured handkerchief in the prescribed manner.

Late that night—or more properly, very early in the next morning—we were tired out but, as the honoured guests, it was not polite for us to leave earlier so it was something of a relief to see some of the people gathering up their dishes in preparation for leaving. Suddenly the drumming stopped, and as we looked up, John Modeste came across to us.

"Thank you for coming tonight, Mr. and Mrs. Billington. You have been good to us and helped us lots, and this is for you." And he held out the drum he had been playing and looked at me expectantly. I was caught completely off guard, and I looked at Muriel and at the drum, and my mind raced. What a gift! I was delighted. I looked up and everyone was quiet and watching. "John," I croaked, then cleared my throat. "John, this is the nicest gift ever, and we are honoured to have it. It will have a special place in our house always, and the honour is big because the drum was used at our feast and given to us by you, the man who played it. Mussi Cho! A big thank you."

We shook hands, John smiled a shy smile, everyone clapped then came forward and shook our hands, saying, "Mussi, Mussi (Thank you, thank you)."

One old lady came and gave me a big hug and said in a loud voice, "Hey, I got only one good tooth in top. I come to station in the morning and you take it out. Maybe next nurse no good!" Everyone laughed loudly at this, and though I laughed, I knew she really meant it because she had trusted me to look after her dental care, which over the years had necessitated removing some of her teeth.

"Harriet," I said, "that tooth is good. You look after it!"

She just smiled and said "Ahh" and walked away grinning.

We left the school and carried our gifts down to the nursing station, the cool night air making a refreshing change compared with the hot and humid air in the school. We felt tired and sad, yet elated by the dancing and with the attitude of all our friends. Such mixed emotions. We talked for a long time that night about our reasons for leaving and of our love for the people of Fort McPherson and their apparent love for us. Were we right to leave, or were we being selfish? On the other hand, would we be denying our children the chance to live "outside" and reap the benefits of a southern existence? But in spite of our misgivings, we knew the die had already been cast, and we would soon be leaving, and before we went to bed we had come to terms with our decision. I slept that night with the memory of the drum beat pounding in my ears, and as I dreamed about dancing to the drum, my legs thrashed out in bed. Muriel later told me it was almost as bad as dancing with me when I was awake.

Several days later, our belongings were packed and we tearfully said our goodbyes for the last time. My heart ached because I was leaving such an important part of my life behind. As the small plane took off, both Muriel and I craned our necks to catch a last glimpse of our home and the people we had grown to love. The Peel River and then the Mackenzie passed underneath the plane, and we saw the cabins and tent frames on the riverbanks. I thought of the exciting history of the area and then, as though to ease the pain of leaving, I remembered that if all of my plans worked out I would be returning in about four months to take part in one last adventure.

35

ONE OF THE MOST FASCINATING and tragic stories of the
north is that of the Royal North West Mounted Police "Lost Patrol," the best and most detailed account of it being found in a book
of that title by Dick North. I first became interested in the story
after seeing the very official-looking grave of the patrol's members
in the cemetery in Fort McPherson. There is one large headstone
with their names engraved on it. A thin chain surrounds the painted
white stones, and I assumed because it stood out spectacularly that
it was part of the current RCMP duties to keep the grave neat and
clean. After my visit to the graveyard, I tracked down William Firth
for details of the event, and he spent a long time recounting the
story to me. Later I was able to visit the cairns that the RCMP had
erected at important points and was privileged to read the actual
account of the patrol directly from the police files.

It was a routine four-man patrol under the leadership of
Inspector Francis J. Fitzgerald that had set off from Fort McPherson
on December 21, 1910, for Dawson City. En route they hired some
natives to guide them over the mountains and then paid them off but
the patrol then became lost. When food began to get very short, the
patrol turned and headed back toward Fort McPherson, but fatigue
and hunger slowed them down, and they resorted to eating their
dogs. One member committed suicide, and the others died one by
one, until finally Inspector Fitzgerald himself succumbed in a rough

camp only 20 or so miles (32 km) from Fort McPherson. The bodies were found the following March just before breakup and taken to the village where they were buried with military honours.

I pored over maps to try and gauge where they may have gone wrong, and over the years I visited some areas where the Lost Patrol had passed and I could imagine their presence in the wind and the snow. I spoke with both Andrew Kunnizzi and William Vittrekwa about the trail and the route, and they agreed it would be a great idea to make the trip "one of these days." Well, "one of these days" came along in 1969 when I was listening to CHAK Inuvik Radio and heard about the Northwest Territories Centennial celebrations. "And would anyone with ideas for celebrating the Centennial with commemorative trips please contact Jim Whelley in Yellowknife." I wrote to Jim outlining my ideas and one week later I was contacted by the officials in the Yellowknife office. They told me that the staff had been feeling a bit despondent because they had not received any applications until my letter arrived. I had suggested a re-enactment of the Lost Patrol that would show the ties the NWT had with the Yukon and would also be a precursor to the planned Dempster Highway, which was to go from Dawson City to Fort McPherson, Arctic Red River and finally Inuvik.

I was asked to head a committee and plan the re-enactment. The Centennial Office would give its blessing and, more importantly, some money to get things underway. A lot of planning and preparation went into the project. Some people laughed at the idea and thought that we were crazy, but others expressed a desire to be a part of the expedition.

The commissioner who investigated the cause of the failure of the Lost Patrol summed up the reasons for the fatalities as: 1) the small quantity of provisions taken; 2) the want of an efficient guide, and 3) the delay in searching for the lost trail. I only wanted to re-enact the successful parts; I didn't plan to eat any dogs or get lost, and with this in mind, I was very happy to be visited by both Andrew Kunnizzi and William Vittrekwa, and be told they would like to volunteer as guides. The Hudson's Bay Company said they would donate dog food as well as food for our patrol members, so in a very short time the most important matters were covered.

From a list of prospective adventurers, eleven were selected. I humbly accepted the position of patrol leader, which was more of a coordinator and organizer as William and Andrew were to be the main guides to actually lead us, and George Robert was to be a back-up guide "just in case" because I was concerned about the age of my two main guides. Andrew was 78 years old and William was 76. George, however, was only in his early sixties!

We held numerous meetings and spent countless hours studying maps. It was decided that instead of leaving in December, as Inspector Fitzgerald had done, we would leave in February when the days were longer and the temperatures had moderated. To make sure that we did not starve, as the Patrol members had, we arranged for two food caches, mostly dog food, to be packed into large metal barrels and flown to two lakes along our proposed route.

But I had one big problem: Muriel and I were leaving the north to go and live in British Columbia, and she was not too happy that I would be leaving her in the south for five or six weeks. Then, as arrangements were continued, she was invited to spend the time with our friends in Edmonton so reluctantly gave her blessing to the adventure. The job I was going to in Vancouver was a newly created position, and I was given the time off, so with a free return ticket from Pacific Western Airlines in my pocket everything fell into place.

I promised everyone in Fort McPherson that I would be back to make the trip, and Bill Antaya, the community administrator, said that he would keep the enthusiasm and arrangements going while I was away and would also look after my dog team and see that they had some exercise in preparation for the 500-mile (800 km) journey. The women of Fort McPherson made caribou skin parkas for the members of our patrol, and for themselves they made long dresses in the fashion of a century ago, the idea being that the community would hold a farewell dance the night before we were to leave.

As the date drew nearer, everyone was filled with excitement and expectation, and we began to wonder if some of them really thought we were going to go "the whole nine yards" and they would never see us again!

There was a large turnout on the night of the dance, and I figured there must be at least 90 percent of the village's population in the school gym. The fiddler and accompanying guitarist were kept busy until the small hours of the morning, and the ladies in their multicoloured, long, full dresses set the scene for the menfolk who, dressed more sombrely, danced a very lively jig. We began the evening dressed in our "lost patrol" caribou skin parkas, but as dance after dance went on we soon shed them in the humid atmosphere.

The weather the next morning was not encouraging. The mercury stood at minus 53 degrees F (-48 C) with a sharp southerly wind blowing. Before we could leave, we had to attend the official send-off ceremony, so we hoped that by the time it was over, the temperature would have moderated. Once again the school gym was crowded, and dignitaries from the government of the Northwest Territories, the RCMP, local government and native leaders all gave short speeches. I was delighted to see the RCMP had stopped in at Arctic Red River and picked up Louis Cardinal and his wife, Carolyn. As old as Louis was, he gave a short speech, which the crowd responded to with loud cheers. Another loud cheer came from the school children who learned that in honour of the occasion, the commissioner, Stuart Hodgson, had declared the day a school holiday.

It was noon before we could pack our toboggans and hitch up the dogs. The food had previously been shared out equally among us. We were very conscious of the reason for the demise of the RNWMP patrol, and we compared our list of food to theirs. They had taken rations for a quick trip; we were not taking any chances and had more than enough food. It was left to individuals to decide what extras they thought their dogs could pull. My extras included a substantial first-aid kit, Mars Bars, a movie camera and two 35mm cameras. The game warden insisted we borrow a short-wave radio to communicate, and I pushed this rather heavy piece of equipment into the top of my sleeping bag.

I said my private farewells and set off for the river where we were all to meet. The total population lined the riverbank to wave us off, and the dogs, seeming to sense they were on show, held their tails high as they trotted by, their colourful dog blankets standing out brightly against the gleaming snow. The dog irons (woollen balls fixed to wires that stand up from the dogs' harness collars) all jiggled in unison as the pace was set by the lead dog. The cold bit into us and we were glad of the caribou skin parkas, which, along with the excitement of the morning's festivities, kept us reasonably warm on the inside.

We camped in a cabin on the first night, and every day after that we started early in the morning while it was still dark. When Andrew called for us to hitch up the dogs, that's what we did, and when he said we would camp in a certain place, we all tied up our teams and helped make camp. Some of the men put up the two tents, some collected pine boughs for the tent floors, and the others found and cut firewood. Before settling in ourselves, we tied up the dogs, gave them each a small bed of boughs to lie on, and then fed them. It was only then that we made our own supper, by which time it was dark so everything was done by candlelight.

After all the chores were done and we could relax, Andrew allowed himself one cigar. As patrol leader, I checked the map to see where we were and wrote in my journal. The other men came from their tent to talk about the trail for the next day, and some of them laughed good-naturedly at me studying the maps and commented that they didn't need maps. This was their country and they knew where they were, but I noticed that they still counted on every word of instruction that Andrew gave them. And within a few days they were all excitedly gathering around the maps each night to see how far we had come and to see exactly where we were. The only people who were not particularly interested in the maps were William and Andrew. They felt confident about where they were because their maps were stored inside their heads.

This was very different from what Fitzgerald's patrol had been feeling after two weeks into their journey as their journal showed: "did not break camp, sent Carter and Kinney off at 7:15 a.m. to follow a river going south by a little east... and Carter said that it was not the right river... Carter is completely lost and does not know one river from another... my last hope is gone and the only thing I can do is return, and kill some of the dogs to feed the others and ourselves, unless we can meet some Indians..."

We were treated to some beautiful moonlight nights, and the dogs seemed to enjoy them, too. They put their heads back and gave out howls that echoed in the mountains around us, then suddenly, as if on cue, they would all stop and the silence that followed was so intense we had to strain our ears to hear if there was any response or to see if we could decipher what it was that so effectively quietened the dogs.

On the sixth day out, William Teya spotted a small herd of caribou, and we waited while he hunted them. He managed to shoot one of them, and we all enjoyed the fresh meat. At William Vittrekwa's insistence, I tried to eat some caribou stomach as he was doing, but I just couldn't get it down and had a piece of bannock instead. William just laughed.

After travelling for 131 miles (210 km), we came to Eagle River, which at that time of the year was a narrow body of ice lying between huge pieces of granite that jutted out as if some giant's building blocks had been dropped there. Spruce trees grew out of impossible places, somehow finding enough nourishment to provide for their stunted growth. In the evening the sky was clear as usual, but while we were on the Eagle River the sky was spectacular. It seemed that the stars were trying to outdo one another with their brilliance, and even before the moon showed its face over the mountains we had enough light to see our way around camp.

William and Andrew were tireless. They worked hard every day, and as our routine developed, the evening chores went by quickly, and we seemed to have more time to relax and talk. We also found everything had a place, which gave us more room in the tent. When the evenings were clear, some of the men would walk on ahead for several miles to break trail for the following day, and in this part of the country Peter Nerysoo (whom everyone called "Neyook") eagerly looked around for signs of old camps. As a boy he had been there with his family when they were trapping, and he had some vague recollection of the area. He told me it was good fur country and offered a lot for the serious trapper, and he showed me the numerous mink and marten trails close to the camp, and then the caribou trails, which meant that meat was available for the trapper.

One of the men had carried a small radio with him but it had been accidentally smashed somewhere on the trail. Then one night he was playing around with it when it suddenly blurted out, "This is the BBC London" then it was silent again, and as much as we fiddled around with it, no one could get anything out of it again. But at least we didn't feel as though we were the only ones left alive on earth even if the others were thousands of miles away.

Our trail-breakers prepare their snowshoes for the next section of our journey.

Very soon we reached a high plateau—Eagle Plains—and we were treated to a spectacular panoramic view of a wide valley with a backdrop of very rugged mountains ahead of us. Pointing to what appeared to be a narrow pass, Andrew told us we would be heading in that direction. We all took a break, and as we were still hot from our climb, we just sat on the toboggans, eating bannock and drinking tea while we surveyed the scenery. The dogs were hot and panted a lot, now and again taking great mouthfuls of snow to quench their thirst. As they panted, it looked as though they were smiling at their accomplishment, and they all deserved a word of praise and a good pat. As we sat there, Andrew stood up, rummaged through his pack and came up with a slab of cheddar cheese, which he had been saving for a suitable occasion, and he handed out pieces of this delicacy.

That evening, Abe Koe, one of our best trail-breakers, cut his foot with his axe and came to my tent for a dressing. After washing it well with soap and water, I decided it should have a stitch or two so that it would not be ripped further by Abe's snowshoe harness, which was made—as all our snowshoe harnesses were made—of lampwick. Abe was not too excited about having stitches in his foot, but I thought he would be quite proud of it later. As there were quite a few men watching the procedure, Abe stalwartly let me inject the local anaesthetic, and when it took effect, I put the first stitch in without him feeling it. He then became quite brave and watched while I inserted the needle for the second stitch. As this was going on, William started to reminisce about treatment for wounds when he was out in the bush as a youngster with his parents. He said that more often than not, a compress of tea leaves was used, and sometimes a small amount of soap was mixed with the tea leaves. If tea was not available then spruce gum was boiled and, when it had cooled down, applied to the wound. For cuts, a piece of beaver guard hair was laid along the cut before the spruce gum was applied to assure there would be no scarring. When Abe's treatment was finished, we all sat around drinking tea and talking, but every time someone new came into the tent we had to wait until Abe had told them in great detail about his "big" cut, which had needed "quite a lot" of stitches to close.

We had now travelled 188 miles (302 km) from Fort McPherson, and we were on the last of our meat supply. I knew that I could go a long time without eating meat if I had to, but I remembered a portion of Inspector Fitzgerald's diary: "… searched tent and cache for food, but none found. Going very heavy. Killed another dog. We now have only nine dogs; the rest are gone for food."

We, however, were more than fortunate to come across a fresh moose track, and George Robert decided to go and find it after we had set up camp for the night. Much later he returned, having shot and gutted the moose and left it to be picked up the next day. I decided that we would have a day of rest while the moose was cut up.

The next morning three dog teams went out to get the moose. The butchering was done quite quickly, and while we were doing it, we roasted some moose ribs by a small fire and sat down and sampled them for lunch as soon as the chores were done, all of us enjoying the unique outdoor barbecue. Again I was reminded of Inspector Fitzgerald's patrol, who had all suffered so much from the severe cold and starvation: "Skin peeling off our faces and parts of the body and lips all swollen and split. I suppose that this is because of feeding on dog meat. Everybody feeling the cold very much for want of proper food."

We loaded the three toboggans with the meat and headed back to camp, and as soon as George had shared it out, everyone started cooking his favourite piece. The rest of the day was spent gorging ourselves with meat and drinking as much coffee or tea as we could hold. It was a very pleasant day off for most of us, but a couple of eager ones said they would eat later and set off to break trail for the next day and didn't return until 7:30 that night.

I kept up my diary every day and on March 3 I noted that "if I thought it was cold yesterday, it was freezing this morning." The stoves in both tents were belching out smoke by four in the morning, but they didn't seem to be capable of throwing off any heat.

Later that morning, as I was taking a turn at breaking trail, I found I was soon covered in frost with icicles from my moustache frozen to my beard. The whole day became a blur of freezing toes, nose and fingers, and when the sun shone brightly into our eyes, we couldn't wear our sunglasses because they froze to our faces within seconds. We passed a bloodied area in the snow, and by the signs we could deduce that a large pack of wolves had brought down a moose and then enjoyed a feast, so we were not the only ones to have been successful hunters in the last day or two.

On March 5 we heard the sound of an engine, but it was difficult to tell the source of the noise, as we were surrounded by hills that echoed every sound. It was not until noon the following day that there was a shout from the man driving the lead team. "A road!" The trail-breakers' job was done. We had reached the new Dempster Highway, which would eventually reach the Mackenzie Delta. Abe Vaneltsi announced he was going to put his "singing snowshoes" away for a rest.

Our teams rest on the incomplete Dempster Highway.

We all pulled up onto the road, which showed recent signs of grader activity, and then after comments and congratulations we stood around rather awkwardly like shy young men at a dance, wondering what move to make next. I called everyone together and told them to be careful in case any big trucks should come down the road at high speed. I didn't want to have come this far only to see the teams wiped out by a semi-trailer truck!

We soon came to the source of the engine noise—a truck that was hauling barrels of fuel oil to a road-building crew to the northwest of us. It was a delight to see the driver's face as we came up to him. He pulled his truck over to the side as we approached, and I really believe he didn't know about any dog teams being in the vicinity. There he was out in the bush on the new road, 100 miles from Dawson City, and he chances to see these 11 dog teams coming at him from goodness-knows-where driven by these dirty, unkempt figures, wearing skins and large smiles! We all waved and shouted "Hello" at him, and the poor man just sat there and stared at us with his mouth open!

Andrew had us camp at an old townsite called Black City (named after the Blackstone River). We set our tents in a small stand of old spruce where there was a little bit of shelter from the wind although a poor supply of dry wood, but as that was all there was, we thought it was better than nothing. In the morning he pointed to the bleak landscape and explained that at one time the whole of it had been covered with trees, but they had all been cut down by the miners for fuel and building materials. He was not quite sure where exactly but he had helped his father to build cabins here, and he pointed to some old blackened stumps and remarked that maybe he had even cut those trees down when he was a teenager.

We had travelled 320 miles (514 km) to reach this location, and as if to mark our arrival to southern civilization, as we sat talking in our tent, we heard the rumble of a large vehicle coming up the road and, dashing outside, we all witnessed a big transport truck thundering by, its twin exhaust stacks smoking and the cab lit up like a city with all sorts of coloured lights. Most of the men with us had never seen a vehicle like this before. Back in Fort McPherson they were used to a couple of miles of road and a couple of pickup trucks. They were suitably impressed by its size and speed while I felt disappointed when I smelled diesel fumes settling over us. We found out a few days later that the truck was taking supplies to a gas exploration camp located on a winter road in the Old Crow Flats area to the north.

The next day we packed up and travelled 30 miles (48 km) down the road and camped opposite a government road maintenance camp. This was, in many respects, the best camp of all because we could have showers. Henry and Barbara Hanilyk lived in a trailer at the camp and invited us to a supper of sauerkraut and spare ribs followed by a special-order dessert. Barbara had asked what food I missed more than anything else while on the trail, and I immediately thought of lemon meringue pie. And so it was that I had several huge helpings of sweet pie, and I just hoped that the Hanilyks understood why we ate as much as a whole road crew together. Al Close (known as "Lugs"), who was the other road maintenance man at the camp, went into town and brought us some Coca Cola, another item I had missed on the trail. By this time we were all beginning to feel spoiled but enjoyed every minute of it. We had passed the test of cold weather, high winds, deep snow, and cold water overflow, and even as we began to relax, so did the weather. The mercury showed the temperature had risen to 27 degrees above zero F (-3 C), and the sun shone out of a brilliantly blue sky.

The day came for us to enter Dawson. We were given a police escort and the children had been given the day off school. The dogs were all restless and excited, seeming to sense that this was a big day and that they had brought us successfully to the end of our journey. They were so frisky that one team tried to get at Bill Antaya and he suffered several bites before the dogs were brought under control. We passed through the ghost towns of Bear Creek and Bonanza Creek, and then with our police escort, we travelled to the RCMP detachment where a commemorative plaque to Fitzgerald had been erected many years ago and now sat on the front lawn.

My lead dog, Silver, behaved superbly and led the teams on the route, never going wrong once. We followed the police cruiser to the post office, where in front of a large crowd, Andrew handed over a sack of mail to the postmaster, and then I was handed the keys to the city of Dawson by Mayor Fabian Salois, which I accepted on behalf of all the patrol members.

The dogs then took us down to the Yukon River, where a place had been prepared for them, and we tied them up and gave them lots of attention along with a good meal, and finally we were wined and dined as guests of the good people of that famed city of gold. The patrol was to fly back to Fort McPherson after all the ceremonies were over, but we were given such a good time and shown so many things that it was several days before we were ready to leave.

The reality of progress was forced upon us when two and a half hours after leaving Dawson City in a DC3 aircraft, we arrived back in Fort McPherson with our dogs. We had covered a distance of 420 miles (675 km), which had taken us 21 days to travel over land only a short time before. I came home tired, but still excited, and more than anything I was proud to have been a part of the patrol that had paid tribute to those pioneers who blazed overland trails in an inhospitable land.

Much to my surprise, Muriel picked me up in a car at the Edmonton airport a few days later, the surprise being that she had learned to drive while she had been in Edmonton! As we drove back to British Columbia, I recounted to my family the adventure of a lifetime.

36

LEAVING FAMILIAR SURROUNDINGS and friends is always a sad experience, but the opportunity to go back home after many years of absence fills people with excitement, anticipation—and fear. Will the physical changes be acceptable? Will I recognize my old friends? Will they recognize me? Such were our feelings when, fourteen years after leaving Fort McPherson, Muriel and I were preparing to return for a visit.

By 1984 satellite communication systems were providing television and telephones to the north, and the new Dempster Highway, deemed one of the top twelve adventure highways of the world, had linked Dawson City to Fort McPherson, Arctic Red River and Inuvik. Well-meaning friends advised us against the trip: "Remember it as it was" they counselled. And pessimists pointed out that the Dempster Highway would only wreck our vehicle. "And," they would add knowingly, "it will be super expensive," but I didn't know of any holidays taken in a vehicle that were cheap. In spite of the warnings, Muriel and I were determined to visit Fort McPherson and renew old friendships that had been kept alive by mail and telephone. As the time of our departure drew close, she started to have dreams about the village and the people and several times woke up in tears, and we were at a loss to understand the reason until we realized it must be a form of homesickness.

On July 1, fourteen years and four months since we had last been in the true north, we packed the truck with tents, sleeping bags and food and, taking some friends with us, headed for the Richardson Mountains and the Land of the Midnight Sun. Our route took us up the Alaska Highway from British Columbia, through the Yukon and into the Northwest Territories, and all of it was through some of the most spectacular scenery imaginable. The youngsters travelling with us clamoured to stop at any body of water to go fishing, and it wasn't long before our food supply was augmented with char, grayling and rainbow trout caught with Red Devil lures and wet flies.

It was exciting to be going to Dawson again, but when we arrived, I found it looked so different to when I had seen it during the winter of 1969-70. Now it was dry and dusty and filled with tourists, but it was also fun to be able to experience some of the activities that had been previously unavailable. We went to the Dawson Visitors Centre to find out what was going on, and it was there I had a very pleasant surprise when I saw Barbara Hanilyk, dressed in period costume, busily attending to the needs of the tourists. I asked if she remembered making a special lemon meringue pie for me, and she looked at me curiously, evidently thinking that I was just another tourist who had been out in the sun too long. In the end I had to remind her of the Dawson Patrol, and I could see the fog lift from her memory and we spent a little time talking about our previous short encounter when the group of eleven of us had had stopped at her road camp for a shower. She said the short dog-team ride we had given her at the camp on the Dempster Highway was the one and only ride of its kind that she had experienced, and she still laughed when she thought about how she had asked us what we had missed most on the 21-day trip and we had requested lemon meringue pie!

We soon began our drive up the Dempster Highway and the first change I saw was the busy gas station at the junction where our Dawson Patrol members had stopped to have photographs taken in front of the highway sign. The sign itself was no longer at its old location but we did find it a few hundred yards up the Dempster

Highway. It was very difficult to recognize the places where we had camped because the road had been altered here and there and the land was covered by fireweed now instead of snow. There was a guiding camp near Black City and at Chapman Lake a tourist sign explained this was a route used by traders and the RNWMP dog-team patrols. I looked out over the blue water and tried to imagine the barrels of dog food sitting in the middle of the lake as I had seen them so many years ago, but it was difficult and I began to wonder if the whole trip was going to be disappointing.

The sight of a lynx by the roadside filled us with expectation of other wild animals we might see, and later we did see moose—one with a calf—a coyote, black bears, and hundreds of gophers, but no caribou as at this time of the year they would be in the barren land calving grounds. The RNWMP had travelled by way of the Wind River, and I had travelled the Blackstone River, but the Dempster Highway branched off to Engineer Creek where the high mineral content of the water stained the rocks brown, and it was in a government campsite at this location where we decided to camp. As I settled down in our small tent at the end of the day, I told Muriel that it seemed only like yesterday that I had been well wrapped up in my down sleeping bag, sleeping in a canvas tent only a few miles from here, and the temperature had been 35 degrees below zero F (-38 C). But I was glad that we didn't have to light a huge fire this time so that we could feed the 56 dogs we had with us 14 years earlier!

We drove through the Ogilvie Mountains, past Eagle Plains, where a gas station, motel and restaurant now stood, and then headed for the Richardson Mountains. The road surface was good with a moderate amount of dust, but other drivers slowed down and the big trucks were never a problem. We all enjoyed the panoramic vistas that were opened to us around almost every turn, and at the Richardson Recreation Park we climbed the nearest hill to look out over a landscape that once in the wintertime I had seen covered with caribou from the Porcupine herd, but for now we had to be content with our imaginations.

The Mackenzie Delta was a green blur on the horizon as we began our descent from the mountains. As we approached the Peel River, we saw a cluster of small white buildings to the northwest and knew we were almost "home." But to reach Fort McPherson now in the summertime it is necessary to take a ferry across the Peel River, and as the law of averages was in effect, we had just missed one. As we waited, I wandered into the bushes and over to a white canvas tent that was pitched by the riverbank. An old lady looked up sharply when she saw me approaching and I recognized her immediately.

"Mary! You remember me?" This was my first meeting with someone from Fort McPherson, and I felt very nervous. Would the people know Muriel and me? Would they care? Mary was the wife of William Vittrekwa and I had spent weeks staying in their camps over a period of many years. She looked at me quizzically for a moment. I could see she recognized my face but could not quite place it. I hesitated a moment then said simply, "Keith."

Mary gasped, "Keith? Keith! When you come here? Where's missus?" and she gave me a great big hug that brought an emotional lump to my throat.

I brought her over to the truck where she greeted Muriel like a long-lost daughter, and then I introduced her to our friends. She shook their hands with a very typical Gwich'in perfunctory handshake, and then she turned to me with a myriad of questions: "Where you stay? Did you see Mary (Firth) yet? Did you know that the old man (William Vittrekwa, her husband) is really poor now and quite deaf? Do you need some fish?" And then without waiting for a reply, she walked back toward her fish house where she was smoke-curing fish. She pulled down a large piece of dried whitefish and a fresh "cony" or inconnu.

"Here, take this. It may be enough for supper. You need more?" She wanted to give us the whole catch but I held up my hands.

"Mary, there is enough in this cony to last us all week!" but I was barely able to restrain her generosity. Someone shouted that the ferry was back, and I told her I must go now but we would see her at

Helen and Stephen's "Jijuu" (grandmother), Mary Firth, in her Mother
Hubbard parka.

her house soon, then giving her my thanks again, I ran back to the truck, climbed in and drove onto the ferry in a vehicle that now had a distinct aroma of fish.

The village of Fort McPherson had increased in area but not in population. We drove down the main street looking at all the new houses, the road, and the vehicles. William Firth had died several years previously, and we had an emotional welcome from Mary Firth who wanted us all to stay in her house, but there were far too many of us so we compromised and pitched our tents in her grass-covered yard. We told her that we would be glad to stay in the house during the daytime and visit, and that seemed to satisfy her. Our visiting was done during the time of the midnight sun amidst hordes of mosquitoes, but they could not diminish our enjoyment as we were reunited with people who were, just like us, older, greyer, and plumper, but all as delightful as ever and as pleased to see us as we were to see them.

Many of our older friends had died, however, and we learned from Chief Johnny Charlie that since 1972 there had been 45 deaths. I was dismayed to find that four members of our eleven Dawson Patrol members had died, too. Returning to Mary's house late one evening, Muriel and I passed through the old graveyard where the members of the Lost Patrol were buried. As we looked at the site, we noticed with some emotion the adjacent graves of some of the people who had almost been family to us: Andrew Kunnizzi, William Firth, Ronnie Pascal, Abraham Vaneltsi, Peter Thompson, Lucy Rat, Harriet Stewart. Some were buried next to their spouses, others were all alone, but all of them were old friends. I held Muriel in my arms as she shed tears for the passing of these friends from the past and it was several minutes and several deep breaths before we felt we could go and rejoin our living friends at Mary's house.

A big change that we had some difficulty adjusting to was the name of the band. When we lived in Fort McPherson the people were officially called Kutchin Indians, and they were the "Loucheux" Band. Our old friend Mary Teya explained that the people didn't

In 1984 the surviving members of Fort McPherson's "Dawson Patrol" of 1970 pose in front of the sign given to Fort McPherson by the people of Dawson City.

like the term "Loucheux" because it meant "slant eye" and "Kutchin" was the European corruption of their name—Gwich'in—to which they had now reverted. But another change that had taken place and showed us the rising pride of the Gwich'in was the new band office, which housed the administrative offices, a local radio station and a craft store. The building was unique in its design, and a far cry from the standardized buildings that had been built years ago by an unimaginative government. And I was proud to see that the sign presented to us by the people of Dawson at the completion of our patrol had been erected outside the new band office.

One day we drove to Inuvik, crossing the Mackenzie River at Arctic Red River on the ferry *Louis Cardinal* run by Dale Clark, old Louis' son-in-law, but we did not stay long and by evening were back in Fort McPherson. Then far too soon it was time to start our journey back, and early one morning we packed up and headed south, our arms tiring with waving to people. Had it been wise to return? Certainly it was well worth the moderate expense for gas and food. Muriel no longer dreams unhappily of Fort McPherson, and I was quite satisfied after having driven a truck over tundra formerly travelled over by dog team. We can never forget the people, their hardiness and their patience, and it still hurts when we hear of the passing of yet another old friend.

Our visit was a happy one tinged with sadness, but isn't it always that way when you eventually go home?